THE BUILDERS ASSOCIATION

THE BUILDERS

ASSOCIATION

THE BUILDERS ASSOCIATION

Performance and Media in Contemporary Theater

Shannon Jackson and Marianne Weems

THE MIT PRESS   Cambridge, Massachusetts   London, England

This book was set in Bookman and DIN by the MIT Press. Printed and bound in China.

Library of Congress Cataloging-in-Publication Data

Jackson, Shannon, 1967–
The Builders Association : performance and media in contemporary theater / Shannon Jackson and Marianne Weems.
    pages   cm
Includes bibliographical references and index.
ISBN 978-0-262-02929-2 (hardcover : alk. paper)
1. Builders Association (Theater company). 2. Experimental theater—New York (State)—New York—History—20th century. 3. Motion pictures in the theater. 4. Video recordings in the theater. I. Weems, Marianne. II. Title.
PN2277.N52B855   2015
792.09747'1—dc23

2015001169

10 9 8 7 6 5 4 3 2 1

To Jackie Jackson,
my mother and
visionary producer.
—SJ

To the company:
without you, no book.
—MW

CONTENTS

ACKNOWLEDGMENTS

This book is a document and testament to the ongoing creativity of a group of artists. The act of writing it coincided with continued acts of theatrical creation. Shannon Jackson wrote in the midst of teaching and administration at the University of California, Berkeley. Marianne Weems worked on the project while teaching at Carnegie Mellon and directing more productions. We ended up adding a new chapter on HOUSE/DIVIDED to what was originally imagined to be a shorter project. Along the way, we had to make hard choices about what productions would not receive a full accounting—THE WHITE ALBUM, AVANTI, INVISIBLE CITIES, SONTAG: REBORN—despite our attachment to them. And we now end this book despite our awareness that there will be future productions, one (ELEMENTS OF OZ) right around the corner.

As a document and testament, it is also a group collaboration with many artists and with many builders who have sustained the two of us. We are both grateful to academic institutions—the University of California, Berkeley and Carnegie Mellon University—that provided us with funding for the preparation of this book and its many illustrations. The seeds of our collaboration were planted when Larry Rinder and Ann Hatch introduced us many years ago, and those seeds began to grow with a 2007 artist residency supported by the Arts Research Center and the Department of Theater, Dance, and Performance Studies at UC–Berkeley soon after. We are grateful to interlocutors at universities and in theaters who have invited us to share early versions of this material, especially Princeton University, Northwestern University, the University of Brussels, and the Association for Theater in Higher Education.

We are indebted to the creativity and commitment of so many artists who have worked with the Builders over time—and to those collaborators who contributed new reflections for this book. In particular, we want to thank company member Moe Angelos for remembering so many details along the way, as well as most names and addresses of those Marianne thought were long lost. Thanks also to Moe and James Gibbs for so carefully tracing the process of creating HOUSE/DIVIDED for this book. Thanks to two collaborators who, while wrapped up in the production process managed to find the time to step out and take so many beautiful photographs—Peter Norrman until around 2003 and James [Gibbs] from there forward.

Over the course of writing this book, student researchers have been vital to the process, organizing reams of material, keeping track of dozens of chapter drafts, and providing good-humored cheer at every turn. From the West Coast, we want especially to thank Ragini Srinivasan who started as Shannon's fabulous assistant before passing the baton to the incredibly diligent and responsive Kate Mattingly. From the East Coast, we want to thank Shannon Sindelar, Michelle Sutherland, and Matt O'Hare, who provided Marianne with early help on the project and the astonishingly capable and caring Eleanor Bishop who was critical in bringing the project home.

Our families have been enormously supportive and enormously patient with us throughout the production of this book; Shannon's family—Jack, Daphne, and Michael Korcuska—made trips to various hotels, studios, theaters, and rented apartments in California, Ohio, New York, and Europe, looking on quizzically as we sorted through boxes, attended tech rehearsals and performances, and mined the memories of various collaborating artists. Marianne's family—sister Helen, parents Charles and Sally, and brother Jeff—while also occasionally quizzical, have shown unswerving faith in her efforts with The Builders for two decades.

We close with a heartfelt thanks to the people to whom this book is dedicated and who have sustained us through this process and throughout so much else in our lives: Shannon's mother, Jackie Jackson, and Marianne's company members.

PROLOGUE
Yes, but Is It Theater?

[In the street a crowd of people has assembled, vaguely seen through the trees.
Music of wind instruments is heard far away behind the new house.]

Mrs. Solness: Are we to have music, too?
Ragnar: Yes. It's the Builders' Association.

Henrik Ibsen, *The Master Builder*, act 3[1]

Over the last twenty years, our audience members have frequently asked two questions: how did you make it, and how much did it cost? The answer to the second question is simple: "it cost much less than it looks like because these shows are pulled together by the sweat and blood of these collaborators and a cottage industry of hacked-together gear." The answer to the first—much more relevant—question can be found, I hope, in this book.

How did we make it? Through incessant conversation—in dialogue with past and present theater artists, in a broader discourse with the visual arts and conceptual art of the 1990s and 2000s, and deeply in discussion with each other. The bottom line is that the work is done well when every collaborator commits to being in the room and in the conversation for as long as it takes to make the show. Sometimes this means years. Often it means enduring breakdowns (people and equipment), usually in an industrial space (sub-zero or sweltering), while attempting to keep the train on the track.

This conversation asks, "What is happening now? How can we reflect and reflect on the way we live?" Our attempts to answer these questions have led to some extraordinary, highly impractical responses—building a full-scale house and then tearing it down (MASTER BUILDER), traveling around the world to make a film where every place is the same place (CONTINUOUS CITY), collaborating with the UK-based company motiroti so that we flew countless times across the Atlantic and topped it off with a trip to Bangalore (ALLADEEN), and pulling together a render farm of computers to create enormous animations, generating a film and a production at the same time (SUPER VISION). I could go on.

When The Builders started in 1994, multiple debates were taking place in "Downtown" New York—about politics and postmodernism, new world performance and old world theater, visual art and both of those, found material and playwriting, art and technology—and many times since then, we have found ourselves straddling the divide. In New York in the mid-1990s, it made sense to a gathering of artists that we had almost no interest in "theater" but that we all were there to make something live using architecture, sound design, video design (although it wasn't called that yet), sculpture, lighting, photography, and yes, performance.

New York produces a specific kind of artist—a hybrid mix, and my pre-Builders life is just one example of this. In the mid-1980s, I joined four other guerrilla academics—Martha Baer, Jessica Chalmers, Erin Cramer, and Andrea Fraser—to form a critical art group called The V-Girls. We staged a series of academic panels where we performed papers that delivered feminist critiques of literary criticism and art history. In the late 1980s and early 1990s, I was dramaturg and assistant director with The Wooster Group, and I worked with the radiant performer Ron Vawter as a co-creator and producer of his final show, *Roy Cohn/Jack Smith*. Through Ron, I also met and worked with Susan Sontag, who, along with Liz LeCompte and Jennifer Tipton, modeled what the life of an exemplary artist could be in New York. In the end, watching Ron navigate his extraordinary life and eventual death from AIDS-related complications was an experience that propelled me into the crucible of beginning a company.

So. Much of this work began on the frayed edges of "the theater", and the artists who still comprise the company came largely from outside the theater with expertise in other media. That's what makes being in the room interesting. When we begin with everyone involved and with all of their tools, each element brings its own language to the core idea, and each informs the entirety of the production. The designers use their tools to frame or magnify or influence a way that an actor delivers a line, the actors play with their performance to a camera and on stage, and we all circle around the key concept, looking for the moment when it all clicks. As our dramaturg James Gibbs says later in this book: "When this happens, we've found a moment in the show. The shows are made by finding these moments and then scoring them into a whole."

Again and again in the making of this book, I have been struck by how the idea of design as dramaturgy has come forward—how we stage media to create meaning and vice versa. This is recapitulated in the book's epilogue, MEDIATURGY, and there is testimony throughout to this intense dialogue between form and idea.

Each chapter in the book concludes with a piece called *Artist's Voice* written by a collaborator who was deeply at the center of creating that production. I asked each to write about what the show was like from their vantage point. Drinking is mentioned fairly often. There are perfect, uproarious, illuminating moments in each voice.

Every chapter also includes a short piece from a *Guest Voice*, and some of these contributors you might expect to find in a book about theater (playwright John Jesurun and performer/director Kate Valk) and some you wouldn't (economist Saskia Sassens and essayist Pico Iyer). I remembered speaking with each of them after a performance and thinking with relief, "They got it!" The endnotes for each chapter contain other ephemera. *Afterparty* includes tallies of drugs ingested on tour and producers' contracts signed in blood, for example. There is also an alarming amount of *Source Material* listed for each production—clearly that's what took us so long.

The creation of the book has been a true collaboration between Shannon and myself, with contributions by all of The Builders and many other key thinkers. Knowing that I would have Shannon as a collaborator gave me the courage to do hand-to-hand combat with twenty years of source material—including notes on bar napkins and in journals, storyboards, photographs, programs, reviews, VHS tapes labeled "NOT BLANK," etc. As this mountain of material took shape, Shannon wrote the critical prose, often in dialog with me, and we have challenged and educated each other all along the way. Shannon's breadth of knowledge and truly interdisciplinary approach make her one of the few people able to trace the conversations among theater, "new" and "old" media, social theory, the visual arts, and all of the discussions that follow. The Builders have been honored to receive her attention and effort—and grateful to her for allowing archival boxes to chase her from Berkeley, to New York, to Paris, to Liege and back.

One of Shannon's keenest insights is her emphasis on the labor of running a nonprofit theater company. Her crucial interest in questions of the practical yet often unrecognized means of support led her to propose a section titled Operating Systems, an archeology of the formation and duration of a company. In line with this, I need to thank the producers and administrators who have worked in our various offices (from my apartment to Soho to Brooklyn)—Claire Hallereau, Erica Laird, Renata Petroni, Lexi Robertson, and Kim Whitener; The Builders' past and present board members—Susan Sontag until her death in 2004, Susan Cahan, Sharon Connelly, Erica Levin, Louise Neri, Andrew Rasiej, David Sternbach, Ellen Salpeter, Rich Sullivan, Duncan Webb, and Kim Whitener; the main presenters who have made working possible—Philip Bither, Chuck Helm, Joe Melillo, and Mike Ross; and many others.

This book begins with the building of a house and the building of a company while building the house. It opens up to look at the ideas found in various rooms, some of which expanded into virtual space while they still were grounded in the lives of the artists in the house. It could be related to the Memory Theater, a guide to memorization in which rooms of an imaginary house are associated with certain names, events, or ideas. To recall these names, one searched the house to find the place where they had been deposited by the imagination.

Downtown New York still exists, and artists still ask each other, "What are you doing?" It is a great privilege to dig deep and be able to reflect not just on what we have been doing but also on what we have been building. One lasting image: on the evening of the last performance of ALLADEEN after more than two years of touring, I spotted my long-time collaborator Dan Dobson before the show sitting at the sound board, quietly tweaking a track, adding a new sound deep inside the already incredibly layered score. Still working, still building.

Finally, here are my truly heroic collaborators, almost all of whom have held this conversation for over twenty years—Moe Angelos, John Cleater, Dan Dobson, James Gibbs, David Pence, Jennifer Tipton, and Jeff Webster. Countless other key artists have contributed their time and effort including Peter Flaherty, Moira Driscoll, Allen Hahn, Chris Kondek, Rizwan Mirza, Laura Mroczkowski, Peter Norrman, Heaven Phillips, Ben Rubin, Tanya Selvaratnam, Joe Silovsky, Harry Sinclair, Austin Switser, and Neal Wilkinson. Many other artists are identified in the chapters that follow, all of them were critical to the life of this company.

Marianne Weems, New York, 2014

INTRODUCTION
"New" Media
for "Old" Theater

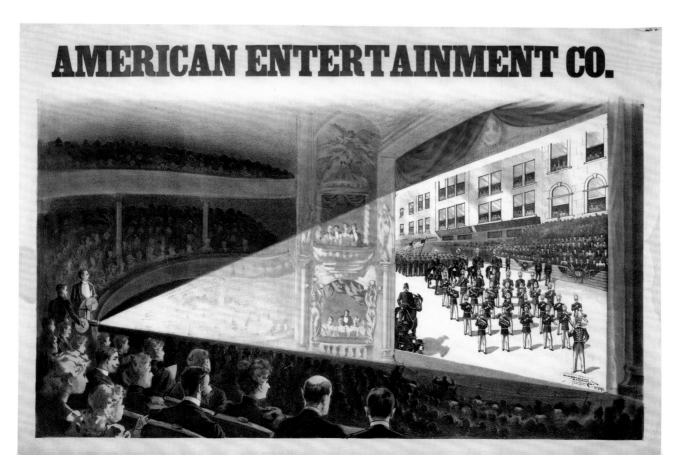

The spectacle of film in the theater. Donaldson Lithograph, 1898.

*The business of workers in the theatre is, as I see it, to express a timeless theme
by means of the tools of one's own time.*

Robert Edmund Jones

This quote appears at the top of an early script for XTRAVAGANZA, a show made by The Builders
Association just as the twentieth century gave way to the twenty-first. The Builders' previous show,
JET LAG, had been celebrated for (and accused of) bringing "the future" to theater. The group's use of
screened, computerized, and digital technologies seemed to transform the traditional theatrical stage.
The Builders made XTRAVAGANZA directly after JET LAG, in part to let everyone know that the "future
of theater" was not their primary interest and that they were equally interested in theater's past. In
excavating that past, they reminded themselves and their audiences of theater's deep imbrication with
the history of technology. Theater has continually reimagined itself with "the tools" of its own time.

A staple of American theater history, Robert Edmund Jones's work[1] could also be a staple of
cinematic history and the history of design. By placing him out front as a reference, not only for
XTRAVAGANZA but also for their work in general, The Builders honored a theatrical innovator in part
by showing his relationship to tools well beyond the theatrical medium. Jones can be looked at from
the vantage point of engineering, architecture, early screen practice, or popular performance history.
Each perspective yields a different insight, but collectively they reveal that an icon of theater
history could have intermedial significance. Jones is thus a figure of artistic interdisciplinarity, and
as such, he is a predecessor for The Builders Association as well as the many artists and designers
with whom The Builders collaborate. Even if some artists are most often remembered by specifically
theatrical histories, they are part of a large group of innovators who have worked across media and
who share a variety of contemporaneous "tools."

The Builders Association, co-founded by artistic director Marianne Weems, is often called an
intermedia performance company. The members develop their work in extended collaborations with

a range of artists and designers, working through performance, video, architecture, sound, and text to integrate live performance with other media. In an artworld context that is preoccupied with issues of collaboration and relationality, The Builders Association has consistently used the project-based nature of theater as a vehicle for integrating visual art, performance, and screen practice. The list of artists who have worked with The Builders Association is unusually broad: some have worked almost every show, others collaborated for one, and others come, go, and return. They include installation artists such as Ben Rubin, sound artists such as Dan Dobson, video artists such as Chris Kondek and Peter Flaherty, lighting designers such as Jennifer Tipton, and architects such as James Gibbs and dbox, John Cleater, and Diller + Scofidio. They have worked consistently with particular performers— such as Moe Angelos, David Pence, and Jeff Webster—and at other times have collaborated with particular performance groups, such as postcolonial intermedia arts ensemble motiroti. This book seeks to document and analyze these varied collaborations, examining how or whether the space of performance enables both cross-media and cross-arts redefinition.

The Builders Association's work is interesting, not only its crossing of media forms but also for how that formal crossing simultaneously addresses different kinds of content. Its productions adapt and rework textual materials, both fiction and nonfiction stories, to reflect on the impact of new media in contemporary culture. Early pieces such as MASTER BUILDER, IMPERIAL MOTEL (FAUST), and JUMP CUT (FAUST) restaged and rearranged classic tales across unorthodox architectural assemblies of screens and bodies, a practice of postdramatic retelling to which The Builders returned in their recent restaging of HOUSE/DIVIDED. In other pieces, their central stories derive from contemporary events and found documents, often addressing the difficult negotiation between identity and mediatization. With this kind of lens, they have explored subjects as varied as contemporary travel (JET LAG), global corporate outsourcing (ALLADEEN), dataveillance (SUPER VISION), and the struggle to remain connected in a digital world (CONTINUOUS CITY).

The Builders Association has received national and international awards and grants from both theatrical and visual art organizations. The Builders have presented over a dozen original productions in prestigious theaters, museums, and festivals throughout North America, South America, Asia, Australia, and western and eastern Europe. As this book chronicles, they have created their innovative performance technologies in collaboration with leading centers for new technologies, including the Studio for Electro-Instrumental Music (STEIM) in Amsterdam, V2 in Rotterdam, and the National Center for Supercomputing Applications at the University of Illinois at Urbana-Champaign. Along the way, The Builders Association has had its moments of success and its moments of struggle. Each production was about the development of an intermedial aesthetic practice, but each production also involved efforts to raise funds, schedule rehearsals, assemble a cast and crew, and make sure that bills were paid. The Builders Association's history is largely about the relation among art forms and media in our contemporary moment. But it is also a story of how a group makes the risky decision to make art—and how that art and its itinerant ensemble can be sustained for twenty years.

OLD AND NEW MEDIA THEORY

To research The Builders Association is to be surrounded by boxes—boxes of letters, contracts, drafts of scripts, journals, clusters of free-floating newspaper scraps, weathered posters and programs, and stacks of VHS tapes in varying states of decay. To research The Builders Association is also to be awash in windows—windows of downloaded essays, downloaded reviews, and digitized photos; windows that play production trailers, that show e-book quotes, and that tell researchers that they have to subscribe before reading more.

Both of these scenarios are familiar to anyone who has ever researched performance or much of anything. But both contexts have a particular resonance when it comes to defining the problem of writing about intermedia performance. The first scenario places the ephemerality of performance in tension with traditional archival processes, reckoning with the material traces left from the material processes that its making requires. The second scenario places the much-touted liveness of performance in tension with newer mediatized and digitized systems of documenting it. In either "old" or "new" research domains, however, performance makers and performance researchers find themselves embroiled in storage systems and recording processes that seem to contrast with the live and ephemeral processes that propel the act of performance. On the face of it, the two different scenarios exemplify the differences between old and new research domains. Windows are an index of a new media world that has facilitated and, in the minds of some, deskilled a research process that used to rely on stored boxes. In the context of theater, the same oppositions between old and new circulate as varieties of proponents celebrate the technological remaking of theater's mise-en-scène while others lambast the cheap techno-thrills of the contemporary mediated stage. New technologies are rarely cheap in the economic sense. Criticism of new media theater often derives from its apparent collusion with multibillion euro/dollar capitalist industries that count on the new in new media to sustain the illusion of "growth" in economic growth.

But whether one mourns "the way we were" or welcomes "the way we live now," the reification of new media forgets the ongoing historical construction of the new—that today's old was once new and that today's new will soon be old. More pointedly, the term forgets its dependence on relational contexts that define newness and that need us to believe that newness is even possible. This point is made repeatedly in collections and colloquia that address issues of media and technology. Sometimes it is used to fight the facile connotations of newness, and other times to surrender to a collective, ill-defined sense that we know new when we see it. This point is made by Wendy Hui Kyong Chun in her introduction to *New Media/Old Media: A History and Theory Reader* when she echoes Slavoj Žižek's *Did Someone Say Totalitarianism?*[2] with a question of her own: "Did someone say New Media?" Both words serve, says Chun, "as an ideological antioxidant, taming free radicals in order to help the social body maintain its politico-ideological good health…. Although new media is clearly different from totalitarianism, it too can function as a stopgap. The moment one accepts new media, one is firmly located within a technological progressivism that thrives on obsolescence and that prevents active thinking about technology-knowledge-power."[3] Invoking Descartes's early speculations on "the passionate state of wonder or surprise" that underpins the perception of the new, Chun laments uses of the term that seek to "dispel surprise or to create it before an actual encounter."[4] The label of the new thus too often neutralizes wonder, domesticating the most recent as much as it constructs the obsolescence of the less so. The new is not a surprise so much as a brand.

Such a state of the affairs makes a research project on The Builders Association exciting and potentially over-determined at once. In the last decade, hundreds of reviews have celebrated The Builders as "the future of theater," an appeal to futurity whose calibrations of old and new made them uncomfortable. Reviews that are negative about their work criticize them in almost exactly the same terms, lamenting their collusion with a future of new technology that leaves the tradition of theater behind. Alisa Solomon summarizes the protheater, anti-technology discourse in a *Village Voice* review of The Builders Association: "Live performance is dying, lamenters have been saying for a century at least. Strangled by the more alluring glitz of ever expanding technology. First it was radio, then the motion picture, then TV, and now the 'digital age' that have been blamed for mesmerizing audiences and drawing them away from the finer forms of the drama, thus depriving spectators of the communal, even mystical, powers of theatrical presence. In this alarmed discourse, technology is always the enemy of the theater, an all-consuming colonizer of the superior art form."[5] Those impulses do not incorporate the long history of technological incorporation and cross-media redefinition that constitutes the global history of theatrical innovation, whether media are aligned with bodily systems of coordination and care, with mechanical systems for transforming a scene, or with incandescent systems for lighting it. As Solomon said in anticipation of XTRAVAGANZA, "technological wizardry has always been a part of theatrical spectacle: the deus ex machina floating down to the rescue on ancient Greek stages; the elaborate 17th century cloud machines and scenic transformations of Indigo Jones's masques; the intricate panoramas of 19th century America."[6] Once we remember the history of technology that is embedded in the history of theater, it becomes impossible to polarize the live purity of performance with the mediatized impurity of technology. They have been in each other's pockets from the start.

Scholarly debate within the field of new media performance has largely rejected these kinds of oppositions between old and new and between live and mediated. An oft-cited conversation between

Peggy Phelan and Philip Auslander shows Auslander critiquing what he understands to be Phelan's misguided emphasis on the unmediated liveness of performance.[7] He used a Derridean frame to argue that the perception of liveness is itself a product of the mediatized structures that produce it as opposite: the concept of a live original is an effect of the copy. The exchange was helpful, and its terms have been reinvoked in the work of scholars such as Matthew Causey, Steve Dixon, Nick Kaye, Jennifer Parker-Starbuck, and Chris Salter. Arguably, however, the critique of the live/mediated binary can become as routinized as the opposition it seeks to dismantle. Phelan's project in her book *Unmarked: The Politics of Performance* is complex and preoccupied with the mediating work of psychoanalytic frames, the dialectical relationship between trace and disappearance, and performance artists located at some distance from the theatrical apparatus.[8] The specifics of these pursuits become diluted when Unmarked is cast bluntly as a celebration of liveness. In thinking about these questions with regard to The Builders Association, it seems important to analyze liveness-making as a practice and an effect. At the same time, Builders performers use elements such as affect and embodiment, inhabiting and coordinating the experience of a copresent, partially real-time medium. Surely the analysis of such performance-based techniques can occur without being perceived to have a liveness fetish.

The response to Jay David Bolter and Richard Grusin's book, *Remediation: Understanding New Media*, sparked another discussion in the emerging field of new media performance scholarship. The concept of remediation emphasizes the already mixed nature of our medial world, offering a conceptual model that refuses hard and fast declarations of the boundaries or originality of apparently new forms. Such a perspective further loosens oppositions between old and new media, emphasizing reuse and intertextual mingling across the history of the arts, media, and technology. Scholars such as those listed above have made ample use of their terms, as have those collected in texts such as Freda Chapple and Chiel Kattenbelt's *Intermediality in Theater and Performance*.[9] The remediation discourse allows scholars to track "intermedial" histories of practice in avant-garde art, popular performance, and early cinema, long before anyone began using the phrase "new media." Additionally,

Bolter and Grusin's frame unsettles fixed oppositions between the so-called live and the mediatized or what they call "immediacy" and "hypermediacy." For them, "immediacy" is a placeholder term for a mode of perception that "leads one either to erase to render automatic the act of representation, [however,] the logic of hypermediacy acknowledges multiple acts of representation and makes them visible."[10] These perceptual effects often exist in a dialectical relationship: "hypermediacy makes us aware of the medium or media and (in sometimes subtle and sometimes obvious ways) reminds us of our desire for immediacy."[11] In other words, consciousness that the desire for immediacy often occurs in a space that foregrounds its own mediation, the most interesting hypermedia work comes clean about its dependence on a representational process. This dialectic is essential to the analysis of The Builders' oeuvre. Even if they only occasionally use a neologism like "hypermedia," their work trains its attention upon the highly mediated space that produces the perception of—or the desire for—its opposite. Theirs is a constant effort to "make us aware of the medium" at the precise moment that we most want to revel in its pleasurably automatic effects.

When working in The Builders' archive, we need to be vigilant against prebranded frameworks—of old or new, live or mediated, or culture industry or avant-garde—that keep us from noticing how their work deploys technology and also interrogates the apparatus of technology. Tracking their work from the first rehearsals of MASTER BUILDER to the most recently completed piece, HOUSE/DIVIDED, means tracking a continual process of technological transfer. From show to show, they explore, move, and rewire backstage technologies to place them into the foreground, making the technology visible and available for critique. In almost every rehearsal process, we find Weems or another collaborating artist looking into the wings, up into the booth, or out into a social world beyond the space of the theatrical mise-en-scène. There they discover their and our own dependence on new apparatuses of technological support that they place under the theatrical spotlight when rehearsals for the next show begin.

This is also a domain where the terms of hypermedia theory resonate with the central terms of political theater history as well. Bertolt Brecht exhorted theater makers to critique the political apparatus of society by deploying techniques that exposed the apparatus of theater itself, and The Builders attempt to make their own technological dependence visible, heeding Brecht's exhortation for a different contemporary moment. This process of post-Brechtian technological transfer—beginning when Weems watched Chris Kondek's early work as a video designer (before the term was coined in the theater) behind the scenes of The Wooster Group and continuing all the way through to HOUSE/DIVIDED's reuse of old and less old "new" technologies—is a constant theme in their production history. As such, The Builders Association is one site in which to consider what a post-Brechtian theater could mean today.

ACROSS THE ARTS AND ACROSS MEDIA

The Builders Association can be seen as an opportunity to join media theory and political theater, but new blindspots are created by this way of framing the intersection. Even a remediated perspective on intermedial art can have the tendency to filter its analysis through disciplinary lenses. Although The Builders Association has been appropriately contextualized as a place where new media and theater meet, analyzing that meeting can sideline a variety of artists and media makers whose work has contributed to and been remediated by The Builders' aesthetic. Builders history is embedded in a range of aesthetic and media histories that can become siloed by scholarly habits that track intermediality from the medium-specific histories of particular forms, including architecture, cinema, sculpture, institutional critique, theater, and dance. Weems's seven-year turn as the dramaturg and assistant director for The Wooster Group—and dramaturg and producer of Ron Vawter's *Roy Cohn/Jack Smith*—is part of The Builders Association's better-known theatrical history.

Less emphasized and just as significant, however, is Weems's eight-year turn as a member of The V-Girls—a feminist critical art group including Martha Baer, Jessica Chalmers, Erin Cramer, and Andrea Fraser—aligned with the origin stories of "institutional critique" in visual art history. Similarly, Weems's status as a board member of Art Matters—an arts foundation that advocates for experimentation in all art forms—greatly informs the aesthetic and the production history of The

Builders' work. Other art and media histories emerge when the significance of architectural practice in their work is recognized, a preoccupation with the doing and undoing of space that is found in the Matta-Clark set of MASTER BUILDER, the Diller + Scofidio maquette of JET LAG's stage, and the distributed windows of a digital network spatialized in CONTINUOUS CITY.

The tendency to homogenize these and other artistic genealogies under the rubric of "new media" can both obscure influences and rob us of critical traction. The language of interdisciplinarity or intermediality does not in itself combat professional and scholarly habits that tell intermedia stories from medium-specific locations. As different kinds of artists pass in and out of Builders rehearsals— an architect reimagining the nature of a set, a sculptor the nature of a prop, or a video maker the nature of character—intermedial moments challenge the skill sets, habits, value systems, and working patterns of whole fields of inquiry and art practice.

This book is in part an attempt to expose but also to loosen the medium-specific frames and skills that underpin aesthetic and social discourses on new media performance. As artists and designers who create formal responses to a changing cultural landscape, The Builders are grappling with new "distributions of the sensible" in our culture by exploring what it means to adapt old but always remediated forms to a differently remediated moment now. Speaking of such aesthetics in the language of "sensible distributions" invokes the complex and oft-cited critical project of Jacques Rancière. It helps us to notice the role of something like theater in Rancière's aesthetic theory and to reposition the role of politics within the aesthetic act. Rancière's conceptual terms place aesthetics and politics onto a symmetrical plane, a model that has an analytic rigor but also a kind of enabling simplicity that is akin to the simplicity of Robert Edmund Jones's philosophy:

The arts only ever lend to projects of domination or emancipation what they are able to lend to them, that is to say quite simply, what they have in common with them: bodily positions and movements, functions of speech, the parceling out of the visible and the invisible. Furthermore, the autonomy they can enjoy or the subversion they can claim credit for rest on the same foundation.[12]

In Rancière's paradigm, aesthetic responses within these distributions occur in a space where they have "become foreign" to themselves. Practices that are called aesthetic constitute a "fold" in a distribution of sensibilities and knowledges that they share with society. Emerging and consolidated forms—whether they are called theater or painting, architecture or cinema—cannot operate clearly against a political scene and cannot be clearly critiqued for being corrupted by it. Rather, art forms develop media to address the sensible distributions of their time that have affected the social landscape in which they are received and the resources that they have at their disposal. This seems a helpful way to plot the relation between so-called new media theater within a much wider and much longer intermedial history. Tracking global and technological systems as sensible distributions, The Builders' work necessarily shares a foundation that "projects of domination and emancipation share with each other"—that is, distributions of embodiment, visibility, and speech and sensible registers of space, duration, and sociality. The Builders Association is thus part of an aesthetic process that "makes foreign" the same sensibilities, bodily positions, functions of speech, and parcels of visibility that it shares with other arts and with contemporary society—even when those positions, functions, and parcels happen to register as new technology.

Rancière can be useful in reorienting thinking about media, theater, and the variety of forms with which they are always already embedded and in reflecting on a contemporary distribution of the sensible and its relationship to different art disciplines. To help with that reorientation, consider the unorthodox reading that Rancière gives to modernist art discourse. Visual art discourse announced modernism's commitment to a "medium specificity" in painting and sculpture that encouraged forms to mine the attributes that are unique to individual media. From there, modernist art critics hailed "flatness" as the ur-condition of modernist (abstract expressionist) painting.

Rancière knows this history of modernist art theory and medium specificity but places its specifying in a different kind of network. By setting this discourse within a larger analysis of new distributions of the sensible, Rancière sees the preoccupation with flatness as paradoxically coming from outside a discourse of painting: "To a large extent, the ground was laid for a painting's 'anti-representative revolution' by the flat surface of the page, in the change in how literature's 'images' function or the change in the discourse on painting, but also in the ways in which typography, posters, and the decorative arts became interlaced. The type of painting that is poorly named abstract, and which is supposedly brought back to its own proper medium is implicated in an overall vision of a new human being lodged in new structures, surrounded by different objects. Its flatness is linked to the flatness of pages, posters, and tapestries. It is the flatness of an interface."[13] Rancière thus finds a cross-media history supporting the discourse of medium specificity that sees the elevation of painting's flatness in a much broader relation to a typographic, paginated, and postered distribution of the sensible in the twentieth century.

Rancière's modernist art example has many other implications, some of which are discussed in later chapters. But here it offers a sample thought structure whose stance on aesthetic sensibilities resonates with that of a perpetually remediated worldview. If apparently singular and autonomous art forms such as painting turn out to be propelled by the media histories of other forms, then Rancière's principle joins that of others that conceive intermediality not as a joining or combining of forms that were once discrete but as a revelation of the lack of discretion in the first place, a principle for understanding the places where the arts are already joined. Rancière's paradigm might help us conceive newer distributions of the sensible in a technologically networked age, especially as artists, designers, and citizens self-redefine within it.

This is a world that structures our perceptions of speed, space, and proximity, our impulses to plan or not to, and our understandings of what constitutes delay. We perceive certain conditions of human accessibility via cell phones or the Internet, and as a result, we also experience ourselves as exceptionally vulnerable to being found. These technological redistributions also affect how we experience the real-time, shared space of performance. It affects how we experience what we might call the performance of "conversation" in a social frame or "theater" in an aesthetic one.

Rather than imagining such realms as old antidotes to new technologized forms of interaction, we might instead examine how the social codes and corporeal conventions of those realms have changed together with technologies themselves. Changes in perceptions of speed, proximity, materiality, and sociality become sensible when we recognize that a copresent rendezvous occurs not by planning a meeting but by counting on the consistency of cell phone contact to find each other. Such changes become sensible when we examine the conventions of private disclosure between face-to-face conversation, email writing, letter writing, texting, Tweeting, or Instagramming to find that no particular medium has a lock on the authenticity of human connection. A face-to-face conversation might change depending on how an interaction on Facebook has been transpiring.

These and other changes become sensible when certain forms of interaction or creation are unable to match the speed and voluntarism to which we have become habituated in digital or wireless realms. Inside inconvenient domains, access is not assured with a point and a click, and resolution, if it does arrive, happens after what now feels like a lag. Having to find a plug, wait for a bus, and take one's turn are all medium-specific experiences that continue to occur, but our sensibilities for enduring them are attached to different distributions of the sensible—that is, to different techniques for defining opportunity and obstacle and to different barometers for gauging freedom and burden.

Finally, such changes in perceptions of speed, proximity, materiality, and sociality might also become sensible when we examine the felt structures that propel us toward newness and nextness here in the twenty-first century. There are projective impulses toward the next window or link where information is sought, speculative impulses toward investments whose offline referents are unclear, and consumptive impulses that are sustained when nextness is strategically deferred. In trying to isolate some of the ways that a redistribution of the sensible manifests itself, we can build a vocabulary with which to understand aesthetic response. For Rancière, "The important thing is that the question of the relationship between aesthetic and politics be raised at this level, the level of the sensible delimitation of what is common to the community, the forms of its visibility and of its organization."[14] Such an orientation cannot support a paradigm that pits "live" theater against mediated interaction or "actual" theater against virtual space. The artistic practices that call themselves theater or performance exist in a world where global technologies have affected the sensible apprehension of our world. Theater that does not call itself "new media" is affected by these technologies as much as theater that does.

The Builders Association still calls itself a "theater" company and is linked to new media. Other phrases and terms describe The Builders, too, including now obsolescent phrases like "multimedia theater" or "hypermedia theater," as well as "intermedial theater," "cross-media theater," "media spectacles," and "digital performance." In The Builders' brand of theater, aesthetic response more directly announces an interest in grappling with the effects of new technology by staging those new technologies themselves. "I'm not interested in the stage apart from the screen," said Weems in an interview: "We all spend a good portion of our day in front of one, whether it's a computer, TV, or movie, and this affects the way we see the world."[15]

The difference between using screen technology, viewing screen technology, and staging screen technology proves to be an animating question. Even so, The Builders continue to pursue their questions of new technology most often from within the architectural space that calls itself theater. Questions about screens and digital space still take place within the inherited bicameral space of what is, with some notable exceptions, almost always a traditional proscenium stage. Those questions occur with the coordinated help of theater's traditional technical apparatus, from the grid of its light plots to the embodied work of its running crews. These questions take place in a venue that asks audience members to do something that is increasingly rare—to show up physically together in a designated space at a designated time. This call to "show up"—which is slightly different from an appeal to presence—is a call to be inconvenienced, plan ticket buying in advance, arrange babysitting, and find the right bus or train. It is thus a medium that differs from the drop-in model of the museum or the read-it-when-you-feel-like-it model of a book. Despite its engagement with new technology, The Builders' theater is not an experience that is downloadable.

What does it mean to make forms under the umbrella of theater at a time when prevailing distributions of the sensible are altering our conceptions of speed and proximity, delay and inconvenience? Theater's processes of time and space coordination use these new digital networks, but they also stall them, introducing a degree of friction, inconvenience, and delay—exposing the frictions of a digital world that presents itself as frictionless. Without using the polarizing language of the live and mediated to theorize this phenomenon, we can think about cross-medium theater as the management of these competing claims that define inconvenience and comfort and that offer contradictory definitions of what it means to move and to stay, to be far from someone and to be near. The Builders' processes and productions respond to these distributions, but they also constitute a fold within them, making inherited forms "foreign to themselves."

THEATRICAL OPERATING SYSTEMS IN A GLOBALIZING AGE

The Builders Association is also an index of other theatrical negotiations in a changing, technological world in both the content of its oeuvre and in the production histories that have sustained it as a US-derived company working in the decidedly mixed economies and postsocialist societies that support an international art circuit. When we speak of theater's relationship to "the sensible delimitation of what is common to the community … and its organization,"[16] we must speak of theater's themes, its mise-en-scène, its artistic technologies, and also the movement of theatrical processes within social organizations with varying commitments to local and international audiences and with varying commitments to supporting apparatuses such as health care, housing, salaries, or other infrastructures that sustain the arts as a form of labor. The sustained life of The Builders Association thus depends on an ability to interface with the apparatus of whatever appears new in new media and also on an ability to present themselves within an international arts world that values a theater from elsewhere.

The Builders' artistic livelihoods also depend on grappling with a political economy of international arts programming by contending with the serial form of collectively coordinated contract labor that is the international tour. This cultural and economic reality is also a place where sensibilities of proximity and difference are newly distributed as theaters and nations decide whether the world is postnational, a question that affects perceptions of familiarity and foreignness and that restructures the boundaries that divide the world's citizens from each other. The economy of the tour also depends on distributions that value the new, the limited run, and the temporary contract. The tour is thus a place where the philosophical celebrations of nomadic citizenship meet the economic precarities of flexible citizenship. It is a model of theater making that cannot count on the value of home-grown theater sustained by a community over time—the repertory model of theater. The politics and human costs of making a life within structures that put that life on tour will be increasingly thematized in The Builders' work. The politics of globalization—in both its cultural and economic associations—are addressed theatrically in their mise-en-scène in part because of how globalization is lived as an itinerant Builder on a limited contract.

In creating a book that tracks The Builders' oeuvre from its earliest experiments to its most recent tour, we feel it is important to give both a conceptual picture and a pragmatic picture of the various "operating systems" that they have used to keep their work going. The phrase operating system is drawn from the computing field, but critics such as Johannes Birringer draw on the analogy to consider the technological networks and support systems of media choreography.[17] To these electronic and aesthetic associations, I add social and economic ones as well, using the term to offer examples of the kinds of labor negotiations, stage management, and production systems that are required to sustain the living work of The Builders and their working lives as artists. Throughout this book, the phrase operating system thus provides a space to gather and document all elements of The Builders Association's production history, providing clues into its inner workings as well as insights into the fitful experience of being an emerging international artist group at the turn of the century.

The Builders Association takes on questions of global technology in a theatrical space whose genealogies are located in time and space contingencies that are not simply predigital but arguably preindustrial. They juxtapose an apparently unfettered, though occasionally pixilated world of electronic connection with the highly fettered space of the theater, where the actor onstage has always been obligated to show up at a certain time. Thinking about digital connection in performance requires juxtaposing the apparently noncontingent world of the digital with the avowedly contingent dimensions of performance, all to expose the supporting actions that produce the experience of seamlessness. The digital world cannot do without the analog any more than immaterial economies can do without the materiality of servicing bodies. The apparent autonomy of globalizing technology is juxtaposed against the inconvenient heteronomy of the theater. New media theater might be most interesting for its juxtaposition of the apparently unencumbered next to the avowedly encumbered, a combination that is not always captured when the language of live or mediated and real or electronic is used to characterize the conjunction of performance and technology.

If the feeling of volitional mobility characterizes the digital world, then theater's anachronistic territoriality might be the most interesting thing about its operating systems in our contemporary moment. It is in such a space, the immaterial experiences of information, affect, volition, excitement, and service show their dependence on the materiality of humans, spaces, and objects. Whether imagined in cargo, in technologies, or in bodies, the friction and gravitational contingency of social formation makes itself felt. Post-Brechtian theater "shows its seams" in a context where the technological fabrication of seams has changed enormously. It also means being skeptical of the ability to imagine resistance or critique as something that exists purely outside social institutions and culture industries. By recalibrating our relation to the technologies that we use, experimental forms can make new use of old theater, placing a frame around and a stage underneath the technology that supports us.

STORYBOARDS AND THE POSTDRAMATIC

In addition to its Operating System sections, nearly every chapter of this book includes a Storyboard section that invokes the assembly process of cinema but also the reassembly process of a postdramatic theater that may or may not be postnarrative as well. The postdramatic is Hans-Thies Lehmann's catchall phrase for a brand of experimental theater that took hold in a European and North American avant-garde performance circuit.[18] His work followed and was succeeded by that of a variety of other contemporary theater scholars who tracked a brand of theater making that remade the basic building blocks of the medium. The post- thus refers to a kind of dismantling but also a reuse, a resistance to convention that nevertheless must always cite the forms that it seeks to resist.

Meanwhile, the elements resisted might vary for different artists and for different conceptual frames. Some forms might be more explicitly postcharacter, an emphasis that is developed in the critical work of Elinor Fuchs, who tracks the "death of character" as a biographically stable and emotionally coherent figure on the contemporary stage.[19] In some cases, the postdramatic is equated with the posttextual, particularly a mode of playmaking that places the textual script as the origin and propeller of the theatrical act that it inaugurates. This frame questions the authorial supremacy of the playwright as a primary author. Both the postcharacter and posttextual references can be further distinguished from other post-s. Some theatrical experiments might be called postproscenium, extending the spatiality of the art event outside of the confines of a theatrical building.

Often, however, the word postdramatic seems to stand in for something like postnarrative, a frame that aligns the dramatic with particular conventions for stylizing duration into something like story or plot. Classical theories of dramatic narrative celebrated the well-paced story along with its revelations, cartharses, and denouements, but the word postdramatic refers to a genealogy of practice that questions such staples of the genre. Sometimes, this means deploying a strategy of interruption, perhaps for Brechtian ends. Sometimes, this means deploying a strategy of repetition, refusing to allow a narrative sense of temporal advancement by reproducing (à la Gertrude Stein) the same words and gestures again and again. Sometimes, postnarrative techniques challenge the conventional speed of storied forms, whether in the aggressive reduction of pace emblematized by Robert Wilson or in aggressive speed-ups of pace that limit the capacity for sense making.

Along with this wide array of formal experimentation, postdramatic theaters still refer to conventional or classical narrative. The conceptual pleasure of experiencing a deconstructed narrative depends on one's familiarity with the narrative in the first place. The post- in postdramatic is thus very much about the reuse of the dramatic, a disassembly that often assumes an audience's prior knowledge of a story. Furthermore, as the professional networks of experimental theater become increasingly international, the reuse of familiar narratives—the myths of classical Greece or the plays of canonical authors—ensures that international audiences can have a basic sense of what narrative was being dismantled in front of their eyes.

As The Builders' work developed, they made different uses of many of the techniques described above. Some pieces involve extended research into the structures and plots of inherited canonical narratives, including the works of Ibsen and John Steinbeck as well as various retellings of the Faust tale. With a production like JET LAG, however, the storying process began with conceptual questions about travel and speed and involved collecting real-world stories that allowed their exploration. This changing relation to narrative—as something that already exists and is waiting to found—means that the storyboarding process in each show could be different as well. The chapters' Storyboard sections thus have a slightly different character than the rest of the text and also appear in earlier and later portions of each chapter. Throughout, the hope is to convey a varied set of approaches to the creation of something like "text." Although The Builders often hired playwrights to assist as collaborators, they also had to find writers who were comfortable with seeing their words reassembled.

The Storyboard foregrounds a sculptural and visual sense of arrangement. The link between each frame might be based on the continuity of an image. It might have a kind of seriality that does not build narratively but invites other visual or repetitive pleasures. It might jump from association to association without a logic of catharsis or denouement that rationalizes the leap. There is a modernist legacy to the storyboards of postdramatic theater, and we could say that that legacy animates the work of The Builders as well. But this sense of assembly also appears in the popular histories of intermedial practice. As soon as we begin to investigate the elemental components of the "cinema of attractions" and other intermedial forms, the genealogies of intermedia assembly turn out to resonate with the genealogies of postdramatic assembly. And in the Storyboards of The Builders Association, we find an illuminating site of convergence.

AS THIS BOOK UNFOLDS

This book has been produced as an attempt to balance several potentially competing goals. It seeks to use The Builders Association as a kind of testing ground for integrating a variety of disciplinary conversations. If—as critics such as Hans-Thies Lehmann, Elinor Fuchs, Henry M. Sayre, Peggy Phelan, Amelia Jones, and Rebecca Schneider[20] argue—innovations in postdramatic theater have reused the tools of literary, cinematic, and visual arts, The Builder Association's work shows that process of retooling in action as artists come to terms with medium-specific understandings of stasis and duration, image and support, aesthetics and politics. If—as critics such as Wendy Hui Kyong Chun, Thomas Keenan, Lev Manovich, Steve Dixon, Susan Kozel, Alexander Galloway, and N. Katherine Hayles[21] argue—the analysis of new media requires conceptual and political vigilance in our definitions of the new, The Builder Association's highly nuanced integration of old theatrically embodied media in a digital sphere offers critical traction for such a conversation. Finally, if—as social theorists such as Arjun Appadurai, Saskia Sassen, Hal Foster, Pamela M. Lee, Dennis Kennedy, and Janelle Reinelt[22] argue—our global imagining needs to consider the asymmetrical political consequences of international networks on local practices, both the form and content of The Builder Association's work show the opportunities and limits of globalized connection.

In addition to reconciling a variety of scholarly perspectives, the book also documents the pragmatics of their reconciliation in the Builders' processes themselves. The documentation shows creative exchange in action, providing a window into the opportunities and hazards of cross-arts collaboration and showing how new technologies revise theatrical and visual displays. By incorporating critical reviews that celebrate and also critique the deployment of new media, this book offers an arena in which to debate the social and aesthetic effects of new technology in a twenty-first-century society of the spectacle. The creation of the book has itself been a collaboration with Shannon Jackson, Marianne Weems, and a variety of Builders collaborators and thinkers who offered their stories. Shannon Jackson has written the analytic prose of all of the chapters and speaks of Marianne Weems in the third person throughout. Weems has contributed to each chapter, gathered the supplemental texts, curated the archival documents and images, and assembled the appendixes that are necessary to give a full picture of The Builders Association's process. The authors themselves have also undergone a process of re-self-definition by testing their thoughts, educating each other about the frames they think are most important, and sometimes allowing differences in their approaches to remain visible as an ongoing conversation.

Chapter 1, MASTER BUILDER: The Aesthetics of Building, focuses on MASTER BUILDER (1994), Marianne Weems's first collaboration under the umbrella of what became The Builders Association. The collective excavation of Ibsen's classic was a year-long process of experimentation in which radically disparate artists produced an innovative performance installation, working across the domains of architecture, sound, sculpture, video, and performance. This chapter also documents the professional relations among collaborators, anticipating the complex negotiations that sustained the organization over the next twenty years. The deconstruction and reconstruction of the Faust tale take up chapter 2, FAUST: Theater as Postproduction, which also focuses on the live screen as both a contemporary and a historical phenomenon in intermedial practice. In IMPERIAL MOTEL (FAUST) and JUMP CUT (FAUST), The Builders Association artists devised live films onstage by theatricalizing the studio practice of postproduction to show the apparatus of screen technology. This project marked the first step toward The Builders' interest in substituting a mediascape for the traditional set. Chapter 3, JET LAG: Still Moving, takes on the poetics of speed and stasis through a study of JET LAG (1998). This chapter continues and complicates the theme of cross-arts collaboration by analyzing The Builder Association's collaboration with Diller + Scofidio. Performing the global experience of duration, it documents The Builders' imagining of a new media landscape of bodies and space, as well as their move from the concept of the set to the concept of a network as a central staging metaphor. Chapter 4, XTRAVAGANZA: Old Media and New Theater, returns to the roots or at least one part of a wider intermedial practice that can be found in the history of popular performance. Focusing on the scale and techniques of early popular spectacles, this chapter on XTRAVAGANZA (2000) addresses a variety of signature theatrical spectacles and technical mechanisms. This performance project questioned a discourse that divides old from new media by engaging a longer intermedia theater history, simultaneously contributing to debates about the fetishization of the new and the live in new media experiment.

Chapter 5, ALLADEEN: Global Servers, examines The Builders Association's collaboration with international arts organization motiroti on ALLADEEN (2002) to address the globalization of technology. Using research and filmed interviews of the Indian call-center industry, ALLADEEN explores the racial politics of authenticity in a project that took shape as a touring theater piece, an interactive website, and as a video installation for the Whitney Museum's exhibit on *The American Effect: Global Perspectives on the United States, 1990–2003*. Their next project took up themes of surveillance in a landscape of pervasive data management. SUPER VISION investigated issues of dataveillance and identity to explore the politics of the datasphere as a system of economic distribution, consumption, affect, and identity formation. Chapter 6, SUPER VISION: Surveilling the Audience, looks at SUPER VISION (2005) to continue following The Builders' exploration of the global politics of new media, focusing particularly on the insidious forms of surveillance made possible in a data-driven world. CONTINUOUS CITY (2007), the subject of chapter 7, CONTINUOUS CITY: Distance Yearning, examines the role of social networking technologies as vehicles for linking and distancing cities and individuals across the globe. This project focused on the notion of the social network and explored how the apparently frictionless space of digital connection redefines our relationships to the local geographies that we inhabit. The website portion of this show developed new software to create an interactive structure among differently linked in users. In HOUSE/DIVIDED (2012), still on tour as this book goes to print, The Builders address one of the most pressing consequences of a contemporary economic crisis—the foreclosure crisis affecting homeowners throughout the United States and beyond. The Builders recall the prescience of Steinbeck's *The Grapes of Wrath* by juxtaposing the passages about the book's Joad family with recent interviews with former homeowners, bankers, property developers, corporate traders, and federal policy makers. Each tries to find and defend a rational place within a chaotic economic environment as they voice their stories within a precarious set that recalls the Gordon Matta-Clark house that was split in The Builders' 1993 production of MASTER BUILDER.

1 MASTER BUILDER
THE AESTHETICS OF BUILDING

Gordon Matta-Clark, *Splitting*, 1974. © 2014 Estate of Gordon Matta-Clark/Artists Rights Society (ARS), New York.

The Builders Association, set for MASTER BUILDER, 1993.

OPENINGS

The theater was not exactly a theater; nevertheless, the audience behaved with a familiar combination of hush and excitement as they waited for something to begin. It was cold in the enormous Chelsea warehouse where an assembled audience of artists, critics, and experimental art supporters shifted in their folding chairs. The theatrical "set" before them was a rebuilt house, or more accurately, a rebuilding of an "un-built" house created in a photo collage by Gordon Matta-Clark in 1974. The warehouse's expanse of unstructured space extended around the three-story house of windows, walls, stairs, and gables. Lighting came from the house's interiors, radiating outward from a room's precarious ceiling and in bluish tones from television sets. The audience that waited had come for different reasons. Some were friends of participating artists. Some knew director Marianne Weems and performer Jeff Webster from The Wooster Group; some knew the sound and video installation designer, Ben Rubin (pre-*Listening Post*). Maybe they were there to see the handiwork of architectural designer John Cleater or the table that artist Eve Sussman had made for the set, a hybrid form that she would later call "sculpture for theater." Maybe they were there to see Tony Smith's wife and Kiki Smith's mother, Jane Smith, play a figure of stalled maternity, that is, Henrik Ibsen's Aline Solness. Maybe they came to see why the extraordinarily successful lighting designer, Jennifer Tipton, was taking time away from her international career to hang lights for this show. Or maybe they simply saw a flyer somewhat surreptitiously circulated to announce a new production of Henrik Ibsen's *The Master Builder* in an illegal loft. That space later became the upscale Chelsea Market, but on that night, it was a derelict warehouse and the site of the first production of what became The Builders Association.

It was not entirely clear when the production began. A carpenter walked into the foreground of the stage and gestured at a table filled with tools. His name was Joel Cichowski, and he was listed in the program as a cast member and as Head Carpenter for the show. "I have two tools to talk about this evening," he said: "they are both saws and they come from a similar family. They are both reciprocating saws." To launch MASTER BUILDER, this master carpenter began to describe the features of the two saws—the Sawzall and "its sister saw" the jig saw: "I want to talk about the differences in their power and strength and also how those differences correspond to their appropriate tasks." He held up the items in question and made controlled swipes in the air. In describing the merits of a Sawzall, he noted that it is "Mainly used for demolition, sort of a subtractive tool. Maybe a more polite way of saying it is that it is a carpenter's editor." He talked about its capacity to cut through even the most important structural parts of a building: "There's a real freedom of movement with it." The audience chuckled with bemused interest as he talked. Cichowski offered his prologue and demonstration while jazz music played in the background, cheering him gently along until he had concluded an oddly earnest lesson in the mechanics of making and unmaking a home.

STORYBOARD

The first production of The Builders Association set Ibsen's play *The Master Builder* in a house "split" by Gordon Matta-Clark. That is a shorthand description of the proposition that Marianne Weems used when she discussed the show with possible collaborators and supporters. Wooster Group actor Jeff Webster recalled the beginnings of the project when Weems, then a Wooster Group dramaturg and assistant director, had begun to imagine a project of her own. She and Webster had already developed Ibsen's *Hedda Gabler* in her former loft located in the Meat Market and begun thinking about future iterations of Ibsen. Webster had just heard a radio interview with Susan Sontag, who described a small-town childhood with "one bookstore that had a few shelves in the back of the store where they kept a neglected collection of classics from the Modern Library."[1] Webster had bought another "neglected classic"—the collected plays of Ibsen—in his own hometown bookstore, and he stuffed the text into his suitcase before he, Weems, and the cast and crew of The Wooster Group toured with *Brace Up!*: "During the tour I would read sections of Master Builder to Marianne using the full panoply of idiotic voices. In London, the last stop on the tour, Marianne went to the Serpentine Gallery where there was an exhibition of work by Gordon Matta-Clark. Matta-Clark's work became central to the development of MASTER BUILDER."[2] Listening to Webster try out voices, Weems made hasty drawings of a two-story house beneath a pitched roof, writing in her journal: "'This Old House' idea—set/rooms

being destroyed. Plaster, dust, walls falling—skeletal building. Electric saws, hammering."[3]
In the process of assembly and dis-assembly behind any experimental work of theater, there are always moments of chance encounter that prompt new ideas for experiment and juxtaposition. This one stuck.

Performer Jeff Webster in rehearsal.

The plan to remount—and to re-site—*The Master Builder* continued and revised many of the central techniques and spatial experimentation of a New York performance scene in the early 1990s. Groups and artists such as Reza Abdoh, Meredith Monk, and several En Garde Arts productions had all pushed the concept of "setting" in performance to one of "siting," lodging classic and original texts in meat markets, on New York piers, and in other found spaces. The Brooklyn Academy of Music had been exposing young artists to experimental theater and dance, presenting Pina Bausch, William Forsythe, and Robert Wilson as "artists working on the edge of their media." They appealed to Weems because they worked on "a scale not available to many American companies."[4]

The use of a "neglected classic" for this venture was also in keeping with the dramaturgy of an experimental theater practice found in the United States and in many of the experimental troupes that toured on an international theater circuit. The reuse of a classic gave new companies something to "deconstruct" (an over-used term), but it also gave their international, multilingual audiences something to hang onto in the midst of experimentation. The alternate theatrical use of dramatic text had been and continued to be a signature feature of what Hans-Thies Lehmann later called "postdramatic theatre." In the late twentieth- and early twenty-first-century theater defined by this roomy term, the text of "the drama" finds itself in an equivocal place with regard to the staging of theater. The dramatic text is no longer positioned as an authority to be followed as much as material to be mined. "Since it became conscious of the artistic expressive potential slumbering within it, independent of the text to be realized," writes Lehmann, "theatre, like other art forms, has been hurled into the difficult and risky freedom of perpetual experimentation."[5]

Marianne Weems had also been working for seven years with a company whose brand depended on this sense of "risky freedom." Whether excavating Arthur Miller, Anton Chekhov, or other classical playwrights, The Wooster Group[6] had made its mark by selecting, dismantling, and reconstructing the bones, themes, and language of canonical texts, in some ways self-animating their own dramaturgy through the aura exuded by what Walter Benjamin might have called "the recently outmoded."[7] The Wooster Group's artistic director, Elizabeth LeCompte, preferred the term *construction* to *deconstruction* in describing her process and, as Elinor Fuchs argued in 1996, was and remains a key innovator in the postdramatic use of the dramatic: "More than any contemporary American theater artist, LeCompte has announced performance itself as the field of raw material. She forages among classic texts, and performance, film, television, and dance styles, for material from which to compose her own highly worked constructions."[8] Weems, Webster, and other collaborators kept trying to imagine what a postdramatic, alternatively sited production of *The Master Builder* could be.

The Master Builder is not just any old "neglected classic" but one whose themes were presciently resonant for the occasion. It was one of Ibsen's last major works, written after his name had been made in Europe and internationally. It follows the trajectory of a man who is successful in his field, a builder and architect named Halvard Solness. While enjoying local fame as a residential builder throughout the region, Solness experiences daily dread as he ponders the past and wonders about his place in a personal and professional future. His aging longtime associate, the subordinated Knut Brovik, is a guilty reminder to Solness of the shoddy collegial ethics with which he has built his career. Meanwhile, Knut's son, Ragnar Brovik, has designs on taking over the architectural office. Solness's wife, Aline, wanders throughout a house that doubles as home and office, in perpetual mourning for the twin boys she lost after a house fire long ago. Solness also suffers from a strange case of vertigo and is never quite able to inhabit fully the imposing structures that he builds. Halvard Solness flirts pompously and pathetically with his bookkeeper, Kaia, who is herself surpassed when Hilde Wangel enters the scene. As a young woman who witnessed Solness's early exploits when she was a little girl, Hilde brings her own memories and prompts many more as the play forces Halvard to articulate his ambivalent relation to his career, family, home, sexual desire, and now a future generation of master builders that may not have a place for him. Goaded by Hilde, who teases that "my master builder will not—cannot—climb as high as he builds," the play culminates when Solness ascends to the top of the village tower that he built and family members, associates, and villagers watch in horror as the master builder falls to his death. "You are the younger generation," he tells Hilde in a scene before this climactic one. "That younger generation that you are so afraid of?" she inquires. Ibsen writes that Solness "nods slowly" before responding, "And which, in my heart, I yearn towards so deeply."[9] Halvard's actions spring from the fear that he too will become a neglected classic.

PENCE

1

MASTER BUILDER
JUNE '94 COMPILATION SCRIPT
(FJELDE AND MEYER TRANSLATIONS)

ACT ONE

[A plainly furnished workroom in SOLNESS's house. Folding doors in the left wall lead to the entryway. To the right is a door to the inner rooms. In the rear wall a door stands open on the drafting room. BROVIK and RAGNAR in drafting room. KAJA in workroom.]

Scene 1a

— PHONE CALL
— LED ZEP

BROVIK: (comes forward into the doorway.) No I can't go on with this much longer. *(Note: combine with Ron's tape.)*

— D: "what's going on"

KAJA: (moves over to him.) It's really bad tonight, isn't it, Uncle?

— D: Coco? C: Just a minute...

BROVIK: Yes, it seems to grow worse every day. (Vehemently) But I'm not going to go until he gets back. Tonight I'm going to have it out with -- with him. The master builder! *D: O Jesus, I have a line in this scene*

C: Just a minute, David

KAJA: Oh no, please, let it wait!

D: Now? C: Yes now!

RAGNAR: (having risen and approached them.) Yes, Father, wait a while.

BROVIK: I can't afford to wait very long.

KAJA: Shh! I hear him down on the stairs.

(All three return to work.)

Scene 1b

SOLNESS: (in the doorway, points towards the drawing office and asks in a whisper) Are they gone?

KAJA: (softly, shaking her head) No.

Scene 1c
(Brovik comes into the workroom and shuts the door.)
BROVIK: May I have a word or two with you?

SOLNESS: Certainly.

BROVIK: (dropping his voice.) I don't want the children to know how ill I am.

R&D

Summoning her skills as a dramaturg, Weems embarked on a wide-ranging research process. She read secondary literature on Ibsen and on modernist theater history more generally. In the visual arts, she was immersed in the work of Matta-Clark and other artists in the Anarchitecture group that assembled at 112 Greene Street in New York, a site where artists challenged each other to work on the edge of their respective media. She saw work by Laurie Anderson, Robert Ashley, Richard Foreman, Jenny Holzer, Joan Jonas, Barbara Kruger, and Robert Smithson, all of whom were finding theatrical and technological means for unsettling inherited visual art forms.

The biggest conceptual question of the project centered around its architectural engagement, a pursuit that was given more traction with input from architects such as Sulan Kolatan and Hani Rashid. When the production began, architect John Cleater—who had studied with Daniel Liebeskind and Sulan Kolatan and worked for Asymptote Architecture—joined the MASTER BUILDER team, a move that challenged the definition of *set design*. In conversations that took place in person and over fax, they studied source material that unhinged architectural stabilities in a number of different ways. Weems's interest in expanding the scale and reach of the theatrical proscenium found a touchstone in Rem Koolhaas's writings on the possibilities and perils of what he called "BIGNESS." Weems's journals show that she read and highlighted quotes from Koolhaas's disquisition on scale:

BIGNESS is where architecture becomes both most and least architectural: most because of the enormity of the project; least through the loss of autonomy—it becomes an instrument of other forces, it depends.... Beyond signature, BIGNESS means surrender to technologies; to engineers, contractors, manufacturers, to politics; to others. It promises architecture a kind of post-heroic status ... it can be achieved only at the price of giving up control, transmogrification. It implies a web of umbilical cords to other disciplines whose performance is as critical as the architect's: like mountain climbers tied together by life-saving ropes, the makers of BIGNESS are a team ... it gravitates opportunistically to locations of maximum infrastructural promise.[10]

This kind of quote makes the match between architectural and theatrical sensibilities clearer. Both art forms work with an awareness of their own dependency and find themselves surrendering to collaborators. Like architecture, theater is always already enmeshed in an interarts web, with "umbilical cords to other disciplines." But if architects and theater-makers can find unexpected kinship, they also have things to learn from each other. What would it take to train a theatrical cast to be architecturally "opportunistic," to search for "maximum infrastructural promise"? How would an architect respond to the extended "charrette" of theatrical rehearsal, with its relations of dependence among humans, designers, actors, and carpenters? Cleater decided that none of these questions could be answered unless he attended rehearsals each day, watched the ensemble build, un-build, and re-build through movement and speech, and tried to anticipate where these interdependent forms wanted to go next. Together, architects and theater-makers had a forum for experimenting with how to stage BIGNESS and how to imagine theatrical space as a macro-system that supported the micro-interactions that it could never fully contain.

Other architectural unsettlings came from different technological directions, including those that anticipated the "new media" aesthetic for which The Builders would become known. Weems, Cleater, and other crew members began to experiment with early versions of a multiplayer real-time virtual world called *LamdaMOO*. A precursor to more complex forms such as *Second Life*, this multiuser dwelling (MUD) enabled participants to coauthor an experience of space online. (*LambdaMOO* gained some notoriety when Julian Dibbell, the husband of Weems's long-time V-Girl collaborator, Jessica Chalmers, wrote a book called *My Tiny Life* describing his experiences there.) The goal, said Weems, was to get all collaborators—directors, actors, designers—to "think of architecture as a material but also a virtual space."[11] Cleater and Weems began spending time together on the *LambdaMOO* site, where users composed performative prose that described existent space and brought new space into being. Users wrote collectively from inside an imagined interior, and their own experiences were adjusted as others described the space that they imagined inhabiting: "The small foyer is the hub of the currently occupied portion of the house. To the north are the double doors forming the

11th November '94.

Dear Marianne

I thought you might like this picture of Buster Keaton.

I was speaking to the director Richard Jones the other night + he was telling me about this great show in New York set in a house that Jennifer Tipton had been telling him to go + see.

I think I'm going to be in N.Y. beginning of December. I hope there is something I can see — I'll call you when I know my dates — hope all is well — much love Stewart xxx

Note from designer Stewart Laing to Marianne Weems, featuring a Buster Keaton production still from *One Week*, 1920.

main entrance to the house. There is a mirror at about head height as well, just to the right of a corridor leading off into the bedroom area." Sometimes the online prose changed from the apparently descriptive to the urgently directive, in one case anticipating the ascent of Halvard Solness: "You climb up. You are at the top of the trellis now. The roofline is tantalizingly close. Indeed, you could probably scramble up the drainpipe! You make a daring leap off the top of the trellis to the roof!" At other times, the urgent tone could find itself inside prose that seemed an odd parody of *Architectural Digest* or an episode of *This Old House*: "This section of roof appears to date back to the original house. The craftmanship inherent in the wooden shingles tells the story. To the north and east of you, the roof has been raised a good six feet, but it looks like you can grab the gutter and haul yourself up. To the south is a sheer drop that looks down onto the Hot Tub deck."[12] Most important, the sense of space as a dynamic and embodied structure came forward in this experiment with a new technological platform. Users imagined themselves moving, stopping, looking, talking, and touching in a performatively conceived environment. In a process that would have its parallel in future uses of ever "new" technologies, The Builders' new media engagement provoked and heightened the "old media" effects of performance.

The major source of architectural unsettling came from the 1960s and 1970s work of artist and conceptual architect Gordon Matta-Clark. Developing what he named an anarchitectural practice, Matta-Clark collected found spaces in the way that other artists collected found objects. In processes that initially appeared "destructive" (such as throwing rocks and cutting walls), Matta-Clark arguably made new constructions that exposed spatial possibilities and challenged definitions of function, structure, and decor. In his most famous work, *Splitting* (1974), he and a group of curators and collectors secured permission to slice a New Jersey home in half. Various critics and artists responded to the action with awe, including Laurie Anderson, who chronicled "the spectacular effects" of the splitting, "as sunlight knives through dark rooms like a brilliant blade."[13] His own text read as both a score for a large-scale event performance and as documentation of an action that had past:

"322 HUMPHREY STREET / AS IT WAS LEFT / ABANDONED." "CUTTING THE HOUSE IN HALF / TWO PARALLEL LINES / ONE INCH APART / PASSED THROUGH ALL / STRUCTURAL SURFACES / BEVELING DOWN / FORTY LINEAL FEET / OF CINDER BLOCKS / TO SET HALF THE BUILDING / BACK ON ITS FOUNDATIONS." "REMOVING INTACT / ALL FOUR CORNERS / AT THE EAVES."

The documentation of *Splitting* is now famous. Photographs and videos capture the split as a fragile object and the act of splitting as its own form of time-based art. Matta-Clark's Sawzall both enacted and enabled a "freedom of movement," as Joel the master carpenter later noted. The photographic documentation underscored just how much the split equalized spatial elements that were usually differentiated. The same one inch of light cut through a wall, a window frame, a door, and a floorboard, drawing an equivalence between the supporting wall and the surface drywall by showing their shared vulnerability. The splits created new quadrants within single rooms and formed passages between rooms that had once been starkly divided. The supporting wall could become the surface; undermounting suddenly appeared to be mounted.

For many—and for The Builders' collaborating lighting designer, Jennifer Tipton—the effect of the splitting on the distribution of light was revelatory. The light projected into quadrants that usually did not have it and came from directions that were wholly unconventional. The split created singular lines of light that outlined new spaces within a room. Pamela M. Lee notes that the effects of light further dynamized the building as the day wore on: "Functioning like a sundial, the house clocked the passage of the day, internalizing light to enact the pressing sense of its incongruities."[14] In the cutting, an abandoned space that might have been called lifeless was revealed to be teeming with sentience, one palpably felt in the moment of its wounding. Matta-Clark then cut the four corners off the house, creating new rectangular holes next to the rectangular holes conventionally called windows, provoking a moment of uncanny confusion about what exactly made one hole a window onto the exterior world and another hole an invasion by it.

If there were relationships to be found between Ibsen's *The Master Builder* and Gordon Matta-Clark's *Splitting*, then they took shape on a number of fronts. Watching Matta-Clark work on the

Gordon Matta-Clark, *Splitting*, 1974. © 2014 Estate of Gordon Matta-Clark/Artists Rights Society (ARS), New York.

edge of his medium gave theater artists fodder for thinking about how to work on the edge of theirs. To undo the architectural was, in many ways, to re-approach the sculptural. Matta-Clark famously said that the difference between sculpture theater and architecture was "whether there is plumbing or not."[15] In slicing through the plumbing, he pursued this proposition, effectively turning a building into a precarious sculpture. In the New York experimental theater scene of the late twentieth century, artists of performance had parallel pursuits, creating collaborations that allowed them to ask whether dance could be painting (Simone Forti and Robert Morris) or whether theater could be sculpture (Robert Wilson). If the concept of the set had been the architectural ground of theatrical figuration, then its destabilization provocatively destabilized the theatrical act.

At the same time, placing human bodies in Matta-Clark's unbuilt house allowed artists to see what would happen to the sculpture when sentient bodies re-inhabited it, presumably requiring the plumbing to be restored. Additionally, relationships linked to the project appeared in what Tom McDonough has called the "performative" dimensions of Matta-Clark's work, which are both its theatricality and its status as an action in the world. In the "spectacular effects" of the slices of light, in the human histories evoked by the layers of wallpaper and tile, and in the high drama of one side of the house moved back onto its foundation, the work achieved a kind of catharsis, what Anne Wagner calls a "mini-apocalypse" for the hungry lens of the video documentary.[16]

After watching rehearsals day after day, Cleater and Cichowski began to transpose *Splitting*'s unbuilt house into something rebuilt for MASTER BUILDER's set. They inserted levers and hinges down the center of the house so that it could be split in half on cue. As Solness's life unraveled in the story, the house cleaved apart, reincarnating Matta-Clark's mini-apocalypse each night. Just as intriguingly, however, Matta-Clark's actions underscored the rhetorical sense of the performative as a constituitive act of doing, a series of coordinated acts and actions that make the world to which they simultaneously refer. Knowledge of the labor of world-making is something that both theater and architecture share with philosophers of the speech act. It means that the mini-apocalypse is achieved through something that "looks distinctly like work," to continue Wagner's point, and that such effects coexist with the effort "at getting something done" to continue McDonough's.[17] In theater and architecture, a one-of-a-kind performance depends on the repetitive labor of the performative. Theatrical mastery and journeyman action go, literally, hand in hand.

Although cross-media and performative connections made the Ibsen/Matta-Clark partnership a resonant one, the combination also surfaced the latent gender politics of each of these works. With a childless wife, a devoted assistant, an upstart young woman, and the potent memories of girlish adulation activating his imagination, Halvard Solness's self-preoccupation as master is acutely gendered. Matta-Clark's decision to select an abandoned house for his most famous project invoked themes of domesticity, privacy, and care that are associated with the gendered domain of the house.

Wagner's retroactive assessment of *Splitting* could have been a byline for The Builders' reproduction of Ibsen: "through montage the interior regains an impossible dollhouse wholeness, even while the cut ensures that its private spaces have been rigorously exposed and inspected. Never has a domestic domain been more thoroughly anatomized; never did its restoration seem more willfully dreamlike, a more fragile effort to reassemble a (scarred) whole."[18]

Weems came to Ibsen with a strong interest in the feminist analysis of space. In conducting research for the production, she returned to what she had learned about the feminized space of domesticity from professors at Barnard College, Nancy Miller among them. She also read Daphne Spain on *Gendered Spaces* and others such as Beatriz Colomina and Laura Mulvey.[19] Weems also began collecting images from novels and films about women in hystericized space—Daphne du Maurier's *Rebecca* (1938), Alfred Hitchcock's *Notorious* (1946) and *Vertigo* (1958), Shirley Jackson's *The Haunting of Hill House* (1959), Fritz Lang's *Secret Beyond the Door* (1948), and Charlotte Perkins Gilman's "The Yellow Wallpaper" (1892). She read Marilynne Robinson's *Housekeeping* (1980), Joy Melville on "domestophobia," and excerpts from issues of *The Practical Householder* magazine (1950s). Matta-Clark's cuts had exposed the felt relationship between identity and space, and Colomina made the point that such exposure was gendered: "Architecture is not simply a platform that accommodates the viewing subject. It is a viewing mechanism that produces the subject. It precedes and frames its occupant"[20] In one of the key passages that Weems highlighted in her journal, Laura Mulvey provides a foundation for thinking through the gendered significance of what she was trying to do with both Ibsen and Matta-Clark:

The melodrama takes place in the literal and psychological space of home and family, turning the narrative space inward, lifting the roof off the American home like the lid of a casket, opening its domestic space into a complex terrain of social and sexual significance—the opposition for instance, between upstairs/private and downstairs/public space, the connotations of stairs, bedroom, kitchen. And this interior also contains within it ... the psychic spaces of desire and anxiety and the private scenarios of feelings, a female sphere of emotion within the female sphere of domesticity ... its emotional reverberations and its gender specificity

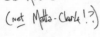

"This Old House"
(not Matta-Clark!?)

street. Unfortunately the main was buried six feet deep, and its route lay right under the steps to the vestibule, a cement walk, and another flight of brick steps, which led down from the lawn to the sidewalk, with massive stone retaining walls on either side. All the brick and cement and some of the stonework had to come up.

We had to wait until spring finally came and the ground thawed before we could begin. Even then it took more than strength and a sledgehammer to get through those heavy masonry obstacles. We had to hire a backhoe and expert operator to do the job. Sometimes even the most independent rehabber has to admit that hiring a big gas-guzzling machine to work for him saves time, money, and his back.

are derived from and defined in opposition to a concept of masculine space: an outside, the sphere of adventure, movement, and cathartic action in opposition to emotion, immobility, enclosed space, and confinement.[21]

A feminist sense of the gendered environment thus raised the stakes for what it meant to cut and split—to foreground the gendering of time and space in Ibsen's world, where movement is assigned to men and stasis to women. The latent gender politics of the split structured MASTER BUILDER's conception of the space and production. Weems, Cleater, and other designers also collected images from *This Old House* and other home shows that documented processes of demolition. In looking at the layers of peeling wallpaper and paint that offered a pentimento onto various life histories, in seeing the exposed studs, rusted wiring, and demolition holes that offered new views into rooms that were formerly private, they began to construct an image of a set-cum-installation. The images of *This Old House* created an uncanny equivalence between an everyday building process and an artistic one: did Matta-Clark aspire to *This Old House* or the reverse?

Weems also found ways to empower the women of *The Master Builder*, developing central imagery around Solness's memories of the young girls who gathered a decade before to celebrate his construction of a central village tower: "Ideas centered around young girls in the 'house' (and in pop culture etc.) as sexualized, threatening, haunting, secretive creatures."[22] Eventually, she cast performance artist Kyle deCamp as Hilga and fifteen-year-old Emma Strahs (Liz LeCompte's niece) and Sheryl Haiduck as "gogo angels" who lived in the secret attic spaces of the house. In her production journal, Weems anticipated their behaviors: "The girls should have increasingly ominous activities—begin with banal acts, making the bed, then progress to smoking and dancing, etc." These "girls" thus provided an affective and abstract counterpoint to Solness's machismo. "Don't you agree with me, Hilde," Solness asks his assistant before he decides to make his fateful climb, "that there exist special, chosen people who have been endowed with the power and faculty of desiring a thing, craving a thing, willing a thing—so persistently and so—so inexorably—that at least it has to happen? Don't you believe that?"[23]

If such "chosen people" seem only to be those of the masculine variety, Weems found herself moved to explore the possibility of a different kind of volition within the household. Her V-Girl collaborator Martha Baer supplied a personal memory of her own childhood that opened up the possibility of a differently gendered view and a differently gendered power:

I learned to listen upward. That is, I listened from the downstairs, to the upstairs floor. This is because my father, in a rage, moving about up there, made the ceiling reverberate. I listened, not just to know if he was heading in our direction or if the rage was about to peak or ebb, but also to prevent the floor from collapsing. In those early years, I learned to give my faculties and sensations active powers. The sheer exertion of my seeing or my feeling the tension in my neck and the concentration of my eyes could hold the roof up. I learned to keep the walls upright with my fear.[24]

OPERATING SYSTEMS

... Strange and hard that paradox true I give,
Objects gross and the unseen soul are one.
House-building, measuring, sawing the boards,
Blacksmithing, glass-blowing, nail-making, coppering,
    tin-roofing, shingle-dressing,
Ship-joining, dock-building, fish-curing, flagging of sidewalks
    by flaggers,
The pump, the pile-driver, the great derrick, the coal-kiln
    and brick-kiln,
Coal-mines and all that is down there, the lamps in the
    darkness, echoes, songs, what meditations, what
    vast native thoughts ...

Walt Whitman, "A Song for Occupations"[25]

If the resonance of the "recently outmoded" suffused MASTER BUILDER, then it was an appropriate beginning for a theater company that would steadily incorporate and critique ever "new" media inside its theatrical aesthetic. At the same time, it highlights The Builders Association's simultaneous preoccupation with the low-tech infrastructure that is required to sustain anything that appears to be high-tech. Having imagined a rebuilding of Matta-Clark's unplumbed house, artist/designers such as Dan Dobson, Chris Kondek, Peter Norrman, and Ben Rubin rewired it with visual and auditory technology. Weems had served as assistant director of Richard Foreman's *Symphony of Rats* and been compelled by his use of television screens as vehicles for inter-character interaction. The video installations and performance work of artists such as Reza Abdoh, Gretchen Bender, Gary Hill, and Louise Lawler provided inspiration. As assistant director and dramaturg throughout The Wooster Group's rehearsal of *Brace Up!*, she watched video designer Chris Kondek, whose systems of

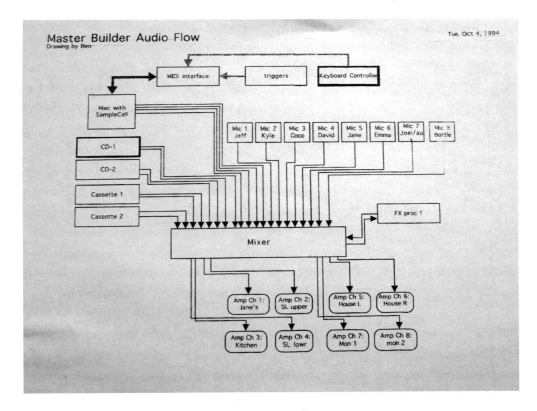

Ben Rubin, sound system design for MASTER BUILDER, 1994.

monitors and cameras projected and embodied actors spontaneously. "Chris was creating a language right in front of me," recalled Weems.[26]

Gradually, the designers drew diagrams (sometimes on cocktail napkins) that inserted "cameras" and "monitors" into the main five quadrants of the house. (Says Weems, "there's a cocktail napkin behind the design of every show.")[27] Rubin's rewiring included outlets for microphones, monitors, cameras, and other "triggers" to be used by the actors who animated them, creating a mediated landscape within the unsettled architecture. Adding microphones and televisions to the nineteenth-century house created its own juxtaposition of old and what in 1993 was "new" in new media. Architect Sulan Kolatan free-associated with Weems in imagining actor interaction in this newly wired if simultaneously un-built house:

Are some rooms more private than others? It strikes me that all of the spaces seem equally exposed (except for the kitchen and bathroom, I suppose) … if one of the roles of the telephone conversation is to bring in contemporary threads, could that also involve contemporary spatial references? … since the phone is not linked to a place, one of the callers could be seen continually on the go—never at home—but always desperate for advice on interior decoration.… I wonder if the public/private coding could be related to the on/off conditions of the players rather than the spaces.[28]

Their musings anticipated the juxtaposition of technology-driven movement and stasis within contemporary spaces of travel and rest that later became part of The Builders' vocabulary. Along with Cleater's drawings of the house structure, Kondek and Rubin began imagining the audio flow and video flow within the house and the necessary networks of wires, screens, computers, and speakers. The cocktail napkins and other rough sketches plotted relations among wires, sockets, screens, cameras, and triggers, anticipating a house where the background structure of supporting technology would be moved into the foreground. Matta-Clark had inversely offered a definition of architecture as "sculpture with plumbing," but this was a mise-en-scène that equally imagined architecture as "sculpture with wiring."

At the same time, the video, lighting, space, and sound designers anticipated actor interaction in this newly wired space. Preceding his formative sound installation, *Listening Post*, this task gave Ben Rubin an early opportunity to think about the nature of wired interaction with humans in proximate space. It also required the designers to divide labor among each other and to commit to new kinds of collaboration. Rubin and Kondek's developing designs had implications for Cleater's task: "John design conduit system to turn cables into house," Weems wrote to remind herself to convey this newly urgent need.[29]

Weems and the designers worked to locate the triggers of technological effects in the actors' actions as much as those of the operators backstage. To integrate the actor into the overall operating system of the show, they imagined "lures" that would entice actors into interaction. Weems recorded ideas in her journals as they thought of them: "Headphones connected to a CD or tape player they control. Create a space where they can really 'hang out' un-self-consciously. GET NINTENDO GAME. 'Lures' for the performers—a shelf with objects. Mini-drawer w/compartments—create 'comfortable' zones in this uncomfortable space."[30] Some of the lures were definitely old media: "leave a notebook for them to write in. Give them a reason to involve themselves in the house." The concept of the "lure" was transformed into a "trigger" as their conception of the project evolved, conveying the image of an enlivened space that capitalized on theater's status as a relational and action-based art form: "Video monitors, microphones, and a computer-controlled sound track will be integral to the production, allowing the 19th century 'voice' of Ibsen's *The Master Builder* to 'speak' through the apparatus of current technology. Eight performers will inhabit the 'house,' which will contain MIDI triggers, activating sound effects and musical phrases stored in a computer/sampler, transforming the house into an 'instrument' which the performers will 'play.'"[31]

Working with the idea that the "public/private coding" of the space would depend on the "on/off conditions of the actors"—that is, that space would become place in the action of performing it—the team began to sketch "Traffic Patterns in House," plotting the ways that exits, windows, rooms, and foyers would themselves be triggered by movement within it. To install television screens was also to think about the different ways that a so-called screen could be placed in this mise-en-scène— sometimes as background, sometimes as television, sometimes as window, sometimes as surveillance

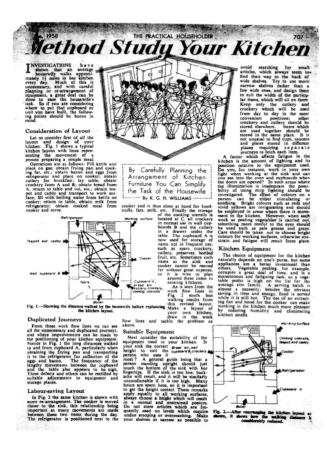

Source: *The Practical Householder*, 1958.

camera; sometimes projecting a scene, sometimes projecting an actor who functioned as scene partner, object, and gazer.

The "sound" was not necessarily ambient background but itself a kind of character, triggered and invited in at different times by actors who initiated it. Dan Dobson, David Pence, Jeff Webster, and others created the soundscape in conjunction with the scenescape, making lists of prerecorded sounds from films and other found recordings: "Lamp Moths, Vertigo, Fan, Swimming Pool, Sprinkler …" as well as other environmental sounds yet to be found: "Ting, Siren, Motor, Pitched Thunk, Cuckoo, Boing, Ry Cooder, Glasses, Electric Buzz, Ticking Bomb, Saws, Crickets, Bulb Breaking, Door Opening, Hammer, Doorbell, Knocking, Knife Sharpening, Phone Ringing, Light Switch, Door Opening."[32] Some were musicological (such as Ry Cooder and Ticking Bomb), but most contributed to the soundscape of household labor, a sonic amplification of what it meant literally and metaphorically to build the master's house.

As the technological operating systems emerged, Weems worked on financial and interpersonal domains of the project. She typed up budget lists, hoping to pay actors as much as possible while honoring design and materials fees.[33] She rented the Chelsea loft less than legally for $1,000: "We were in a space that was completely unregulated."[34] She also assembled a circle of collaborators, including lighting designer Jennifer Tipton. Writing from her East Village apartment (at that time, The Builders' production office) to Jennifer Tipton "c/o The Guthrie Theater," Weems apologized for not being able to send "sketches" and hoped to arrange a conversation among herself, Tipton, and Cleater. After recounting their "great fortune" in securing rehearsal space in the 70,000 square foot space that "Reza Abdoh used last winter, and that Elizabeth Streb is using now," she acknowledged to Tipton that the lighting design process was going to be a little unusual: "Unfortunately there isn't really a grid." Additionally, Weems admitted that the rhythms of the development process were nontraditional: "We're planning a rehearse/build/rehearse/build schedule, so that there'll be a dialogue between the performers and the construction of the set."[35] In other words, the exploration of the technologies of "building" meant that set-building was not an autonomous process and that "tech week" could not be conveniently scheduled just before opening. The "set" and its technology were copresent actors in the space, hence both sentient and nonsentient components of the "dependent" ensemble needed to be conceived simultaneously. By placing "building" at the center of the production, MASTER BUILDER anticipated another of The Builders Association's working methods. In The Builders' process, as Weems has often said, "every week is tech week."[36]

Under "other news" to Tipton, Weems reported that she had a possible lead on a producer—an aspect of administrative and infrastructural coordination that she was anxious to find "so that the piece could have a 'life' beyond what I could provide." By the end, she apologized again: "I'm sorry that this is heavy on administrative details and light on the fun part—but that is why I need a producer. Anyway, we'll have fun as soon as we meet."[37] In the absence of a producer, Weems continued to work on project development for MASTER BUILDER even as she finished old projects: "Dearest Valerie: Thanks so much for calling. I have been running like a chicken with its head cut off (do you say that in Scotland?) because we are trying to finish the film edit of *Roy Cohn/Jack Smith* this month.

Not. (Do you say that in Scotland?) Anyway, I truly appreciate your ongoing interest in MASTER BUILDER…. I can't say that I will have anything ready to show at Tramway in June…. Should we consider the possibility of a residency?"[38] In working with international presenting organizations, she hoped to find access to an apparatus of production and rehearsal support, asking if a "presenter" could become a "producer," turning the pursuit of the final product into a resource to support its R&D and the development of its Operating Systems.

REHEARSAL/ASSEMBLY

With its deeply imbricated processes of acting and design, MASTER BUILDER's rehearsal and performance process pushed the bounds of interdisciplinarity. Following the "umbilical cords" of an interarts collaboration, artists found themselves engaging with other artists who had only a vague understanding of their respective forms. Some were there to act and to dismantle a canonical dramatic text. For others, the project was primarily a design puzzle, whether in architectural, filmic, or sonic terms. Weems found herself amid "all these people who didn't know how theater was supposed to work," supporting the process of actors in an increasingly complex apparatus: "It was almost like I was stealth staging."[39]

But using this precariously rewired house as a set also meant changing actors' processes. Weems composed a game structure that, "as a staging device," did not allow any actor to occupy bodily the same "room" at the same time as another actor. Scenes were played as actors occupied different quadrants of the house, some delivering their lines in direct address and others acting with the screened presence of a live video feed from another room. The structure provoked a question about how proximity and intimacy could be created by joining the projective acting technique of a performer with the differently projective screen techniques of a video system. Here is one more place where techniques of theatrical acting and techniques of mediating technology developed coincidentally.

In addition to the ongoing creation of a script, the troupe slowly developed a scene-by-scene video score for where actors stood in space, how they should direct their gaze, and how their gaze would be

captured, projected, or distributed across different quandrants of the space. The skills of acting for the camera thus had an early incarnation in this first production. In later productions, the theatrical mise-en-scène required actors to hit their marks in a way that mimicked the work habits of a film studio as much as a theater. Technical operators mixed live bodies and screened presence on the spot so that the whole house became an expansive editing space. The preproduction process of theatrical rehearsal thus integrated and depended on the postproduction process of the cinema.

Balancing acting styles in a multiperspectival space brought new challenges, and the actors worked with Weems to modulate their performances. "Work on making all lines extremely conversational & natural—think transcript audiotape of real conversations," Weems wrote in her journal: "Kyle [deCamp] and David [Pence] are ungrounded & surfacey, too many conflicting styles."[40] Actors tried new techniques to maintain their ground in a space that was coming apart. Coco McPherson, who played Kaia, joined David Pence in an improvised warm-up before every rehearsal. She placed herself underneath the house, while he sat in the attic on top of the space. From there, they used microphones as they improvised dialogue with each other, asking, describing, and performatively creating a world that they were not exactly cohabiting. Their sequences focused on themes of agoraphobia ("I have been having a really hard time leaving my house") but spun out in different directions, recalling a couple who "moved again and again to keep their marriage alive," a family with "five sons, one daughter who lit herself on fire," speculations on the discomfort of "a gallery opening where no one comes," and questions such as "did I ever tell you about the time the house fell on my friend?" or what can be done when "there is a hair in your contact lens?" By creating the interactive trust required of successful improvisation, they and other actors overcame spatial distance to create an oddly amplified intimacy.

The improvised sequence proved so resonant that they integrated it into the beginning of the show. After Joel the master carpenter introduced his tools, house and stage lights came down, and Coco and David begin to speak in the dark. David's question became the first line: "Did I ever tell you about the time the house fell on my friend?" "Yes," was Coco's matter-of-fact reply, pressing further to learn more about the story but eventually reminding David that he would need to start acting soon: "We are right at the top of the first act, David, and you have lines coming up." After this sequence, the familiar lines of Ibsen's canonical play did indeed come up, welcomed in by the rising chords of Led Zeppelin's "Houses of the Holy," whose lyrics—about gardens, houses, Satan's daughter, and "heeding the Master's call"—resonated with the play's themes.

Performer David Pence rehearses with a "bottle mic" created by Ben Rubin.

Dancers Emma Strahs, Coco McPherson, Jeff Webster,
Kyle deCamp.

Performer Coco McPherson improvising dialog while stationed under the house.

The actors interacted with the image of their scene partners on monitors and sometimes seemed to respond to a presence sensed and felt in the atmosphere, even when the actual body was located in another room of the house. This spatial technique offset the metaphors of intimacy and domesticity already embedded in Ibsen's text. Halvard Solness opens his conversation with his assistant and sometime mistress, Kaia, on separate floors of the house. When he asserts that "I need to have you close to me every day," their physical distance heightens the urgency of the assertion but also questions its sincerity. In a later scene, Solness conducts a heated conversation with Dr. Herdal about his health, his work, and his future. A line like "It's so obvious to me, Doctor, that you come here to keep an eye on me," had an eerie resonance amid television screens that seemed to double as surveillance systems. And when Miss Hilde Wangel enters the house, her presence is all the more menacing and compelling for being out of reach. In her earlier scenes, she forced Solness to recall the vertigo that besieged him atop his own magnificent tower as well as the kiss he scandalously pressed on her that day when she was not quite thirteen. In these and later scenes, Kyle deCamp's Hilde stalked Solness as he came to terms with his obsessions, following him as an image on a screen, seducing him as a presence felt on the other side of the wall. "I know what you'll build next," she urged him toward self-destruction, "a terribly high tower."

MASTER BUILDER's assembly of bodies in space also underscored the gendered assumptions and gendered anxieties of Ibsen's text. While performances of Ibsen's text often naturalize the roles of mother, whore, helpmate, and temptress in the play's female characters, their presentation inside the divided home and among the spectral screens of MASTER BUILDER suggested that they were also the projections and fantasies of Halvard's imagination. Inspired by her readings of Mulvey, Spain, and Colomina, Weems staged her young female actors to hide throughout the house and then settle at the top of the house in an attic space. From there, they embodied the devil angels that preoccupied Solness, ominously giggling, sighing, or calling in terror in response to the action below.

Underneath this depiction of hormonal hysterics, Weems placed Aline Solness, the childless mother and long-suffering wife of Halvard. Jane Smith played Aline from her second-floor bedroom and never moved from that location. Embodying the conventional stasis of maternal domesticity, Aline spoke resolutely from her immobile position. At some moments, she recalled all that she lost in the fire, and at others, she was silent but present, acting as a stoic witness even as her husband carried on with Kaia or Hilde in other parts of her house. In the final scene of the play, Aline learns that there will be a ceremony to celebrate Halvard's latest edifice and that he intends to climb to the top

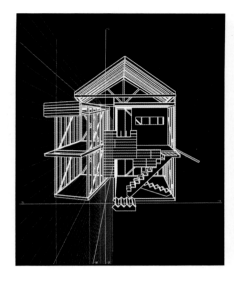

Early design sketch for MASTER BUILDER.

Installation at the Storefront for Art and Architecture, New York. After the involuntary closing of MASTER BUILDER, the company installed one room of the house in a gallery setting in 1995. The scene between Jane Smith and Kyle deCamp was reframed in a fragment of the structure of the house.

of the tower. Alarmed by the news and sure that his vertigo will overpower him, Aline knows that she must leave the house and join the dreaded ceremony as part of her duty to her husband. Anticipating danger in the midst of festive celebration, she asks Ragnar, "Are we to have music, too?" "Yes," he replies, "it's the Builders' Association."

CLOSINGS

The building of MASTER BUILDER came to an abrupt end in the winter of 1994 when some unexpected visitors interrupted rehearsal in the Chelsea industrial space. "Some realtors who looked 'real' came into the building," recalled Weems, "and asked 'what the hell are you people doing in here?'" Whether realtors, property managers, or prospective developers, these guests told the artists that they needed to leave immediately. The property was about to start a process of rehabilitation and revitalization—and eventually became the upscale Chelsea Market. MASTER BUILDER's timing thus

The ensemble in 1994.

coincided with that of another building process that gentrified the neighborhood with a new "creative" identity that required artists to leave.

In this case, the artists managed to convince the agents to allow them a few days to load out. They used the borrowed time to spread the word that they would hold two surreptitious evening performances. About two hundred audience members came each night. Some sat close to the house, and others sat on the sides or farther away. The performance unfolded as planned—Cichowski's Sawzall monologue, the improvised phone calls, and Ibsen's text performed by actors who kicked through walls, smashed triggers, and performed both live and on live camera. The sonic triggers, the architectural tricks, and the musical loops cohered into a precarious assembly. The performance culminated in the final moments of the master builder's downward plunge. Kyle deCamp's Hilde waved and yelled, describing his rise and fall with mad delight; Jeff Webster's Solness spun wildly on a rotating wall. And as the master builder fell to his death, two young women emerged from the house to claim the power to dismantle it. They pried apart the structure from the middle, and when the house opened up, a blade of light came through the interior. As the young women pushed the house open wider, the light expanded in white luminescence, engulfing the stage in a theatrical version of a mini-apocalypse.

After the performance, the audience was invited onto the stage and into the house. As guests at an art show that was about to come down and as fellow makers curious about the how-to's of the set, audience members tapped on sound triggers, investigated trap doors, rotated walls, and followed wiring to figure out which live camera led to which room. After two shows, the house was pulled down. Some parts were packed away, and others were donated to a Boy Scout camp (where the lumber eventually was used to build a stage). For Weems and other artists, the experiment had been crucial, allowing them a chance to adapt artistic strategies drawn from different places as well as to follow through on some new aesthetic propositions. Weems's mentor Susan Sontag offered a morale boost that Weems recorded in her journal: "Sontag was divine after the show. She said it was more subtle, elegant and funny than she had ever pictured it from my descriptions. She said that I would have to defend myself against 'charges' of similarity to The Wooster Group ('people talking to tv's') but

Performer Jeff Webster falling down the stairs of the house.

that at some point someone invented the proscenium stage too and that they weren't the only ones to use it. She said the difference was that it was 'more emotional, more moving' (!) I think she meant more psychologically-based which would make sense—Liz = formal abstraction, MW = return to more psychology, but with a twist."[41]

At the same time, Weems recorded the sadness of seeing the experiment coming to an end before it had time to live. She wrote in her journal:

The piece has found its skeletal structure and now the performers can go deeper into it and live in that world. I can't believe we have to stop now. All the wheels are just beginning to turn—the group is coalescing, the word-of-mouth is working. I am beginning to finesse the structure and it all has to come down. I feel sick.[42]

Of course, the experiment of building was only just beginning. The "coalescence" of a new group of artists would continue, even as some of its members changed and returned for different projects. The word-of-mouth communication about the MASTER BUILDER experiment circulated well past the two days of its limited run, emboldening Weems and collaborators to do more. In honor of the play that launched the group, Webster suggested they adopt the name The Builders Association. Luckily, they had been working with Michael Meyer's translation, or they might have been named The Masons Union.

ENDNOTES

Artist's Voice: Jeff Webster, performer/co-creator

The MASTER BUILDER house was split in two with a space maybe a foot wide between the two storied sections. Cleater found this old beat-up overstuffed chair, and he cut it in two and put a half on each side of this divide. I loved to sit in that half chair and feel the life of the house—scenes being rehearsed, barely audible voices from the upper floors, people clomping around on the floor directly above, images on the monitor screens. It wasn't like being on a set, and it allowed the performers to emerge into the performance layer and then recede into this other intimate, almost private layer.

I remember that once in the early rehearsal period of MASTER BUILDER, before the giant house was built, we had set up some scaffolding to stand in for the set. One day, David Pence and I got up on the scaffolding, and for some obscure and long-forgotten reason, we belted ourselves into these plastic bucket-type chairs and tried to improvise a scene. There wasn't a lot of room on this scaffold, and when one of us moved or turned, we would practically knock the other one off the scaffold. Of course, nothing from that particular inspirational moment made it into the show, but the accumulation of many, many such moments greatly informed the spirit of the performance. The early rehearsals had this feeling like when you were eight years old and the summer stretched out ahead.

In the first stages of rehearsal for MASTER BUILDER, I began making tape loops on an old reel-to-reel tape recorder. It was ridiculously cumbersome—splicing blocks and cellophane tape, endlessly trimming tiny bits of tape to try to make the loop work rhythmically: something that would take seconds on a computer today. Some of the loops were so long they stretched out of the bedroom down the hall into the living room and back again. I'd have the tape propped on various improvised sticks and mic stands and broom handles to keep it from getting tangled. Then I would let the loop play for thirty or forty minutes while I recorded it on cassette.

In the MASTER BUILDER, Jane Smith played the role of Aline Solness, Halvard Solness's long-suffering wife. She sat in one of the upper rooms of Cleater's two-by-four house like a queen locked away in some remote tower. Her voice was commanding yet fragile, even brittle. She had the most incredible presence, and her performance was breathtakingly beautiful. I've carried her performance with me all these years as a kind of barometer that I've aspired to—simple, elegant, direct, abstract, but also deeply personal.

In rehearsal, it quickly became clear that we were desperate for a sound designer/operator. After making some inquiries, Dan Dobson emerged as the leading candidate for the job. Marianne and I met with Dan, and it was clear that he was perfect for the job because (a) he played guitar and (b) he was thinking about going to cooking school. Of all the decisions made during those early days of The Builders, hiring Dan was the most important and prescient. His work and dedication shaped the company and elevated the esthetic more than anyone other than Marianne.

Rehearsing and performing The Builders' work are often compared to working on a film set, but for me it's more like being in some odd little orchestra. You have your own part of the score to perform, and it's supposed to intersect or augment or harmonize with half a dozen other elements or scores. Like in an orchestra, when everyone is playing their part of the score, coming in exactly on cue with the correct intonation and dynamic, it sounds great. But when the elements get slightly off, there is a cascade that is difficult to get back on track.

One of the oddities of touring with The Builders Association is that there seems to be an assumption that the company, because of the name, will be most comfortable in close proximity to a construction site. On a tour to Singapore, I remember arriving exhausted in the middle of the night and being very excited because the hotel looked quite promising. I went up to the room, and it was fairly large, with the requisite minibar and so on. One end of the room was covered by a large curtain, and when I opened the drapes, the view was of an entire city block under construction—work continuing apparently around the clock.

The apotheosis of this phenomenon was in Rennes. Of course, the hotel was under renovation. And one morning, I went down to breakfast, and when I returned to my room, it had disappeared. All that was left was the four walls and the plumbing stubouts. While I was at breakfast, the construction had removed everything in the room—bed, furniture, sink, bathtub, everything.

Artist's Voice: Jennifer Tipton, lighting designer

Only when human beings become angels is there a possibility of Utopia:

But I recently worked on a project done despite overwhelming odds by young people, a play about young people tearing down a house and rebuilding a new one on the foundation of the old, based on Ibsen's *The Master Builder*. I had quarrels with the final production but it was important work. My students adored it, saying "This is the kind of theater we should be doing." And the teenaged friends of two of the actors loved the production. The people involved were deeply concerned and committed to what they were doing—to process, not just product. I felt privileged to be working with them. If there is an ideal situation, this was it. Now wouldn't it be wonderful if we supported such work?

[Source: "Utopia Forum," *Theater* 26 (1995).]

Susan Sontag
470 West 24th Street
New York, New York 10011

October 14, 1994

Dear Marianne,

You've asked me to put in writing some impressions of *Master Builder*, which I'm glad to do.

I think *Master Builder* is one of the most valuable and original theater projects being done anywhere in this country. Even at the early work-in-progress stage at which I saw it this autumn, I could see more than potential. I saw a work that seemed to me brilliantly conceived and already articulated in such a way as to communicate intensely with an audience.

You have splendid actors, you have in Jennifer Tipton the best lighting designer in America, and you have an enthralling set and visual design. I was very taken by the text you've written, and the way it intensified and updated the themes of Ibsen's play. I was enthralled by the use you made of the scenic language of the Wooster Group. There is nothing derivative in your use of this language: the television monitors, etc. You have used this scenic language to take it one step further---toward a greater intimacy of effect.

There is very little in the contemporary American theater that I admire or that seems to me to contribute much in the way of pleasure or thoughtfulness. What you are doing is really outstanding and I hope with all my heart that *Master Builder* gets the support it deserves.

As ever,

Susan

People

Directed by Marianne Weems

Set design by John Cleater

Sound design by Dan Dobson

Video design by Ben Rubin

Lighting designed by Jennifer Tipton

Performed by

Jeff Webster—Halvard Solness

Jane Smith—Aline Solness

Kyle deCamp—Hilde Wangel

David Pence—Doctor Herbal, Ragnar Brovik, Man on phone

Coco McPherson—Kaja Folsi, Woman on phone

Emma Strahs and Sheryl Haiduck—The Young

Joel Cichowski—Carpenter in prologue

Paul Lazar—Special guest

Video associates: Peter Norrman, Amber Lasciak

Lighting associate: Allen Hahn

Original female vocal music: Frank London

Camera operators: Amber Lasciak, Aimée Guillot

Analog loops: Jeff Webster, David Pence

Film and archival footage: Rebecca Baron

Lighting board operator: Georg Bugiel

Technical director: Michael Casselli

Assistant director/stage manager: Matthew Dawson

Assistant to the director: Aimée Guillot

Audio system: MacPherson Audio

Production assistant: Amanda Exley

Rigging/engineering consultant: Bill Ballou

Set construction: Henry Buckingham, Joel Cichowski, Yoma Karim, Richard Herbet,
    Greg Meriweather, Rhett Russo

Table design: Eve Sussman

Production documentation: Peter Norrman

Project consultant: Melanie Joseph

Management: Sue West

Venues

1993–1994   Industrial space, 460 West 16th Street, New York, NY

1995   Storefront for Art and Architecture, New York, NY

Afterparty

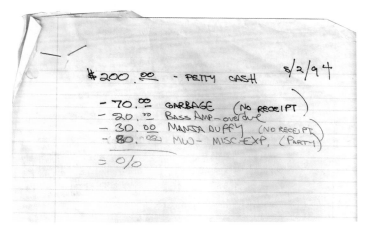

Budget for MASTER BUILDER.

SOME SOURCE MATERIALS FOR THE PRODUCTION

Books

Archer, William, ed. *From Ibsen's Workshop: Notes, Scenarios and Drafts to the Modern Plays.* New York: Scribner, 1913.

Bachelard, Gaston. *The Poetics of Space.* Boston, MA: Beacon Press, 1994.

Bahman, Reyner. *Theory and Design in the First Machine Age.* Cambridge, MA: MIT Press, 1960.

Carver, Raymond. *Cathedral.* London: Vintage, 1981.

Clurman, Harold. *Ibsen.* New York: Macmillan, 1977.

Colomina, Beatriz, ed. *Sexuality and Space.* Princeton, NJ: Princeton Architectural Press, 1992.

de Certeau, Michelle. *The Practice of Everyday Life.* Oakland: University of California Press, 1984.

Gilbert, Sandra, and Susan Gubar. *The Madwoman in the Attic: The Woman Writer and the Nineteenth-Century Literary Imagination.* New Haven, CT: Yale University Press, 1979.

Gilman, Charlotte Perkins. *The Yellow Wallpaper.* 1899. Reprint, Washington, DC: Orchises Press, 1990.

Harbison, Robert. *The Built, the Unbuilt, and the Unbuildable: In Pursuit of Architectural Meaning.* Cambridge, MA: MIT Press, 1991.

Hubbard, William. *Complicity and Conviction: Steps toward Architecture of Convention.* Cambridge, MA: MIT Press, 1982.

Ibsen, Henrik. *The Master Builder.* Translated by Edmund Gosse and William Archer. London: Heinemann, 1893.

Jackson, Shirley. *The Haunting of Hill House.* New York: Viking, 1959.

Levy, Mattys, and Mario Salvadori. *Why Buildings Fall Down: Why Structures Fail.* New York: Norton, 1992.

Matta-Clark, Gordon. Various writings.

Meyer, Michael. *Ibsen: A Biography.* London: Hart-Davis, 1967.

Robinson, Marilynne. *Housekeeping.* New York: Farrar, Straus and Giroux, 1980.

Salinger, J. D. *Raise High the Roof Beam, Carpenters.* New York: Little, Brown, 1955.

Smithson, Robert. Various writings.

Spain, Daphne. *Gendered Spaces.* Chapel Hill: University of North Carolina Press, 1992.

Vitruvius. *The Ten Books on Architecture.* Translated by Morris Hickey Morgan. Cambridge, MA: Harvard University Press, 1914.

Films and Television

The Atomic Man. Directed by Ken Hughes. London: Merton Park Studios, 1955.

The Dick Van Dyke Show. Various episodes. CBS, 1961–1966.

"The Free Paint Job." *Green Acres.* CBS, 1971.

Home Improvement. Various episodes. ABC, 1991–1999.

Home Shopping Network. Commentary by Lucy Sexton. HSN, n.d.

The Innocents. Directed by Jack Clayton. London and Los Angeles: Achilles, Twentieth Century Fox Film Corporation,1961.

Izzat Ki Roti. Directed by K. Pappu. Delhi: Inderjit Films Combine, 1993.

Matta-Clark, Gordon. Various films.

Notorious. Directed by Alfred Hitchcock. Los Angeles: Vanguard Films, 1946.

Picnic at Hanging Rock. Directed by Peter Weir. Sydney: Australian Film Commission, McElroy & McElroy, Picnic Productions, 1975.

Playtime. Directed by Jacques Tati. Paris: Jolly Film, Specta Films, 1967.

Poltergeist. Directed by Tobe Hooper. Los Angeles: Metro-Goldwyn-Mayer, SLM Production Group, 1982.

Rebecca. Directed by Alfred Hitchcock. Los Angeles: Selznick International Pictures, 1940.

Sacrifice. Directed by Andrei Tarkovsky. Stockholm and Paris: Svenska Filminstitutet, Argos Films, 1986.

Secret beyond the Door. Directed by Fritz Lang. Los Angeles: Diana Production Company, Universal Pictures, 1947.

The Shining. Directed by Stanley Kubrick. Los Angeles and London: Warner Bros., Hawk Films, 1980.

Suspicion. Directed by Alfred Hitchcock. Los Angeles: RKO Radio Pictures, 1941.

This Old House. Various episodes. PBS, 1979–2014.

Songs

Blue Öyster Cult, "(Don't Fear) the Reaper"

Led Zeppelin, "In the Light"

Led Zeppelin, "(Living Loving Maid) She's Just a Woman"

Led Zeppelin, "Kashmir"

Led Zeppelin, "Nobody's Fault But Mine"

Led Zeppelin, "No Quarter"

Led Zeppelin, "Whole Lotta Love"

Other

Brontë, Charlotte. *Jane Eyre.* 1847. Longmeadow Press, 1983. Jane Eyre's monologue from the ramparts.

Children's consciousness.

Faulkner, William. *As I Lay Dying.* 1930. New York: Vintage, 1991.

Ibsen, Henrik. *A Doll's House.* 1879. New York: Dover Thrift Edition, 1991. Nora's lines.

The Practical Householder. Magazine, 1933–1963

Woolf, Virginia. *To the Lighthouse.* 1927. San Diego: Harcourt Brace Jovanovich, 1993. Mrs. Ramsey.

2 FAUST

THEATER AS POSTPRODUCTION

Performers onstage and onscreen, Theater Neumarkt 1996.

OPENINGS

When lights came up in Zürich's Theater Neumarkt in October of 1996, it could have been a night at the movies. The only luminescence in the darkened theater came from the projection on-screen. The title "ROUTE 66" appeared on the screen, followed by a rear shot of a man sitting behind a car steering wheel and the sounds of the man mumbling to himself. An ominous wind blew in the background. "Dear one ... dear one," he said as he drove down the highway that spread out before him. For a moment, the rear-view mirror appeared to be a screen within a screen, showing the furrow of the man's brow as he muttered:

Dear One, I'm writing you from an airplane above your country. The computer breakdown continues over most of the hemisphere. The nation's in a coma.

We're just about over the border now. I don't know if you'll ever get this. As we move away, we see only smoke and light. It's hard to tell if it's fog or exhaust or light from the city, but I hate to tell you that your city is destroyed while you're still in it. But then, you may know that already. Then again, we both know it's true and you're just a photograph in my hands now. And your city is smoke and vapor.[1]

As the monologue continued, the rear-view mirror began to expand, reflecting the fixed stare of the driver's eyes as he recounted a horror story—the bombing of a city, perhaps the bombing of Dresden?—in which he seemed to have taken part. Suddenly, the back of a woman's head dressed as the devil appeared behind that of the driver, and he registered her face looking at him in the rear-view mirror. It was at that moment when the screen cut to a title image—"ROOM 202"—and lights came up on what appeared to be a film set placed in the theater. Suddenly, the audience realized that the screen was in fact perched on a truss that enclosed a stage set made up to look like the film set of a generic hotel room. The car driver, Faust, played by performer Jeff Webster, was now live onstage, and he paced before a lone bed and table, looking at himself in a small mirror as he made his deal with the devil: "If he will give me four and twenty years, letting me live in all voluptuousness, to have thee ever to attend on me, and give me whatsoever I command, on these conditions, I resigneth to."

Above him, the devil, played by Kyle deCamp, sat quietly with a small camera mounted on her chair. Faust looked into the mirror while viewers—the theater audience members and the cinematic spectators—saw Faust seeing both his own reflection and also the superimposed image of the female devil who enticed him. "Then Faustus," she declared, gesturing into her camera, "stab your arm courageously, and find your soul, so that at some certain day, great Lucifer may claim it as his own." The audience saw what Faust saw and also witnessed the technological magic that made the devil appear in the mirror's frame.

STORYBOARD

Despite its truncated run, MASTER BUILDER generated enough postshow excitement to give its collaborators the hope that there would be a next show. A few next shows were proposed, including a staging of the Beatles' *White Album* that came to fruition in a workshop production created with students at New York University's Experimental Theater Wing. However, The Builders Association's next full-scale effort produced a pair of distinct but related pieces. IMPERIAL MOTEL (FAUST) and JUMP CUT (FAUST) reimagined the Faust myth for a contemporary technological age and experimented with different conceptual questions as the cast and crew moved across technological and performance laboratories in the United States and Europe.

Although MASTER BUILDER produced an animated buzz about a new, young, cutting-edge New York theater company, The Builders received their next offer of production support not from the United States but from Europe. The pattern reproduced one familiar to young theater companies that are discovered as the next great "American theater company" by European producers before many American producers seem to know about them. Producers at the Theater Neumarkt in Zürich were keen to talk to Marianne Weems and her collaborators about a next project. After they exchanged faxes and phone calls, she flew to meet them to begin to hammer out the details of a new piece that Theater Neumarkt would fund if guaranteed the premiere. Weems was already clear that she wanted to continue to juxtapose stage and screen, building on the concept of live editing as a kind of performance form that The Builders had begun to explore inside the house built for MASTER BUILDER. She and collaborator Jeff Webster proposed to Neumarkt producers Stephan Müller and Heiner Volker a few possibilities, including a deconstructed reenactment of *Mildred Pierce* or *Who's Afraid of Virginia Woolf?*

When they also suggested *Faust*, Müller and Volker jumped. The possibility of a young and brash American company taking apart one of the most canonical texts of European literature was too provocative to pass up. At their brainstorming session, Müller and Volker began to list source material that they hoped Weems would explore, including a classic Faust film by Gustav Gründgens. They revealed the surprising news that the actress who had played a young Gretchen in the Gründgens film (Ella Büchi) had retired nearby in Zürich. Perhaps she could be persuaded to join a reenactment now? Like all presenters concerned about funds, they had to limit the size of the cast to four to five performers, and they asked for two to three to be cast from within their Swiss pool of actors. Weems made notes about necessary follow-up, promising to send resumés and a preliminary budget and to research Faust historiography. Before leaving, Müller and Volker promised to support financially a process of research and rehearsal. In true Faustian spirit, they sealed the deal with a drop of blood.

IMPERIAL MOTEL (FAUST) and its successor JUMP CUT (FAUST) continued The Builders Association practice of using a classic text as primary source material. Weems commissioned the playwright John Jesurun to reconstruct the Faust story in order to dismantle it in postdramatic fashion. In a group packet of research prepared for the cast and collaborators, Weems shared the long history of the Faust story, which dated to the Simon Magus legends before the fourth century. Her summary included aspects of the legend that were most important to her. The notes described legends that "center around an individual who has a reputation as a practitioner of black magic, is known for a career of remarkable feats, and dies under mysterious circumstances."[2] By the early 1500s, there were many historic citations of a living Faust, a self-invented "conjurer, sodomite, and global traveler" and often "a doctor, a trickster, and charlatan ... some versions told that he had sold his soul in exchange for knowledge and magical power."[3] These early tales paved the way for a series of classic retellings, including puppet plays, Christopher Marlowe's *The Tragicall History of the Life and Death of Doctor Faustus* (1592), and Johann Wolfgang von Goethe's magnum opus. In Goethe's *Faust* (1808– 1831), which took half a lifetime to write, part 1 tells the story of Faust's pact with Mephistopheles and his seduction of Gretchen, and part 2 expands the Faust tale to meditate on the fundamental cosmological, scientific, and ethical questions of Weimar during Goethe's lifetime.

In researching Goethe's *Faust*, Weems, with the help of several dramaturgs, found the abridged transcripts of the trial of Susanna Margaretha Brandt, who had been Goethe's inspiration for the character of Gretchen. After Brandt scandalized her village by reportedly murdering her illegitimate child, her defense argued that she had been possessed by the devil. In Goethe's adaptation of the tale, Susanna becomes Gretchen, a woman who is corrupted and possessed by Faust's dark magical powers. Weems gave the trial transcript to Jesurun to inspire his own engagement with the story, and his text mixed epic lyricism with punctuating contemporary references. Jesurun had a habit of keeping his radio tuned to pop songs while writing, and after listening to the Beach Boys' "Help Me Rhonda," he titled the script "The Trial of Rhonda Gretchen Kindermoerd." Other musical catch phrases populated the text, including fragments from the Beatles' "Across the Universe."

Faust was in many ways a kind of Rorschach exercise, a vehicle through which each period's social ideals, anxieties, and corruptions could be vetted or disavowed. Max Reinhardt's production (1909) endured Nazi criticism, and F. W. Murnau's film version (1926) reportedly depoliticized some elements of the story to avoid Nazi retribution. The Faust character came across as corrupt in some versions and misguided in others, responding to the contextual needs of the moment. Jesurun tried for a script that mixed linguistic styles and left his own allegiances unclear. A *Village Voice* review describes the result: "Jesurun's floods of language, with their never-ending shifts of allusion from antique poetry to 60's pop [were] given carefully measured areas in which to bloom, like demented verbal sunflowers."

Trial of Susanna Margaretha Brandt

question 5

Had she not after this felt the life of a child, or contractions or abdominal pains and furthermore had she not felt her breasts swell?

reply

Until the birth she had neither felt contractions nor the life of a child inside of her. There was something occurring insider of her though, it was something hard, like a stone, falling once to the right, then to the left, which she had not known to be a child, otherwise she would have reported of it to her mistress and to her sisters whom she had visited many times about four weeks prior.

...

question 7

Why had she not taken someone to be with her, or called for someone?

reply

The wash-house was some distance to the back of the house, she had been exhausted and the pains had overcome her at such impetuous hurry that she had not been able to call out.

question 8

Whereto did she take the child from Mrs. Bauer's wash-house?

reply

When the child had dropped out of her and onto the ground, she picked it up from the ground by the neck. There was a croaking in its throat, otherwise she could make out no other signs of life, as far as she could remember. Thereafter she carried it into the stable and covered it there with a little hay and straw,

Source: Birkner, Siegfried. *The life and death of the child murderess Susanna Margaretha Brandt.* Frankfurt: Insel Verlag, 1973.

Goethe's Faust

MARGARETE. What can I do, I'm in your power.
    Only let me nurse my baby first.
    All night long I hugged the dear creature;

    taking hold of the chains to unlock them]

MARGARETE. *[On her knees]* Headsman, so
    early, it isn't right.
    Have mercy on me! Too soon, too soon!
    You come for me in the dead of night –
    Isn't it time enough at dawn?
    [Stands up]
    I'm still so young, too young surely –
    Still I must die.
    How pretty I was, that's what undid me.
    He held me so close, how he's far away,
    My wreath pulled apart, the flowers
    scattered.
    How rough your hands are! Please, won't
    you spare me?
    What did I ever do to you?
    Don't let me beg in vain for mercy,
    I never before laid eyes on you.
    They took it from me out of spite
    And now they say I murdered it.
    And I'll never be happy, no, never again.
    They've made up songs to sing about
    me. It's wicked of them.
    There's an old fairy tale ends that way,

The Trial of Rhonda Gretchen Kindermoerd by John Jesurun

M:
We have here this signed testimony from you yourself Miss Kindermoerd.

F: (*indecisive throughout scene*)
It was drug induced
And so it cannot be admitted as evidence.

M:
I'll read it anyway.
The defendant was asked:
Why did you wait so long to confess?
She replied:
I killed the kid
I'm glad I did.
She was then asked:
Was it painful?
She replied:
It was not at all painful. I was overjoyed to do it!
I was haunted, taunted by this baby.
This prickly lilly in me.
I wanted to wilt it.
            so I kilt it.
I was glad I willed it.
            spilt its
Blood where ever I could.
Redeemed it.
Creamed it.
Turned the spud into a dud.

Three texts from Weems's dramaturgical research: Transcript of Susanna Margaretha Brandt's 1772 trial; Johann Wolfgang von Goethe, *Faust* (1828), John Jesurun, "The Trial of Rhonda Gretchen Kindermoerd" (1996).

After the initial pitch and blood-bound agreement with the Swiss producers, The Builders held a workshop in an abandoned office building on Broad Street in the Wall Street area of New York. In 1995, the year preceding the premiere, the United States was in the midst of an incredible story with a possessed man at its center. On April 19, 1995, in Oklahoma City, bombs were detonated in the Alfred B. Murrah Federal Building, and 168 people lost their lives, including nineteen children. Investigators soon found a prime suspect, a former army gunner named Timothy McVeigh who had strong ties to neo-Nazi groups. Reporters chronicled his fraught childhood, his military aspirations, and his affiliations with white supremacist groups. Fellow soldiers retroactively interpreted odd behaviors in the barracks, including McVeigh's propensity to keep a large store of guns on hand at every moment. In what *New Yorker* writer Michael Kelly called "The Road to Paranoia," the country gradually formed a picture of a man whose sense of superiority was stoked by a bloated fear of government conspiracy, a mixture that rationalized in his mind the necessity of violence.[4]

Weems was struck by a *New York Times* article that described McVeigh's vigil of several weeks in a southwest motel room where he hid alone with the curtains drawn until the day of the attack. Company members Ben Rubin, John Cleater, and Weems eventually made a pilgrimage to this motel—the Imperial Motel in Kingman, Arizona—which became a central touchstone for the show. If there was a loose analogy to be made to Faust, it lay in the possibility of Timothy McVeigh's pact with a dark spirit amid a life of "solitude and obsessions" that recalled the hermetic life of Faust in his cryptic library of dark magic and corrupted wisdom.[5] Investigators uncovered eight months of planning, including the rental of storage units to house more and more explosives. They retraced McVeigh's movements between the Dreamland Motel of Junction City, Kansas, and the Imperial Motel in Kingman, Arizona, where, sitting alone for days on end, he resolved to keep up his end of the deal.[6]

R&D

While the McVeigh intertext formed a contemporary and ominous storyboard in juxtaposition with the Faust tale, the R&D behind IMPERIAL MOTEL (FAUST) brought forward other analogies to

Faust's history as a magician, trickster, and global traveler. Advancing a theme that followed most of their work, The Builders saw Faust as a metaphor for theater's long history of collaboration with new technology, an exchange that can appear to some as the selling of a theatrical soul. What began to intrigue Weems was the fantastical history that theater shared with early cinematic invention, including the cinematic experiments that propelled Georges Méliès's *The Damnation of Faust* (1898) and Murnau's *Faust*.

In reading early critical treatises, from Frederick A. Talbot's *Moving Pictures: How They Are Made and Worked* (1912) to recent scholarship, such as Tom Gunning's "The Cinema of Attractions: Early Film, Its Spectator, and the Avant-Garde" (1986), Weems and her collaborators identified their interest in the role of the stage as a platform for performing technology. For Talbot and contemporaries such as Méliès, the appeal of the cinema lay most crucially in its capacities to trick the eye and challenge optical possibility. The tools of "cinematographic chicanery" expanded in the use of double exposures, reverse motion, size expansion and contraction, and splices and cuts that made people seem to appear and reappear, shrink and expand.[7] The appeal also lay in watching the apparatus perform such tricks. Long before the highly sutured cinema that repressed its own apparatus, the placement of early screen practice in an open theater provided a venue to watch those tricks in action. As Janet Staiger later wrote:

the spectator is never permitted to forget that a theatrical performance is being observed. The dream is the center of attention and like his predecessors—the magician in the Méliès films truc and the sketch artists in early animation films—he is the on-screen presence who creates and then beholds his own magical, impossible creation....The almost obsessive desire to reveal the mechanics of trick photography to the audience ... should be apparent to anyone leafing through trade journals of the day. In contrast to the magician's code of secrecy, these films revel in making known their secrets.[8]

Artists' research trip to Imperial Motel, Kingman, Arizona, 1995.

Imperial Motel signage reconstructed outside Theater Neumarkt, 1996.

George Méliès, *L'Homme à la Tête en Caoutchouc*, 1902.

Gunning elaborated on the significance of this hybrid history of stage and screen, showing how the "cinema of attractions" was primarily an assembly of visual tricks with sound accompaniment displayed by an able showman. Quoting a contemporaneous critic, Abel Gance, on the capacities of the cinema to attend to "the matter of making images seen," Gunning noted that this visual spectacularization of technology was the key attraction: "early audiences went to exhibitions to see machines demonstrated."[9] Weems linked her research to the show in her journal, where she wrote, "Faust is a fascinating character, a kind of sorcerer and he does some incredible tricks. This explains why silent film directors felt it was such an ideal opportunity for them to play with their magic lantern. Our show also plays with this magic."[10]

This kind of theatrical and cinematic conjunction pointed to a different way of imagining both theatrical and cinematic history. It also provided grist for a theater company of mostly nontheater artists who were interested to learn that its performative engagements with cinematic production had a longer history. Although cinephiles condemned the theater as an early enslaver of cinematic possibility and theatrical purists derided the corrupting influence of cinema on their embodied art form, Gunning pointed to a different kind of theater that had enabled cinematic experimentation:

It is the direct address of the audience, in which an attraction is offered to the spectator by a cinema showman, that defines this approach to filmmaking. Theatrical display dominates over narrative absorption, emphasizing the direct stimulation of shock and surprise at the expense of unfolding a story or creating a diegetic universe. The cinema of attractions expends little energy creating characters with psychological motivations or individual personality ... its energy moves out toward an acknowledged spectator rather than inward towards the character-based situations essential to classical narrative.[11]

Rather than precinema, Gunning's scholarship joined that of others, such as Charles Musser, who used the term "screen practice" as a catchall for the variety of popular performance forms that used early projection and sound technology.[12] Such rhetorical moves countered inherited notions of cinematic progress. Rather than casting the nonintegrated assembly of projection, sound, and showmanship as stumbling experiments that eventually gave way to closed, sutured narrative film, Gunning and others argue that such experiments propelled a modernist avant-garde into a domain where artists "spent little energy creating characters" and were not particularly preoccupied with narrative closure. Although "such viewing experiences point more to the traditions of the fairground than to the traditions of the legitimate theater," the relations of the fairground also inspired—in Gunning's view—the nonnarrative, multiperspectival assemblies of avant-garde art experimentation.[13]

Once we acknowledge the connection between cinema and the theatrical fairground (over and above its connection to the "legitimate" or narratively pre-occupied theater) then a wider, intermedia sense of performance comes forward as well. The fairground aesthetic animated the goals behind The Builders' reenactments of the Faust legend. Georges Méliès himself was a kind of Faust figure in his steady pursuit of technical chicanery that seemed spiritual to some and magical to others. Méliès was aware of so-called spirit photography, a nineteenth-century innovation that "meant photographing a shrouded 'spirit' against a black background and then superimposing the image or scene that the spirit is supposed to inhabit."[14] In films such as *The Triple Lady* (1898) and *The Cave of the Demons* (1898), Méliès adapted this technique to cinematography, searching for new vehicles for imagining new optical tricks. More films invoked themes of spiritualism or magic to provide the pretext for new illusions where heads were severed and figures blurred as camera apertures opened and closed. By the time he made *The Damnation of Faust*, Méliès knew how to construct the piece with all manner of "diabolical trimmings."[15] He characterized his own screen practice as an assembly of tricks rather than as a plotting of a story. Méliès's elaboration made clear that his primary interest was in structure and form over the content and progress of a particular narrative: "You could say that the scenario in this case is simply a thread intended to link the 'effects,' in themselves without much relation to each other. I mean to say the scenario has no more than a secondary importance in this genre of composition." Elsewhere, Gunning quotes Méliès as saying, "as for the scenario, the fable, or tale, I only consider it at the end…. I use it merely as a pretext for the 'stage effects,' the 'tricks,' or for a nicely arranged tableau."[16] His succinct rearticulation of his principles could have been a rallying cry for The Builders' evolving process of assembly: "The story simply provides a frame upon which to string a demonstration of the magical possibilities of the cinema."[17]

While such conceptions could be interpreted as simplistic capitulation to the anesthetizing pleasure of technology, they could also provide a link to the principles of modernist composition. In fact, it was a short step from an aesthetic of composition in which effects are "without much relation to each other" to the aesthetic promoted by Gertrude Stein's modernist landscape, which mixes "any detail to any other detail."[18] If postdramatic theater was an extension of a modernist interest in flattening the references that would normally build a progressive plot, then The Builders' extension of this practice was propelled by the memory of a "screen practice" equally uninterested in narrative as anything other than a pre-text for the assembly of "diabolical trimmings." The live remaking of a film for experimental theater thus recalled the long popular history of theater as a place for the display of screen technology. Weems also was interested in the history of early traveling film raconteurs who presented evenings of remixed bits of film that they purchased from the laboratories of Thomas Alva Edison and Edwin S. Porter and combined to mix narrative and technical effects. Such early intermedia travelers provided an intriguing precedent for a contemporary touring intermedia theater company. Weems wrote to her Swiss producers with a progress report:

what is most compelling to me is the space between theater and film, i.e. the illusionistic, magical world created by Georges Méliès and others. We have expanded the idea of the set to play with all the possibilities in the crossover between theatrical and cinematic space. It has become a space where illusions are produced, a film set. So the task of the performance becomes the production of a film—creating the images below ("hell is production") and projecting the seamless, pristine images of the film-in-progress in the space above ("heaven is the icon"). The audience can follow the process of manufacturing the illusions, the tricks created through the "magic" of cinematography above, and the disjointed, segmented, "real" world of the production of different scenes from Faust below.[19]

Just as Méliès, Murnau, Gründgens, and others had found in Faust a welcome scenario for their own cinematic preoccupations, so Weems's notes show her working out the analogy between Faust and the power of new technology: "Faust enters a world where the promise of technology guarantees transport to a fluid, phantastical universe, where 'information' is the currency and personaes are means of exchange."[20] Critical responses to the versions of Faust in IMPERIAL MOTEL and JUMP CUT suggest that the analogies held, especially those that linked Faust's pact to our own contemporary pact with new technologies. Jonathan Kalb saw a link between The Builders' stance and Christopher Marlowe's original "Mephistophelian idea to seduce spectators with the 'black magic' of theatre effects.... Weems and Jesurun seem to understand this implicitly, constructing every scene around a juxtaposition of live and mediated images that forces us to consider the devil's bargain we have made with the latter."[21] Throughout their research, rehearsal, and production, The Builders collaborators found in Faust the content that served as a pretext for pursuing their own intermedia forms.

OPERATING SYSTEMS

A conventional conception of an operating system places it in the background. Whether imagined as the apparatus of the camera, the technical support of the run crew, or the underlying structure of a computer program, the operating system is most often hidden. Its effects are all the more magical because its workings go unseen. Emboldened by the long history of the cinema of attractions, Builders collaborators sought to foreground this backgrounded operation. In many ways, the assembly process of the cinema of attractions paralleled that of other artists who were working in New York in the 1980s and 1990s. Laurie Anderson, Judith Barry, Richard Foreman, Jenny Holzer, Tony Oursler, Julia Scher, and Krzysztof Wodiczko all influenced Weems and other New York installation and performance art groups at that time. Gunning's scholarship provided a theoretical and historical armature for intermedia performance that recognized that the display of the operating system was one of its key attractions. In imagining a platform for Faust, Weems recorded the blocking of video monitors rolling back and forth on a stage populated by working actors. The "blocking" of such technology and humans would become a significant design element in FAUST. The arrangement of light but also the lighting instruments, the arrangement of projection screens but also the cameras—all of these would become mobile sculptures to be arranged in a stage space with sentient bodies.

Of course, the goal of exposing that apparatus has a significant theatrical pedigree. Bertolt Brecht called on theatrical practitioners to display theater's conditions of production, a move that advanced theater's political potential by unraveling sealed plots and defamiliarizing the emotional life of characters in what Brecht derided as "culinary theatre." By invoking the early fairgrounds of technological display and the refunctioned apparatus of avant-garde political theater, The Builders' aesthetic gradually found a delicate place where both of these popular and modernist genealogies converged. That pursuit placed social and technological operating systems in the center of the stage.

Rather than support for the medium, rather than suppressing the backgrounding apparatus that upheld a foregrounded image, these operating systems were part of the interior of the work, a central character in the storyboard. As such, the line between the interior and exterior of the artwork began to erode as well.

The first rehearsals of what would be IMPERIAL MOTEL (FAUST) involved operators from a variety of fields. Weems combined Jesurun's Faust texts with excerpted sections from others, including Johannes Spies's *Historia von D. Johann Fausten* (the *Faustbach*) (1592), Marlowe's *Tragicall History* (1593), Wilhelm von Hamm, Gotthold Ephraim Lessing, and Guido Bonneschky's *The Puppet Play of Doctor Faust* (1850), along with Goethe's work. Using a loose compilation script that was called "Stations of the Text," actors and designers worked through a structure that moved from pacts made with the devil through to the seduction and betrayal of Gretchen, changing stylistic idioms at unexpected intervals. Having contracted to premiere in German-speaking Switzerland, the text included simultaneous translations of English and Swiss German. Jesurun created a kind of devil assistant that was played by the Swiss actor Michael Neuenschwander, and the young Gretchen was played by Swiss actress Susanne-Marie Wrage. Anticipating the operating system of supertitles that are required in international theater, The Builders and their Swiss counterparts incorporated this bilingual convention into the text itself. The lines of Susanne-Marie Wrage, Michael Neuenschwander, Kyle deCamp, and Jeff Webster slid between English and German—sometimes ironizing the host language, sometimes making fun of English translation, and sometimes using the switch to an alternate language to punctuate the urgency of the scene:

MEPHISTO   IT'S TAKEN ALL THESE YEARS TO SEE WHAT'S REALLY GOING ON IN THE UNIVERSE. AND ALL THIS TIME I HAVEN'T TOUCHED ONE GRAIN OF COCAINE.

FAUST   WAS HAT DAS JETZT DAMIT ZU TUN?

MEPHISTO   WELL, EVERYONE THINKS I'M THIS EVIL, DECADENT PUTRESCENT, DRUG FIEND, EVIL QUEEN, SEX FIEND. LOOK AT ME. WIE SHE ICH AUS? WELCHE GESTALT HAVE I TAKEN TODAY?

FAUST   MAN SAGT YOU CAN TAKE ANY GESTALT YOU WANT.

MEPHISTO   FALSCH, I WILL TELL YOU THIS. I TAKE WHAT EVER GESTALT WHOEVER SEES ME WANTS ME TO TAKE. DU SCHAFFST MICH IN YOUR OWN IMAGE. ALSO WIE SEH ICH AUS? AM I UGLY, REPULSIVE, A TROLL, A CANNIBAL?

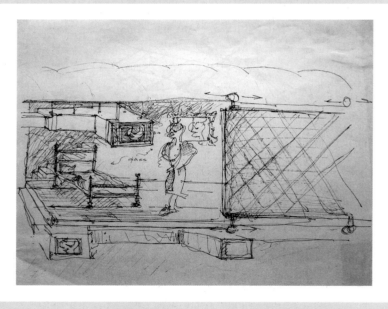

Early sketch (the devil appears in the motel room).

FAUST   ZIEMLICH BEAUTIFUL, A SURFER GIRL

While The Builders excavated the stories, their working process was also significantly Mélièsian in its use of story as a pretext for the exploration of the "magical possibility" of screen practice. The most significant operating system present in the space was the one that was organized to create what Weems called, at the time, "a live film." First Ben Rubin and then Chris Kondek took part in imagining the wired world that its staging would need, arranging cameras around John Cleater's set, positioning them to capture live enactments from one part of the stage so that they could be projected to interact with an actor on another part of the stage. At different moments, those live enactments were mixed on the spot with prerecorded film and then projected. The technical aspects of these early scenes of torment and negotiation between Faust and Lucifer nodded overtly to a history of trick photography. As Faust paced inside the spare Imperial Motel's "Room 202," he found the image of Kyle deCamp's devil following his every move. While deCamp delivered her monologue from atop the truss, Kondek projected her inside the frame of the hotel's mirror. When Faust opened the drawer of his bedside table, his face looked up from inside it. When he reached for the phone, her image was shrunk, inverted, and isolated to fit inside the receiver. The image of the diminutive devil recalled Director J. Stuart Blackton's *Princess Nicotine; or, The Smoke Fairy* (1909), a technical feat that translated Méliès's early twentieth-century trick photography to a late twentieth-century intermedia aesthetic.

While The Builders played with this technological chicanery, embodied elements of the theatrical ensemble were also acutely resonant. Ella Büchi's presence set new parameters and brought new possibilities to The Builders' aesthetic for the Neumarkt's production of the Faust story. In director Peter Gorski's *Faust* (1960), Gustaf Gründgens played the title role, and Büchi played the luminously blonde and innocent Gretchen. Now, decades later, Büchi took the stage once more, serving as a conduit between past and present iterations of the Faust myth. One of the most poignant (or insidious) moments in the 1960 film involved young Gretchen cheerily straightening her home and changing clothes while singing "The King of Thule," a popular and cathecting song for German nationals. For historians of German film culture, the sequence participated in the white-washing of Gründgens's politically radical past, sending fascist audiences into raptures of nationalist nostalgia. The Builders

Trick photography: The Devil (Kyle deCamp) appears to Faust (Jeff Webster).

asked the veteran Ella Büchi to reenact this scene, singing the same song in a slightly lower register as the projected image of her younger self did the same. Together, the young Gretchen and the older Gretchen moved about their respective rooms, reenacting the same movements of undressing and straightening, making it conceptually unclear who was initiating and who was following the actions of the other. As Johan Callens argues, the juxtaposition created a volatile encounter in the present, threatening to unleash the repressed political history of the early film:

The incorporation of Gründgens's Faust actually short-circuited public history (next to Büchi's private one), as a foil to the spatial simultaneity achieved by the video cameras and the collapsing of theater history.... In this manner, Weems forcefully opened up a controversial metatheatrical and political realm, dominated by Germany's traumatic past. The early career of Gründgens was indeed inextricably entwined with the rise of Fascism and its ideological appropriation of Faust.[22]

Similarly, a critic writing for a *Tages-Anzeiger* publication calls it "a dense moment in which the biographical and the historical, the theatrical and filmic combine to produce a mutual commentary."[23] For Peter von Becker, who reviewed the production, the presence of Ella Büchi and Susanne-Marie Wrage trumped the complex technological landscape with their unique viscerality and skill. He singled out other moments when "nothing happens. There is nothing but words. No video. Only a marvelous theater of the moment."[24] For Builders collaborators, the composition of technological machinery and embodied viscerality was the central pursuit. As performers and designers worked through scenes, managing text, bodily enactment, and live video, the interaction between a filmed memorial to Gründgen's Faust and Büchi's enacted memorial produced the most bracing argument of the piece. And as The Builders' aesthetic continued to develop—in JET LAG, XTRAVAGANZA, and ALLADEEN— they devised more ways to stage the dialectical relationship between embodied and technological media.

The set design for IMPERIAL MOTEL (FAUST) juxtaposed a past Gretchen and a present Gretchen inside an interior. After visiting the Arizona motel where Timothy McVeigh had readied himself before the Oklahoma bombings, Builders designer and architect John Cleater recreated McVeigh's room for Faust's own solitary ruminations. Next door to Room 202, a lovely Gretchen circulated in her own room, and Faust listened furtively to her singing from the other side of the wall.

REHEARSAL/ASSEMBLY

When Swiss reviewers and audience members saw IMPERIAL MOTEL (FAUST) at the Theater Neumarkt, many placed themselves in the position of the actors who were working in the midst of the scene. "The actors and actresses are called upon to perform the most difficult and unusual feats," said one, echoing the language of the fairground. He went on to describe the feats required of a media-driven theater that unsettled conventional narrative along with discrete conceptions of character: "We see none of the theatrical realism to which we have grown accustomed, neither imitation nor alienation of characters in obvious situations. What we find instead is a process of co-ordinating what is happening on stage with the film that is running simultaneously."[25] This reviewer missed the fact that the film was not "running" but being created in real time. The response shows the entrenchment of viewing habits that see intermedia performance as the combination of discrete forms—theater combined with cinema—rather than as an opportunity to contemplate a shared process of assembly and dispersion. The sense that acting was a "feat," fundamentally an act of technological coordination, had driven the rehearsal process from the beginning. In many ways, the stops and starts, the lags and sudden inspirations, the frustrations and unexpected coalescences are central to any rehearsal process. For The Builders, rehearsal further mimicked the postproduction process of the cinema. When Weems wrote her progress report to Müller and Volker, the juxtaposition of the messiness of rehearsal with the seamlessness of the final image was very much on her mind. The particular seamlessness of the screen made the juxtaposition between process (the hell of earth) and product (the heaven of the screen) all the more tangible. Later productions—especially XTRAVAGANZA, ALLADEEN, and CONTINUOUS CITY—used this two-tiered presentation of laboring bodies below a digital screen, replicating the base process of labor that supported the seemingly unfettered space of superstructural illusion.

If hell as production and heaven as icon animated the concept of IMPERIAL MOTEL (FAUST), it did so in part because the process of rehearsing presented its own unique challenges. The "acting for the camera" skills that were nascent in MASTER BUILDER rehearsals advanced to another level of complexity in this production. The Swiss actors struggled at different points to hit their marks so that their faces, gestures, and motions would align for the screen as well as for the stage. "I worry that the audience is going to be looking at the screen and not me," said one Swiss actor, a sentiment expressed at different moments by others in rehearsal. The Swiss actors remained anxious about whether the coordinating effort of the production studio would overshadow their technique as actors. In fact, the performance required and developed an expanded set of skills for the actors, something that experienced Builders actors Jeff Webster and Kyle deCamp modeled during rehearsal. In a combination of film and stage acting, they maintained the intimacy of private exchange in a space that greatly magnified it. Webster and deCamp explained that actors had to trust that expansion and to cease worrying about being upstaged by their own projected image. Acting in a Builders show meant managing the introverted effects of one's embodied presence with the extroverted effects of one's mediated image, and it meant doing it simultaneously. The cinematic skills of camera acting and the presentational skills of theatrical acting thus responded to each other and revised each other moment to moment.

Other elements of IMPERIAL MOTEL (FAUST) exploited the effects of a composite intermedia performance. The famous *Walpurgisnacht* (Night of the Witches) scene in the Faust tale started with the four actors on stage somewhat obscured by a blue screen. Above them, however, the screen showed the foursome in an oddly familial exchange as they prepared for a road trip. With the help of video compositing, a detached steering wheel, and Dan Dobson's compelling soundtrack, the four appeared to embark on a drive down a country road. They chatted amiably as the music increased in volume and intensity, with the blue-screen background transforming into a starry sky. Their flight through the *Walpurgisnacht* eerily mixed dread and dark magic with the lovable annoyances of a family drive.

REHEARSAL/REASSEMBLY

The particular parameters of the Swiss production were not reproduced beyond the operating systems of the Theater Neumarkt. For all the excitement and experiment that it generated, this particular assembly of people and technology—especially an aging Ella Büchi—could not easily tour. Without Büchi, the structuring logic of Gründgens's film went as well. Reflecting on the results of IMPERIAL MOTEL (FAUST), Weems also worried that it was "too long, too serious, too narrative."[26] In ensuring that Faust would have a life beyond the Swiss production, Weems began to explore new presenting possibilities, which in turn provoked new aesthetic experiments. The company made a connection with Ellen Salpeter, the director of the Thread Waxing Space. As a downtown New York gallery and performance venue, this space did not reproduce the frontality of a theater viewing situation but was an old loft that extended the depth of the playing area nearly 150 yards. Without the clear bicameral spectatorial relation, The Builders returned to the same Faust material but altered its structure and formal pursuits. They decided to focus entirely on Murnau's *Faust* film, eliminating both the theatrical truss and the motel spaces that had supported the exploration of Gründgens's film and using the storyboard of Murnau's film as their structuring device. What eventually was called JUMP CUT (FAUST) took over the entire gallery space, and the motions, angles, sounds, and marks of actors, cameras, and designers were orchestrated to create a film in real time before the audience.

The decision to eliminate conventional theatrical structures further advanced the experiment of creating a live film where postproduction was truly the central event of the theatrical production itself. The coordinating works of focusing, marking, splicing, and assembling were the central composition techniques of JUMP CUT (FAUST). The pleasure and violence of a jump cut provided the central drama of the piece. By rendering the fragmented actions below into "seamless, pristine images" above,

JUMP CUT (FAUST). Performers fly in the *Walpurgisnacht* scene with the use of blue screen. (l. to r.) Heaven Phillips, Moira Driscoll, David Pence, Jeff Webster. Thread Waxing Space, 1998.

the piece also created an analogy to the black magic of Mephisto. In moving to the next iteration of Faust, these techniques—these "operating systems"—were pushed even further, so much so that the operating system—the jump cut—itself would title the show. The challenge of siting the work in an art gallery thus provoked new deconstructions of a narrative theater apparatus. The elimination of the theatrical truss was also accompanied by the erosion of the narrative "stations of the text" in favor of an assembly of actions that mimicked that of a studio set where the primary "story" lay in watching actors and designers make a project together. Jesurun's script was significantly trimmed, and instead of Gründgens's version, Murnau's *Faust* film was the primary intertext for JUMP CUT (FAUST). Murnau's own tricks and directorial interventions set the scene for new tricks and interventions for The Builders, too.

Murnau rendered the pivotal exchange between Faust and Lucifer on a blackened stage that set off his own luminous cinematic chicanery, and The Builders mimicked its haunted landscape. Using a basic compositing technique, Lucifer (now played by actor David Pence) unfolded a handkerchief to create a blue screen on which the image of Gretchen (now played by Heaven Phillips) appeared. That handkerchief then became a scroll on which the text of an apparently diabolical spell, drawn from the Murnau film, was projected. When Faust (Jeff Webster) crumpled the handkerchief, Kondek distorted the projected text, matching physical and digital disintegration in one gesture. That handkerchief was in turn transformed into a bandage that wrapped the arm of Faust at the moment of their blood-bound contract. "A signature is more binding in blood," hissed Mephisto from performer Moira Driscoll's voiceover located offstage.

In lieu of Gründgens's private dressing scene, Murnau dramatized Faust's fixation on Gretchen in a different way, tracking Faust as he spied on Gretchen in a romantically flowered grotto and following him as he followed her into a crowded medieval cityscape. In their rerendering of these scenes, Kondek projected Murnau's Gretchen above as The Builders' Gretchen mimicked her movements below. As Murnau's Gretchen moved in and out of the framed grotto, Heaven Phillips matched her steps, her turns, and her reentries in the blank space of the studio set below. What appeared romantically tantalizing above came off as a strange and fragmented choreography below. Phillips watched a monitor to time her actions, making sure to hit her mark.

Between each of these awkwardly magical scenes, actors abruptly stopped their actions, and the "film" came to a halt. The beep of a recording device triggered the arrest each time, signaling the end of each "take" of the scene. In the lag time between scenes, actors and operators reset cameras, rolled set pieces on and off, or removed costume pieces. They asked for snacks or requested a technical adjustment of some kind, creating the mundane feel of a studio set in operation. The poignant mundanity of the studio in all its low-tech creativity came forward throughout the piece. The magic of other moments depended not only on the high-tech splendor of "new" media but also on the captivating aura of the "outmoded" technologies of an earlier era.

In another meditative group scene, actors interacted with each other from completely different spaces in the Thread Waxing Gallery. As Phillips sat perched at the back of the Thread Waxing space, the depth of field produced its own low-tech version of optical trickery. Phillips perched in the back of the gallery while interacting with her fellow performers in the front. The distance made her appear to be a small, minuscule Princess Nicotine, delicately suspended not through a trick of the camera but with the optical illusion created by the architecture of the space.

The complex coordination of actors and operators, screens and bodies, voices and soundtracks developed into precisely timed composites. As one reviewer notes, "There is no place for improvisation or spontaneous motion in this kind of theater. And the music is a constant companion—techno, rap, sentimental kitsch, the noise of a plane and a car, etc.—becomes a sort of superior scenery that frames the built frame and the plot."[27] Sound designer and musician Dan Dobson created the entire score, mixing live voices with mediated effects and developing a soundtrack that ranged from the lush score of Richard Wagner's *Tristan and Isolde* (1859) to the paranoiac electronic "room tone" made famous in Francis Ford Coppola's *The Conversation* (1974). For this production that simultaneously arranged the stage with machinery, bodies, screens and sounds, the collaborators were always in tech—that is, incorporating all design elements as well as all designers as interlocutors from the beginning of rehearsals. Just as actors had to learn the skills of operational coordination, the technical operators and designers cultivated the sensibility of actors. Meanwhile, the hypercoordination and chaos of production qualified, but also made more magical, the illusionary effects of the sutured image on screen. This technical operation created a landscape for reflecting on the moral of the Faust myth. As Weems reiterated to a French interviewer: "On stage everything seems chaotic, fragmented, while the

JUMP CUT (FAUST). "The contract signed in blood." Performer David Pence wraps blue screen around Jeff Webster's arm while Heaven Phillips aligns a "bleeding" stunt arm in camera. The composite image on the screen above mimics Murnau's shot of Faust's signature in blood.

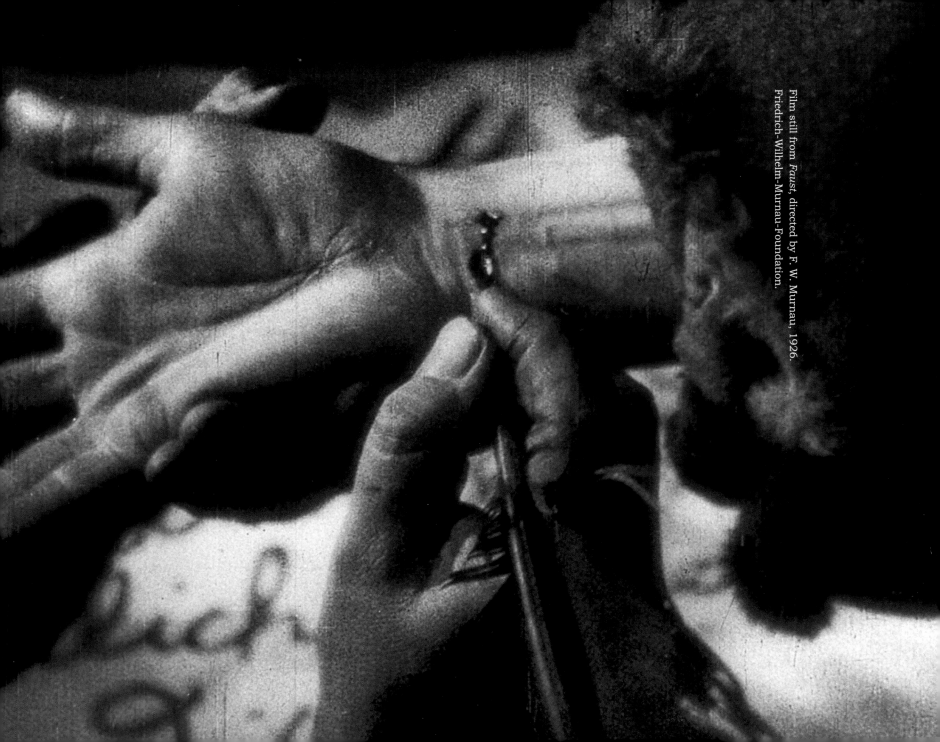

Film still from *Princess Nicotine; or, The Smoke Fairy*, directed by J. Stuart Blackton, 1909.
The Smoker is staged in foreground of camera frame, and the Fairy is staged in the distance.

image that appears on the screen is perfectly clear and focused. It's sort of the hell of production on stage and the paradise of the image on the screen."[28]

Interestingly, just as the actors worried and wondered about their place in this form, so reviewers worked hard to find terms to describe the forms that they were viewing. Perhaps the most intriguing attempt was made by a reviewer for *Le Monde* who described the "trois écrans suspendus au-dessus de la scène renvoient en direct les images des acteur jouant en dessous, un procédé largement utilizé lors de concert ou de meetings politiques" ("Three screens suspended above the scene directly project the images of actors playing below, a process usually used in concerts or in political meetings").[29] While unexpectedly recalling Philip Auslander's arguments on the production of liveness, perhaps the analogy to the rock concert artist or to the scene of the politician alleviated the fears of the actors that no one would pay attention to them.[30]

CLOSINGS

IMPERIAL MOTEL (FAUST) and JUMP CUT (FAUST) effectively transitioned a group that mounted MASTER BUILDER into a new media theater company called The Builders Association. Although the sense of The Builders' newness as a next-generation New York experimental theater company depended in part on their "new" use of media, such experiments had come about entirely through an excavation of the old. Nineteenth-century fairgrounds had been important places to perform the wonders of then-new technology, and the Faust pieces replicated that sense of experimental wonder. Reviewers consistently remarked on the feats of technology—some with a defensive concern for the future of a nontechnological theater but many with an awareness that theater is always already a prime site of technological innovation. For Johan Callens, "Much of the audience's pleasure derived precisely from the fluctuations between the illusion and its disruption, the embodiments and disembodiments of the fiction."[31] Moreover, those fluctuations provoked a respect for the operators and designers who produced them: "Often it was difficult to ascertain which was which, whether filmic action was mimicked or stage action filmed, because of the smoke effects, style copying, and technological processing."[32]

The composite quality of the stage image was compounded by the composite quality of the texts with which it interacted. Given the critical tendency to locate authorship in the figure of the writer, some reviews advertised the production as "by John Jesurun." Some reviewers praised

Performer Heaven Phillips juxtaposed onscreen with a scene from Murnau's *Faust*.

Performer Jeff Webster onstage with effects added on screen. Kaaitheater, Brussels, 1997.

Faust in Amerika – cool und medial

«Imperial Motel», eine theatralische Recherche zwischen Zürich und New York, uraufgeführt in Oerlikon

Ein Abend der Überraschungen in der ABB-Halle. So hat man den «Faust»-Stoff noch nie aufbereitet gesehen. Aus der Zusammenarbeit des Zürcher Neumarkt-Theaters und der New Yorker Builders Association resultiert eine kühle und kühne, eine in ihrer Art perfekte Aufführung. Das Premierenpublikum geizte nicht mit Beifall.

■ VON CHRISTOPH KUHN

Akzeptieren muss man als mit europäischem Kultur- und Theatergut durchtränkter Mensch nur eines, wenn man sich dem Abend in der ABB-Halle hingibt: dass es für eine junge New Yorker Theatergruppe, die eigentlich mit unserem ganzen (Bildungs-)Theater nichts am Hut hat, sich dafür in der Welt des Films, der Videotechnik, der elektronischen Unterhaltungsindustrie (inklusive Musik) bestens auskennt, keine grössere Herausforderung, kein spannenderes Ziel zu geben scheint, als eben unsere Klassiker – Ibsen, Tschechow und jetzt Goethe – zu ergründen und zu spielen. Dass sie es aufs unbefangenste und abenteuerlichste tut, dass sie demontiert, remontiert, transformiert oder, um es philosophischer zu sagen, «dekonstruiert», versteht sich von selber.

Die nagende Frage, weshalb der uralte «Faust» von Johannes Spies (1592) über Marlowe und Goethe bis John Jesurun (1996) wiederbelebt werden muss, um uns eine atemraubende Multimedia-Performance zu zeigen, sei gestellt – und gleich vergessen. Wahrscheinlich gibt es auch unter der amerikanischen Sonne von 1996 keinen besseren theatralischen Stoff als eben diese Sage aus dem deutschen

Direktübertragung ins Zeitalter der flackernden Bildschirme: Faust in Oerlikon.

BILD TOM KAWARA

wie die Schauspieler. Für Improvisation, für spontane Regungen gibt es in dieser Art von Theater keinen Platz. Und die Musik als ständiger Begleiter – Techno, Rap, sehnsüchtiger Kitsch, Fahrgeräusche etc. – wird zu einer Art Überkulisse

brechen sich die Akteure durch den Dialog, der in Fetzen veräussert wird, wobei Herrn von Goethe immerhin der Löwenanteil gewährt bleibt – auch wenn sich der Ehrwürdige Verspottungen, gegen den Strich gebürstete Stilfiguren und einmal

zeitig ablaufenden Film plausibel zu koordinieren, dafür zu sorgen, dass wir im Zuschauerraum die verschiedenen Dimensionen, die gespaltenen Wirklichkeiten auf der Bühne und auf den Bildschirmen mit einem Blick zu erfassen vermögen –

Review of IMPERIAL MOTEL (FAUST), performed in Zurich, 1996.

the modernist assembly of references and his practice of linking "one detail to any other detail." Given the sanctity of the Faust tales in a European context, this postdramatic textual practice was especially provocative, provoking European critics who lauded the way that "Wit, sarcasm, and a cryptic humor flash up in these stripped, compressed, linguistically mixed and newly composed sentences."[33] For others, though, the assembly was received as oddly literal, especially when mounted in a cinematic landscape. Jonathan Kalb read the pop cultural references of the text as a sign of the unintelligence of a population brainwashed by the culture industry: "[T]he cynicism and compulsory empty-headedness of pop and media drain people of the capacity for real thought and feeling."[34] For him, Jesurun's "demented verbal sunflowers" were not intriguing blossoms but confirmation of the deadened incapacities of the figures onstage. "Self-consciously sophomoric dialogue" mixed with "strings of pop lyrics and dumb one-liners like 'Help me, Rhonda'" might have been read as a modernist assembly of dereferentialized signifiers to some reviewers, but others read them as signs of the "empty-headedness" of people onstage.

The different kinds of reception bespeak the different stakes of postdramatic theater, especially one that travels between the European avant-garde and that of the United States, especially one that decides both to incorporate and to critique the effects of screen and sound technology. For some, the expediency of the Faust text was lauded for the juxtapositions it enabled. *Le Monde* argued that "Le mythe de Faust n'est qu'un prétexte aux fantasies verbales de John Jesurun, et à jeu d'incrustations, où l'on perd rapidement pied" ("The myth of Faust is no more than a pretext for John Jesurun's verbal fantasies and for a game of embeddings, where one quickly loses one's footing"),[35] recalling Méliès's language of "pretext" for the enabling of cinematic chicanery. For many European audiences, the deconstruction of the tale and the involvement of new media technology were what made this work an "American" intervention:

For a young New York theater group, which is not really interested in our (educational) theater, but all the more at home in the world of film, of video-technology, and the electronic entertainment industry (including music), there seems to be no greater challenge no aim more thrilling than to fathom and stage our classics—Ibsen, Chekhov, and now Goethe. It goes without saying that they do this uninhibited and adventurously, that they disassemble, re-erect, transform or—to put it philosophically—to deconstruct it.... Probably there is no better theatrical material, even under the American sun of 1996, than this medieval German legend concerning the conquest of the world, the sale of one's soul, and the descent to hell. Is this not flattering enough for us?[36]

The same review applauded the American capacity for "wonderful, pitiless irony" that Europeans could not quite have toward themselves.

If "Faust in Amerika" was "cool and medial," the pleasure and frisson came from the sense that an American company was cheekily taking apart a staple of the European canon, an act of deconstruction that, as any critic of postdramatic theater knows, is always a simultaneous act of homage.[37] Indeed, the international attention that JUMP CUT (FAUST) received helped to launch The Builders on a European avant-garde tour circuit, a form of support and recognition that proved essential to their survival as a company.

Interestingly, the intermedial aspect of the show also signaled "America," even when it was primarily in dialogue with European filmmakers. But the link between Americanization and technological mediation continued as the twentieth century turned and The Builders' aesthetic developed. That conjunction later prompted the group to speculate on the international politics of its own position, especially as artists who found themselves circling the globe to keep working, trying to overcome jet lag at each stop along the way.

ENDNOTES

Artist's Voice: John Jesurun, playwright

FAUST was a play that I originally had no interest in writing. But it's an example of how artists can pull each other into significant directions and situations. My initial reaction was that the last thing this world needed was another *Faust*. Marianne's persuasive sense of enthusiastic exploration lured me into the project even though I would have rather done *Mildred Pierce*. I do remember a kind of conversation with Marianne similar to one I had with Ron Vawter concerning *Philoktetes*. The takeaway was: "You can write whatever you want. We'll just call it *Faust*."

In any case, it was an opportunity to write a play that involved artists I respected, including Jeff Webster, Jennifer Tipton, and Chris Kondek. This trip into the unknown had great appeal to me, and I appreciated the complete freedom I had as a writer. It was a particularly fruitful project for my writing. I loved attending the readings and watching as various technical and esthetic ideas were tried out. I found these readings a great testing of the text. Jane Smith's gentle yet resolute portrayal of Gretchen was particularly evocative in early readings of the play. Her version of the character is still one of the most powerful resonances I retain from among the play's eventual iterations. Over time, all these resonances left their mark in what I think contributed significantly to a template for The Builders' own form. It wasn't an easy script to deal with, and the convergence of the text and design was decisive. This is a good example. It shows that real relationships between artists are what can instigate work that has a relevance that continues to expand. The play has continued to have its own life, including major runs at the National Theater of Mexico.

Artist's Voice: David Pence, performer and co-creator

MASTER BUILDER and IMPERIAL MOTEL (FAUST) were big shows built on translations of classic scripts by Ibsen and Goethe. After those productions, it seemed as if Marianne Weems and Jeff Webster took a deep collective breath and said, "Okay, let's try that once again, but this time...." JUMP CUT (FAUST) was exhilarating and refreshing because essentially it was a remix—Faust, take 2.

Hiring John Jesurun to write his own Faust tale was brilliant. It was like throwing open the windows of a luxurious but stuffy room. Suddenly we were free to play a classical story through a contemporary linguistic fuzz box. John's scenes were designed for maximum theatrical pleasure, and his sentences were written to be spoken at various degrees of high speed and using the widest possible range of sonic frequencies.

Above all, JUMP CUT was fun. It was a blast to perform—a spectacular collision of smarts and goofiness. Gretchen and Faust's mating dance spinning out of the grandiose 1970s radio rocker "Magic Man." Moira Driscoll in Aunt Marthe's hoop skirt and weird fez scooting over to the tech table to mix live video because Chris Kondek needed another pair of hands. The actors taking "front seat" and "backseat" positions in front of a blue-screen highway as I steered our vehicle gripping a twelve-inch film reel fastened to a mic stand. And those words! How many hundreds of words poured forth each minute, goosing this or that Teutonic concern with, say, a phrase from "Help Me, Rhonda"? A gas! Foolish fun.

Then there was another sense of fun, half-lit, as serious matters landed with a twist or a wink and a sigh— evil and good, bargaining for a soul, the unlikeliness of innocence. In 1997, The Builders delighted in using funky mechanical means (alongside digital cleverness) to deliver touch points of the story. One favorite scene involved using live video to recreate a tender image from F. W. Murnau's 1926 film *Faust*—Gretchen in a hooded cloak cradling a baby. On the screen above the stage, the audience sees woman and child, as well as the lovely snowfall that adds the desolate note of the original scene. On the stage, the audience sees me standing behind Heaven Phillips, cranking some white flour through a rusty metal sifter onto her shoulders and head. Another favorite: a poetic dreamscape of drifting white clouds and German rooftops onscreen is echoed by moody video landscapes shot live and eventually revealed to be nothing more or less than a crude miniature city on a table noisily wheeled onstage.

JUMP CUT was a milestone in another way. For the first time, The Builders designed and made a piece that could be shipped and put up and pulled back down in multiple venues, and the group made two transatlantic trips with the show to cities in Germany, Belgium, and France. Moira's and my son, going on two years old, made the trips with us. Some of the sweetest memories of that show have various Builders folding our nuclear family of three into the daily life of the extended Builders' family on tour—playing jumping games on a Paris sidewalk, putting live video of the boy on the stage screens during a Maubeuge rehearsal, making extra room for him to nest on the crowded van floor for a long drive back to Brussels and the flight home....

As years passed, the show took on an old-fashioned sepia glow in my mind, as the wooly analog approach of MASTER BUILDER and JUMP CUT (FAUST) gave way to sophisticated digital methods that allowed a cleaner, more seamless beauty in productions like ALLADEEN and SUPER VISION. However, it turns out that humble tools and materials (like the dusty box fan placed offstage to flap the pages of Faust's book in a keen moment of reckoning) have not been abandoned in a dank corner of The Builders' storage container. In 2012, something of the group's former analog spirit was reanimated when HOUSE/DIVIDED arrived with a motley and soulful collection of foreclosed lumber, newspaper bonnets, plumbing fixtures, reel-to-reel tape, and an old spoon.

IMPERIAL MOTEL (FAUST)

People
Directed by Marianne Weems

Video design by Ben Rubin with contributions by Chris Kondek

Sound design and original music composition by Dan Dobson

Lighting designed by Jennifer Tipton

Set design by John Cleater

Costume design by Ellen McCartney

Performed by
Kyle deCamp and Jeff Webster from The Builders Association

Ella Büchi, Michael Neuenschwander, and Susanne-Marie Wrage from the Theater Neumarkt

Dramaturgy by Christoph Stratenwerth

Assistant director: Rainer Hoffmann

Additional music: David Linton

Devil's tail: Bill Ballou

Voice: Andree Tavares

Technical director: Norbert Marks

Lighting setup: Ueli Duttweiler, Martin Rohr, Franz Windlin

Assistant stage designers: Nadja Fistarol, Cecile Thalmann

Video technical supervisor: Steve Powell

Video operator: Katharina Vischer

Video cueing: Sabine Rosenberg

Cameraman: Rogelio Perez

Directing interns: Anne-Christine Gnekow, Andree Tavares

Make-up: Doris Lohmann

Stage technicians: Franz Fleischmann, Peter Strassmann

Costume department: Kathrin Baldauf, Doris Choudary, Elisabeth Schubiger, Beata Sievi, Elsbeth Vondra, Beatrice Zimmerman

Metalworking: Christiano Remo

Carpentry and joinery: Philippe Anderegg

Paint shop: Vanessa Belz

Decoration department: Michael Severa

Props department: Ueli Zellweger

Makeup: Clara Ferramosca, Anne-Rose Schwab

Stage technicians: Matthias Gutherz, Stefan Stutzer

Lighting: Twist Sopek

Sound: Jürg Breitschmid

Support: René Weber

Venue

May–November 1996   Commissioned by and developed and performed at the Theater Neumarkt, Zurich, Switzerland

JUMP CUT (FAUST)

People

Directed by Marianne Weems

Video design by Christopher Kondek

Sound design by Dan Dobson

Set design by John Cleater

Text by John Jesurun with additional found texts
Lighting by Jennifer Tipton

Performed by
Moira Driscoll
David Pence
Heaven Phillips
Jeff Webster
Lighting associate: Allen Hahn
Video associates: Yvette Mattern, Kelly Reiling
Assistant director, subtitles, and baby *Kindermoerd* voice: Abigael Sanders
Production manager: Eric Dyer
Costume design: Ellen McCartney
Set construction and additional set design: Lorrie Synder
Produced by Renata Petroni with The Builders Association

Venues
October 2007   Speil.Art Festival, Munich, Germany
December 1997   Thread Waxing Space, New York, NY
March 1998   Kaaitheater, Brussels
             Creiteil, Paris, France
             National Theater of Brittany, Rennes, France
             Via Festival, Maubeuge, France

Afterparty

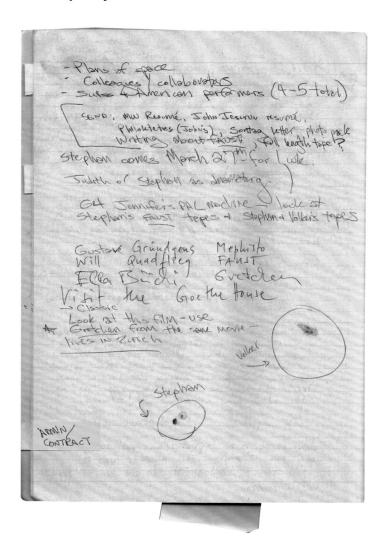

Contract signed in blood by Theater Neumarkt producers
Stephan Müller and Volker Hesse, Zurich, 1995.

SOME SOURCE MATERIALS FOR THE PRODUCTION

Books on Faust

Bonneschky, Guido. *The Puppet Play of Doctor Faust*. 1850. London: K. Paul, Trench & Co., 1887.

Clausen, Rosemarie. *Gustaf Gründgen's* Faust In Bildern. Braunschweig: George Westermann Verlag, 1960.

Goethe, Johann Wolfgang von. *Faust*. Translated by Philip Wayne. New York: Penguin, 1949.

Goethe, Johann Wolfgang von. *Faust*. Translated by Walter Arndt, New York: W. W. Norton & Co., 1976.

Goethe, Johann Wolfgang von. *Faust: A Dramatic Poem*. Translated by Anna Swanwick. New York: A. L. Burt Company, 1905.

Goethe. Johann Wolfgang von. *Faust: A Fragment*. 1790. Zürich: Verlag der Corona; Munich: R. Oldenbourg, 1940

Goethe, Johann Wolfgang von. *Faust: A Tragedy, Part One*. Translated by Martin Greenberg. New Haven, CT: Yale University Press, 1992.

Mann, Thomas. *Doctor Faustus: The Life of the German Composer Adrian Leverkuhn as Told by a Friend*. Chicago: University of Chicago Press, 1969.

Marlowe, Christopher. *The Tragicall History of Doctor Faustus*. 1593. New York: Oxford University Press, 1995.

Melanchthon, Philip. *Explicationes Melanchthoniae*. Parts 2, 4. Berlin: Evangelische Verlagsanstal, 1997.

Mountford, NAME. *The Life and Death of Doctor Faustus*. 1697. La Jolla: University of California Libraries, 1886.

Rudolph, Yvonne. *Faust und Mephisto: Goethes Dramanfiguren auf dem Theater Theatermuseum der Universistat Koln*. Munich: Grin Verlag, 1983.

Spies, Johann. *The Historie of the Damnable Life and Deserved Death of Doctor John Faustus* (the Spies Book). 1592. Notre Dame, IN: University of Notre Dame Press, 1963.

Books on Timothy McVeigh

Calverhall, Randolph D. *Serpent's Walk.* Hillsboro, WV: National Vanguard Books, 1991.

Jeffrey, Grant R. *Prince of Darkness: Antichrist and the New World Order—Startling Bible Prophecies Uncovering the Secret Globalist Conspiracy behind Current Events.* New York: Bantam Books, 1995.

O'Driscoll, Robert, et al. *The New World Order and the Throne of the Antichrist.* The Armageddon Series Part 3. New York: Printing Office, 1993.

Stern, Kenneth. *A Force upon the Plain: The American Militia Movement and the Politics of Hate.* Norman: Oklahoma University Press, 1997.

Articles on Timothy McVeigh

"Americans See Strangers in Their Midst." *New York Times,* May 14, 1995.

Applebome, Pepter. "An Unlikely Legacy of the 60's: The Violent Right." *New York Times*, June 5, 1995.

Belluck, Pam. "Suspect Hoarded Bomb Materials, Affidavit Implies: Months of Preparation." *New York Times*, May 12, 1995.

Brooke, James. "Officials Say Montana 'Freemen' Collected $1.8 Million in Money Order Scheme." *New York Times*, March 28, 1996.

"Conspiracy Theories Impact Reverberates in Legislature." *New York Times*, July 6, 1995.

Hackworth, David H. "The Suspect Speaks: A Prison Interview with Alleged Oklahoma City Bomber Timothy McVeigh." *Newsweek*, July 3, 1995.

Hawthorne, G. Eric. "Dear White Racial Comrade" (assorted letters). *Racial Loyalty*, 1994.

Janofsky, Michael. "Paramilitary Group Leaders Try to Burnish Their Image." *New York Times*, May 26, 1995.

Janofsky, Michael. "Senate Panel Focuses on Internet as a Classroom for Violence." *New York Times*, July 5, 1995.

Johnston, David. "Leg in the Oklahoma City Rubble Was That of a Black Woman." *New York Times*, August 31, 1995.

Kelly, Michael. "The Road to Paranoia." *The New Yorker*, June 19, 1995.

Kifner, John. "Bomb Suspect Felt at Home Riding the Gun-Show Circuit: McVeigh's World." *New York Times*, July 5, 1995.

Kifner, John. "Despite Indictment in Oklahoma Blast, Case Is Far From Closed." *New York Times*, August 13, 1995.

Kifner, John. "Extremist Army Group at War with U.S. Policy." *New York Times*, December 14, 1995.

Kilborn, Peter. "The Nichols Brothers: Seeking Clues along a Highway." *New York Times*, May 11, 1995.

Lapham, Lewis. "Seen But Not Heard: The Message of the Oklahoma Bombing." *Harper's Magazine*, July 1995.

McFadden, Robert D. "John Doe No. 1: A Life of Solitude and Obsessions." *New York Times*, May 4, 1995.

Rosenbaum, Ron. "Staring into the Heart of the Heart of Darkness." *New York Times*, June 5, 1995.

"Strassmeir Uber Alles?" *Village Voice*, July 16, 1996.

Treaster, Joseph B. "For Figure in Oklahoma Inquiry Ties of Blood and Something More: The Sister's Story." *New York Times*, August 4, 1995.

Books on Early Film

Dickson, W. K., and Antonio Dickson. *History of the Kinetograph Kinetoscope and Kineto-Photograph.* New York: Raff and Gamon, 1895.

Eisner, Lotte H. *The Haunted Screen: Expressionism in the German Cinema and the Influence of Max Reinhardt.* London: Secker and Warburg, 1973.

Hopkins, Albert Allis. *Magic, Stage Illusions and Scientific Diversions, Including Trick Photography.* New York: Munn, 1897.

Leyda, Jay. *Before Hollywood: Turn-of-the-Century Film from American Archives.* New tYork: American Federation of Arts, 1986.

Palmer Handbook of Scenario Construction. New York: Palmer Photoplay Corporation, 1922.

Riefenstahl, Leni. *Leni Riefenstahl: A Memoir.* New York: Picador, 1992.

Rovin, Jeff. *The Fabulous Fantasy Films.* New York: Barnes, 1977.Simons, Sarah, ed. *No One May Ever Have the Same Knowledge Again (Letters to Mount Wilson Observatory 1915–1935).* Culver City, CA: Society for the Diffusion of Useful Information Press, 1993.

Talbot, Frederick A. *Moving Pictures: How They Are Made and Worked.* Philadelphia, PA: Lippincott, 1912.

Films

Georges Méliès

The Apparition or Mr. Jones' Comical Experience with a Ghost, 1903

The Astronomer's Dream, 1898

The Ballet-Master's Dream, 1903

The Cave of the Demons, 1898

The Damnation of Faust, 1898

The Famous Box Trick, 1898

Jack Jaggs and Dum Dum, 1903

Jupiter's Thunderballs, 1903

The Magic Lantern, 1903

Le Manoir du Diable, 1896

Melomaniac, 1903

The Spiritualistic Photographer, 1903

The Terrible Night, 1896
A Trip to the Moon, 1902
The Vanishing Lady, 1896

J. Stuart Blackton

Princess Nicotine, 1909

3 JET LAG

STILL MOVING

JET LAG performer David Pence in a stormy scene.

OPENINGS

A man enters from stage left and begins to putter around an assembly of wires, cameras, and screens. He shuffles his hands through his hair, whether to tame it or to mess it up more is unclear. A light turns on as he perches atop a stool. He flicks a switch to turn on a screen behind him, the luminous flat rectangle projects an image of the sea meeting the horizon of the sky. He runs his hands through his hair again, this time definitely to mess it up, and begins talking into a microphone. "Good morning," he says to the camera as his image appears on a large screen center stage, with the sea and sky as background. Suddenly, he starts to talk to himself. "Maybe a hat," he mumbles, leaning over to put on a white boating hat. "Good morning," he says again to the camera and to the audience from the large screen. He stops once more, muttering "No—no hat" and tossing it back down to the ground. "Good morning," he tries a third time: "I've been at sea now for three days, more or less." He speaks into the camera as the small screen begins to rock side to side on an oscillating pedestal. The man rocks slightly on his stool. On the large screen center stage, a man in a boat reports on his days at sea: "First of all, I'd like to begin by thanking Channel 8 for their support of my effort, their interest in me." He smiles broadly and gives a thumbs up to the camera as the boat floats and the sun shines.

JET LAG premiered in 1998 at Kulturhus Århus in Denmark and toured internationally to venues including Trafó House of Contemporary Arts in Budapest and the Barbican Centre in London. This was the European tour of a "new American theater company" that ultimately put The Builders Association on the theater map in the United States. It earned The Builders their first Obie Award as well as official status as a new media theater company, whether or not such a designation was welcome. As the production continued touring throughout 1999, the show found itself framed within millennial themes, including series festivals in France and Quebec organized around the approaching fin de siècle. That might be the reason that questions and anxieties around futurity attached themselves to this production intensely. JET LAG was celebrated as "the future of the theater"[1] and also was critiqued for ushering in a future that many hoped to keep at bay.

R&D

As a collaboration with Diller + Scofidio (D+S), JET LAG upped the ante on The Builders' attempts to unsettle the parameters of theater, a pursuit complemented by D+S's efforts to unsettle the material parameters of architecture. D+S had already garnered acclaim for conceptual works displayed at American Lawn: The Surface of Everyday Life (1998), a multimedia exhibition at the Canadian Centre for Architecture (CCA) in Montreal, and *Refresh* (1998), a twelve-site web project for the Dia Center for the Arts. D+S also experimented with the theatrical form with Hotel Pro Forma (Denmark), and Dumb Type (Japan). In *(Monkey) Business Class* (1996), performers traveled on a vertical trajectory through three media registers—the stage, the screen, and the fly space above the proscenium—"changing their material presence for the audience" by mixing live and prerecorded video in the middle plane.[2] Innovating in a longer tradition of what Chris Salter calls "performative architectures," D+S foregrounded architectural design as a precursor to a built environment and also as its own propositional exercise.[3] Soon after working on JET LAG, D+S created its signature work *Blur Building* (2002), an exposition pavilion for the Swiss Expo at Yverdon-les-Bains that solidified its stature as an architectural team that offered un-built environments as invitations to reflect on the nature of building itself.

The central themes of JET LAG came from several places, including The Builders' physical experience of jet lag, aggravated by being compelled to perform while enduring the fatigue and disorientation of international travel. It also came philosophically from an ongoing dilemma in the contemporary experience of time, particularly in a global landscape whose "perspective geometry" had changed enormously. Paul Virilio's meditations on these changed parameters of encounter were influential, especially his argument that "Everything is being turned on its head at this fin de siècle—not only geopolitical boundaries but those of perspective geometry."[4] The artists appreciated Virilio's analyses of perceptions of speed and space and his use of narrative anecdotes to elaborate them. Virilio wrote about the story of Sarah Krasnoff, who during six months in 1971 crossed the Atlantic in 167 consecutive flights with her fourteen-year-old grandson to elude the boy's father and

The trimaran: found intact with dinghy and liferaft.

Mystery of missing yachtsman

By JONAS SMITH

Donald Crowhurst, the lone round-the-world yachtsman, was feared lost last night only a few days from completion of the voyage.

His trimaran Teignmouth Electron in which he was expected to win the £5,000 prize for the fastest circumnavigation of the world in the Sunday Times Golden Globe race, was found abandoned about 700 miles south-west of the Azores.

There was no sign of the yachtsman nor anything to suggest what had happened to him. Books, papers, films and tapes, and Mr. Crowhurst's log were found intact. The trimaran was hauled

Crowhurst's voyage exposed. *Sunday Times*, July 20, 1969. Courtesy of The London Times.

Flying granny grounded by heart attack

Amsterdam, Aug 31.—An American grandmother, aged 74, with a passion for flying, was temporarily grounded today by a mild heart attack after making 160 transatlantic flights in five months at a cost of about £50,000.

Mrs S. Krasnoff and her grandson, Michell Howard Gelfand, aged 14, both from Cleveland, Ohio, have flown to and from New York and Amsterdam almost daily to the amazement of airport officials.

They usually arrived at Schiphol airport in the morning and returned to New York the same evening without leaving the airport.

Inquiries were answered by the grandson with, "Grandma likes flying", and by Mrs Krasnoff with, "My grandson would like to learn to fly."

American police at Kennedy International Airport, New York, had also observed the grandmother and her grandson, who seldom left the airport before flying back to Holland.—Reuter.

Sarah Krasnoff dies. *London Times*, September 1, 1971. Courtesy of The London Times.

psychiatrist. They never left any airport. After a nonstop chase that lasted nearly half a year, Krasnoff finally collapsed from exhaustion in Amsterdam, and her death was reported in the news as "death by jet lag." Virilio was transfixed by the story as a metaphor for how new technologies (here, the airplane) simultaneously expanded and contracted the experience of time and space. He referred to Sarah Krasnoff as "a contemporary heroine who lived in deferred time."[5]

The other central narrative of JET LAG drew from the story of Donald Crowhurst, a weekend sailor who faked his circumnavigation of the globe in a 1969 around-the-world competition. Driven by the guaranteed publicity of the event, Crowhurst attempted the difficult voyage without adequate preparation, and after encountering severe difficulties, he aborted the race in the first leg, sailed in circles off the coast of South America, produced a counterfeit log, and sent home regular reports documenting a ten-month voyage around the world. When the British press published his fraudulent reports of the journey, he became a celebrated hero. Crowhurst also kept a second log of his journey—a haunting diary that documented his mental deterioration and increasingly delusional episodes. While in the apparent lead of the race, Crowhurst threw himself off his boat and presumably drowned. The BBC provided Crowhurst with a movie camera and recorder to document his journey, and the tapes became a key resource in The Builders' recreation of his story.

These two narratives provided fodder for a meditation on time and space at the fin de siècle. Together they represented different extremes on a time and space chiasmus: Krasnoff moved constantly without progressing, and Crowhurst seemed to progress but in fact barely moved. Moreover, each scenario engaged with a well-established technology—the sailboat and the airplane— that transformed the relationship of people to motion and travel as well as to their sensible connections to each other. Recalling Jacques Rancière's thinking about how experiences of media partake of a shared sensible landscape, JET LAG juxtaposed the time and space effects of technologies that link individuals across the sea and the sky.[6] It asked how such technologies of travel interface with contemporary experiences of mediated travel, especially in a digital landscape that seems to compress the experiences of distance and duration. That compression can have a dizzying effect on the body and perceptual system of global travelers. A reviewer of the show later meditated on the metaphor of the airport as a place of sensible reversal: it "puts a twist on the familiar period-dating question, 'What time is this place?' In airports, we're more likely to wonder, what place is this time?"[7]

We also could say that the distributions of the sensible that are shared in a world of rapid travel—literally and metaphorically, physically and virtually—affect the experience of performance. Intermedia performance thus finds itself responding to and intervening in a landscape where all participants are reckoning with new experiences of time. For Susan Melrose, Virilio's "geometries" of perception have their parallel in alternate forms of "measuring" and assembling time-based work:[8] "Measure can apply both in terms of the technical (metrization or quantization) and in terms of judgments of taste and value, which condition the emergence and evaluation of 'bits' of 'new work.'"[9] Such judgments redefine the temporalities of conventional elements of an artwork and try to hail a spectator into engagement with them: "It is by the measure in both senses, of 'actual discontinuous spatio-temporal structures' (such as 'character' or 'performer' or 'ending'), that 'we' identify 'them' as such. Measure, in this specific sense, where the production of 'new performance' material is concerned, seems to be linked to a capacity, in emergent material, to sustain a certain duration of (inquisitive) regard."[10] JET LAG told the story of individuals who were experiencing a variety of "discontinuous spatio-temporal structures," even as it demonstrated the degree to which the theater was always already discontinuous with itself.

JET LAG captured the attention of an expanded visual art world as much as it did the world of experimental theater. As a collaboration with the architects and media artists Diller + Scofidio, the production prompted a different kind of audience to take notice, especially when it became clear that the collaboration was an opportunity to mine and revise the parameters of the architectural and theatrical simultaneously. If a conventional approach to architecture emphasizes built environment, a theatrical partnership offers a reminder of the people who inhabit it. And if architecture tends to presume material solidity, theater also brings duration and movement to such a space. Influence across media also occurs reciprocally. If a conventional approach to theater assumes the stability of a background set, an architectural partner exposes the contingency of the background. And if theater has a habit of aligning itself with progression in narrative time, architecture encourages the theater to conduct a self-reflexive exploration of stasis. Much of D+S's work focuses on making artistic use of architectural tools, particularly digital software programs created for three-dimensional design. By using such tools, JET LAG occasioned a different kind of cross-media experiment than had been seen with the FAUST plays. At the same time, it extended the architectural excavations of MASTER BUILDER to focus more deeply on the time and space compressions and preoccupations of a millennial moment.

OPERATING SYSTEMS

With great interest, we learned about your project to use our terminal as background for your upcoming "jetlag" play. Thank you for your kind words about our architecture. We look forward to seeing your play as soon as it is on stage in Brussels.

Brussels Airport Terminal Company, April 10, 1998

After compiling research on Crowhurst's story, The Builders assembled resources to create its mediated dramatization. The company borrowed a friend's boat to shoot ocean footage for the Crowhurst sections. The goal was to find stable and consistent ocean landscapes that allowed only an occasional increase in the height of the water line because it would have to be matched by a more extreme rocking of the screen's pedestal. The crew had to venture fairly far out to sea to find a view of the horizon without land. Just as Crowhurst must have avoided any identifying backgrounds, so The Builders sought to create a uniform and unending background of sea and sky.

    After hearing The Builders' pitch for the concept of JET LAG, Kaaitheater in Brussels agreed to support a residency that allowed them to film in the Brussels International Airport, home of one of the longest moving walkways in the world. Weems, Kondek, Diller, and Scofidio created a shot list that

BATC

N.V. BRUSSELS AIRPORT TERMINAL COMPANY S.A.

The Builders Association
187 E 4th street - Suite 5N
New York   NY 10009
USA

Attn. Marianne Weems

ref. COM/JVC/td/98-0473   Zaventem, April 10 1998

00322 755 4229

Dear Mrs Weems

With great interest, we learned about your project to use our terminal as background for your
upcoming "jetlag" play. Thank you for the kind words about our architecture. We look forward
to seeing your play as soon as it is on stage in Brussels.

Kindest Regards and a pleasant Easter holiday,

Jan Van Der Cruysse
Communications Manager

Permission letter from Brussels Airport Terminal Company.

Video shoot for JET LAG, Chris Kondek and John Cleater, 1998.

included black-and-white videos from ostensible surveillance cameras and wide-angle color videos of the airport environment, representing from an omniscient perspective. Kondek trained these cameras on the various environments of the airport—waiting areas, passport control, escalators, and the vanishing-point perspective of the world's longest moving walkway. The shot list anticipated the staging of the footage in the performance, and each shot was storyboarded to support the choreographed movement of the live performers: "Camera moves smoothly at speed of walkway. Shoot going one way. Then the other way."[11] Other directions included, "Make sure to capture Doris and Lincoln on moving walkway looking toward the camera." The shot list anticipated the increasingly depleted trajectory of the travelers who ultimately were undone by their perpetual motion: "Pace surveillance shots to see them in different outfits, in a progression of deteriorating states."

STORYBOARD

The Diller + Scofidio team collaborated with dbox (James Gibbs and his colleagues Matthew Bannister, and Charles d'Autremont) to create the animated backgrounds for the airport—the moving walkways, the airplane, the escalators, and other places where still bodies would need a moving set. This iteration pushed the concept of set design in new architectural directions, combining architecture's interest in space with the conceptual goal of positioning a theatrical set as a digital screen.

The plotting of the "set" of the airplane was a case in point. dbox developed an animation that slowly built the fuselage of a plane. The image started with a row of airplane seats and multiplied wider and deeper to create the illusion of perspective. Building from this repetitious geometry, sound designer Dan Dobson created a deafening soundscape of a plane just before takeoff. This digitized set offered a counterpoint to the arrival of embodied characters. The grandmother and grandson were wheeled in on two airplane seats by flight assistants and then manually elevated to the center of the plane's digitized interior geometry. "Wait. Did you feel that?," Lincoln asked his grandmother: "We were like standing still in the air." In some ways, the seated travelers on the airplane recalled the blue screen of the four passengers in the car of IMPERIAL MOTEL (FAUST). The old-school technique of juxtaposing a moving background with static actors continues to delight. In this case, however, the actors were carried in a "purposely clumsy contraption"[12] to make the physical seats flush with digital seats on the screen, sitting still in the air.

Digital tools also were vital to imagining the arc of the story and its relation to image. D+S used Photoshop software to sketch storyboards and stage ideas for presenting JET LAG's material. This prospective script took form as a kind of deconstructed graphic novel, and using Photoshop concretized the concept of the storyboard in Builders' practice, ensuring a process by which text, image, and sound occupied the same plane as potential artistic materials.

The nature of the story in the storyboard was another question. Donald Crowhurst's ill-fated voyage provided a clear trajectory, but making a story out of a repetitious trajectory like Sarah Krasnoff's travel was more challenging. The use of storytelling was already controversial in the world of experimental theater in which The Builders worked. And JET LAG was the first Builders show that did not deconstruct an existent canonical narrative, such as Henrik Ibsen's *The Master Builder* or

Grandmother (Moe Angelos) and Grandson (Jess Barbagallo) in opening sequence.

the Faust tales. Weems began the process with a question about how the creation of a new narrative would be received:

We had very intentionally set out to tell the story of Donald Crowhurst, in a way without deconstruction. The story is really pretty straightforward. There wasn't a subtext that was undercutting the classical text. I remember feeling that this was an unexpected step toward telling a story, with a beginning, a middle, and an end, and I worried about that. It certainly wasn't the current fashion in "Downtown" theater, and I felt over-exposed in investing in something that could seem so "mainstream." You know, actual story-telling![13]

Ultimately, the intriguing element of these stories was that they barely followed a traditional narrative structure. As tales whose premises were unclear and whose progress was stalled or circuitous, their content was all middle, with beginnings and ends continually deferred. The unusual formal implications of these "real-world" stories made them adaptable to exploration in a mixed-media scene. Narrative was not assumed but under scrutiny. As such, the production of "text" for this show was necessarily a mixed-media process. The text needed to sit in partnership next to serially repeated images on a dbox storyboard, evoking that repetitious seriality in lieu of narrative progress.

Finding a capable writer who was willing to create such a text turned out to be difficult. Having previously navigated this process with playwright John Jesurun, Weems agreed to work with a former collaborator from D+S, Douglas Cooper, who was accustomed to writing for voiceover and informational contexts and might feel comfortable as a producer of textual material. However, his contributions were perceived to be too expository. Weems then turned to former V-Girl collaborator, Jessica Chalmers, with the mutual understanding that her prose was to be positioned as part of an assemblage where text is one component but not the prime mover of a postdramatic practice. Elizabeth Diller also was keen on ensuring that the language was imagined in relation to the "surface"[14] of the show. The language needed to be fragmented and elliptical to reflect the stalled trajectories of these travelers. It needed to be one element inside an architectural installation, something that Chalmers understood.

SCENES | LOCATION
1 | Bath
2 | Airplane
3 | Booth
4 | moving sidewalk
5 | booth
6 | lounge
7 | booth
8 | lounge
9 | plane
10 | booth
11 | lounge
12 | escalator
13 | booth
14 | plane
15 | booth

Writer Jessica Chalmers's ongoing scene list.

REHEARSAL/ASSEMBLY

By focusing on Crowhurst (also known as Roger Dearborn, performed by Jeff Webster) during the first half of the production, JET LAG eased audiences into a narrative structure whose masculinist preoccupations with movement and progression were delivered and simultaneously parodied. The character of Dearborn presented himself to the world as a seafaring adventurer by telling tales to the camera of his dangerous exploits and harrowing confrontations. He talked of the pleasures of being at sea and his near drowning when his boat's hull filled with water. This on-camera self-presentation contrasted with the backstage behavior that was witnessed by JET LAG audiences. Dearborn's movements actually were restricted as he stationed himself in front of a camera with a backdrop of his choosing (sunny or stormy weather, large or small waves). The manly exploits of this self-satisfied persona created illusions of movement that depended exclusively on a stationary arrangement of body and technology where the only actual motion came from a screen that rocked in place.

The Dearborn section of the show recalled the body and technology relationships of past productions, particularly the FAUST plays. Here the aesthetic of postproduction was managed by a single figure whose material embodiment was visible onstage amid all its wires, cameras, and flesh. This figure managed and mixed below to present a perfect image above, eliciting the same frisson in juxtaposing the encumbrances of hell with the pristine qualities of heaven. The process of documenting his journey was exposed as a highly stylized affair. Documenting also involved staging (with a hat and then without) and editing as Dearborn stopped, rewound, and restarted his tale several times until the telling satisfied him. The aperture of the camera served as a conduit that refined the image and edited away any extraneous and compromising background. At the same time, it changed the orientation of a figure from a side view onstage to a frontal view on screen, enlarging him to something beyond "life size" in the process.

As the opening scene progressed, a radio operator at a long table downstage of Dearborn's performance platform tried to open a channel of clear communication with Dearborn. "Roger, this is Nantucket. What is your position?," she asked over the distorting sound of radio waves, conveying a sense of enormous distance across what was, in fact, only a few feet onstage. "Bermuda is coming up on starboard," replied Dearborn of his fictionalized place in space: "too bad I can't stop to take a swim." Dearborn's little joke went unregistered as the radio operator tried to handle the delay in sound travel. Performer Jeff Webster's words were heard live and then echoed a second time to manifest the lag that is inherent in all radio communication. Sound designer Dan Dobson employed this method for all communications between Dearborn and the characters on land (his wife, his agent, the radio operator, and a television anchorman), creating a palpable break in communications as voices overlapped and interrupted each other. "What?," asked the radio operator. "What? We're experiencing some lag," she continued, her words ("some … some … lag … lag") sounding once live and once mediated. The conversation continued as Dearborn loquaciously described the landscape, until his eavesdropping agent suddenly prodded him to turn aimless accounts into cathartic plot: "We're recording, Roger, so can you tell us any more stories, brushes with death, that kind of thing?" In this reverberating soundscape, the would-be seaman and would-be public relations man attempted to make a story from the surround.

In rehearsal: Press agent (Kevin Hurley) and sailor
(Jeff Webster) communicate via radio.

Dearborn's static journey unfolded in the communications between these spaces. The camera on the boat at times witnessed his private recordings of his chronicle, staged and edited in the hopes of being publicly shared. Other times, the camera caught him in moments of anguish as he tried to communicate to his wife (played by Heaven Phillips) his uncertainty about the voyage, ultimately pulling apart the radio, which was his only connection to her. During one scene, Dearborn's wife, seated at a downstage table, was interviewed and almost ruined his act by worrying aloud about the bags of important provisions he had left behind. The anchorman noted that Dearborn's boat started two months later than other boats and hence was not trying to return before them. Rather, his goal was to win an "elapsed time race" that counted only the total time on the boat. Thus Dearborn displayed only slightly different ocean video as background, an undifferentiated landscape without visual markers of where he moved or what he passed. The news anchor tracked Dearborn's fictive progress, unwittingly exposing the contingency of a story that depended on wires, screens, and broadcast technology to verify its source. In these gaps and lags, the nature of liveness was itself under scrutiny, unsettling the veracity of television's "coming to us live" by entangling it with the "already with us live" of theater.

JET LAG continued The Builders' excavation of the relation among mediated technology and performance, and it did so with frames and forms that differed from those of MASTER BUILDER and the FAUST plays. As it toured in cities in Europe and North America, it also became emblematic of some of the formal questions of time and space that preoccupied late twentieth-century experimental theater more generally. It was clearly a meditation on liveness as the FAUST plays had been, and it dramatized Philip Auslander's Derridean argument about the live as a deeply imbricated, mediated effect.[15] But with JET LAG, The Builders also were preoccupied with the perception of speed and stasis in a globally connected world. As figures emerged and receded on stage, the play asked an overriding question about what it meant literally and aesthetically to move. As such, JET LAG participated in a late twentieth-century reinvention of what Elinor Fuchs's has called "the landscape play," resuscitating the questions once asked by Maurice Maeterlinck when he proposed his "slow theater" a century earlier.[16]

That formal interest also built a bridge to the so-called static forms of visual arts—architecture and the stillness and all-over plane of painting. For Hans-Thies Lehmann, JET LAG exemplified the formal preoccupations of what he eventually called postdramatic theater, a catchall term for a variety of practices that challenged the normative temporality of drama. Robert Wilson's slow stages figured centrally in Lehmann's argument. Interestingly, postdramatic theater also extended and revised Brechtian arguments about theatrical politics, proposing that Bertolt Brecht's dialectical terms needed to take seriously the effects of a contemporary mediated environment. "Theater can respond to this," wrote Lehmann, "only with a politics of perception."[17]

The perceptual stakes of postdramatic experimentation were particularly resonant in the second portion of JET LAG, which enacted a grandmother's trek back and forth across the Atlantic with her grandson. Dearborn's scenario was that of a perpetually stalled journey, but the grandmother explored a relentlessly mobile stasis. This section opened with a video projection of a moving airport walkway—again, the longest moving walkway in the world at Brussels Airport. At first, only the walkway itself was visible, with one belt moving toward the camera and the one next to it moving away. The walkway was centered in the camera's lens to create a perfect symmetry on either side as well as a perspectival window as the walkway receded infinitely toward the center of the camera. After several moments, small figures became visible, gradually enlarging as they approached. The faces of grandmother Doris and her grandson Lincoln eventually became visible, along with their luggage, headphones, and traveling paraphernalia. The travelers moved toward the viewer while continuing to stand still. Finally, they were carried, still standing, past the camera and out of the frame.

Throughout the exploration of Sarah Krasnoff's travel story, JET LAG meditated on the landscape of the airport and was informed by the tightly sealed, antiseptic, yet staged space of Jacques Tati's *Playtime* (1967). An airport is a place filled with mechanisms for managing the pace of bodies as they await access to the intense speed of a jet, and the airport walkway became an architectural metaphor for a landscape that alters perceptual conventions of movement and stasis. When the bodies of Builders actors came off the screen to inhabit the stage, the techniques of perceptual play expanded. In a later scene, Lincoln (played by Dominique Dibbell and then by Jess Barbagallo) and Doris (played first by Dale Soules, then by Ann Carlson, and then by Moe Angelos) found themselves on a moving walkway again, this one embodied live on stage from a side rather than front view. Once again, the travelers stood still to discuss their plans and ready themselves for the next trans-Atlantic leg. This time, the actors stood still on a stage and did not move bodily or mechanically across it. Instead, the perception of movement was created by the animation behind them, as the camera moved laterally across the antiseptic airport, passing gate after gate, walls of windows, and parked airplanes. The actors stood still and talked on a walkway that did not move as the projected environment unfurled.

This theatrical use of new media forms crystallized the philosophical conundrums surrounding speed and stasis in JET LAG. The mediated characters appeared metaphorically to move while the literal bodies standing in for them remained in one place. A similar technique was taken to greater effect later in the play when Lincoln and Doris mounted an "escalator." Once again, the actors stood still in the center of the stage while appearing rise. This time, the projected environment moved diagonally and down. Stairs, beams, and windows fell and disappeared as they reached the stage, their diagonal descent creating the impression of the characters' complementary ascent as they traveled through the airport's environs. Throughout JET LAG, a mediated mixture of screens and bodies staged the paradoxical compression of time and space in an area transformed by global travel. Performers and viewers occupied an uncanny space that promised unparalleled speed in the midst of relentless stasis. They were indeed "like … standing in the air."

As they "moved" from location to location, Doris and Lincoln also made contact with performers who were seated at a downstage table, including Transportation Security Administration (TSA) agents, the newscaster, the father, and others. The effect of stasis was created temporally and spatially through repetitive behaviors and environments. The airport is necessarily a fairly uniform space, with security systems, lounges, and gates that provide only occasional opportunities for stylistic or functional variations. The fonts of the gate sign might change from one airport to another; the duty-free shop might be located on the left rather than the right. But the airport landscape is a world whose lighting, desks, chairs, and opportunities to purchase food, liquor, souvenirs, and earplugs remain largely the same. That sense of repetitious uniformity was compounded for Doris and Lincoln, who ultimately made 167 flights between John F. Kennedy International Airport in New York and Charles de Gaulle Airport in Paris. JET LAG dramatized the overwhelming repetition textually and visually. Below the stage, a two security officers sat at their desk, retroactively presenting a review of their security logs and itineraries:

Security Officer #1:
Day 43
Paris, September 30th
Arrived Charles DeGaulle 14 minutes early due to favorable jet stream.

Day 44, Trip 41
Paris September 31st
Departed Charles DeGaulle on Sky Air Flight 84 bound for New York.
Half hour equipment delay due to late arrival of connecting Flight 6009 from Johannesburg.
Additional 40 minute mechanical delay caused by unspecified electrical malfunction.

Security Officer #2:
Same Day New York
Arrived JFK 2 hours and 4 minutes past scheduled arrival time. Further delay caused by air traffic control due to high congestion in the air and on the ground.

Same Day, Trip 42
Departed JFK on Sky Air Flight 603 bound for Paris. On time.

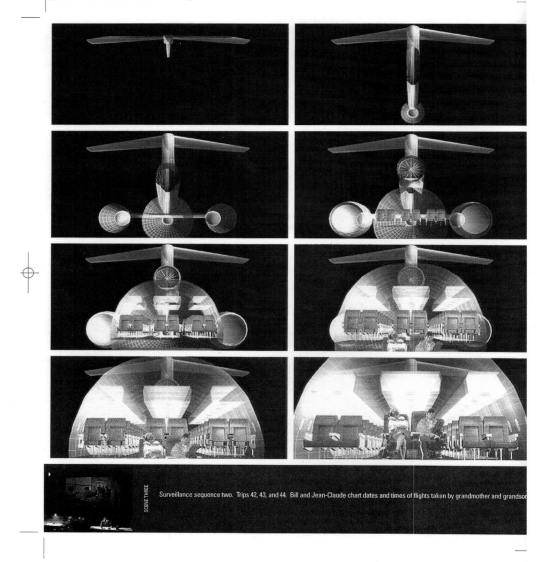

SCENE THREE

Surveillance sequence two. Trips 42, 43, and 44. Bill and Jean-Claude chart dates and times of flights taken by grandmother and grandson

Diller + Scofidio, "Jet Lag," original comp for ec/art S: #1–99: site de recherche et d'expérimentation.

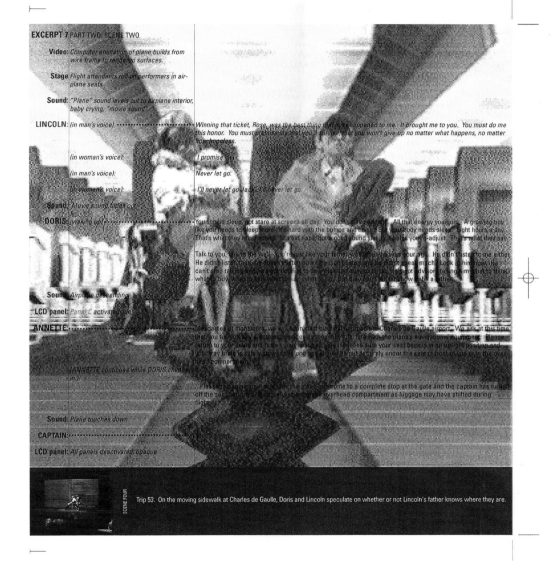

EXCERPT 7 PART TWO: SCENE TWO

Video: *Computer animation of plane builds from wire frame to rendered surfaces.*

Stage: *Flight attendants roll on performers in airplane seats.*

Sound: *"Plane" sound levels out to airplane interior, baby crying, "movie sound".*

LINCOLN: *(in man's voice)* Winning that ticket, Rose, was the best thing that ever happened to me. It brought me to you. You must do me this honor. You must promise me that you'll survive, that you won't give up no matter what happens, no matter how hopeless.

(in woman's voice): I promise.

(in man's voice): Never let go.

(in woman's voice): I'll never let go Jack. I'll never let go.

Sound: *Movie sound fades out.*

DORIS: *(waking up)* You should sleep, not stare at screens all day. You don't sleep enough. All that energy you burn. A growing boy like you needs to sleep more. It's hard with the bumps and noise. But your body needs sleep. Eight hours a day. That's what they recommend. Not just naps, but a good sound sleep. It helps you re-adjust. That's what they say.

Talk to you, talk to the wall. You're just like your father, when he was your age. He didn't listen to me either. He didn't listen then, he doesn't listen now. He didn't listen, and he didn't speak much. Look at him now. He can't stop talking, he never stops. He's on his phone too much, his lot advisor telling him what to think, what to buy, what to sell. There he is, when... But that's your father now. He's a father.

Sound: *Airplane descending.*

LCD panel: *Panel C activated: clear.*

ANNETTE: Mesdames et messieurs, we will soon start our descent to approach Charles de Gaulle airport. We ask at this time that you turn off any electronic devices they may not interfere with the plane's navigational equipment. Please return to your seats and fasten your seatbelts. Also make sure your seat back is in an upright position and your tray table is secured. Your belongings should be put securely under the seat in front of you or in the overhead compartment.

(ANNETTE continues while DORIS chimes in.)

Please remain seated until the plane has come to a complete stop at the gate and the captain has turned off the seatbelt sign. Please open the overhead compartment as luggage may have shifted during flight.

Sound: *Plane touches down.*

CAPTAIN:

LCD panel: *All panels deactivated: opaque.*

SCENE FOUR Trip 53. On the moving sidewalk at Charles de Gaulle, Doris and Lincoln speculate on whether or not Lincoln's father knows where they are.

spreads 12-13 Quark   2/8/99   12:05 PM   Page 1

SCENE ELEVEN

Surveillance sequence six. Jean-Claude announces the death of Doris Schwarz after 167 consecutive transatlantic flights.

EXCERPT 11 PART TWO SCENE TWELVE

Video: Computer-generated moving sidewalk

Sound: "tinkle pulse" loop with bass added. (ambient) lobby noise.

Stage: JFK Airport moving sidewalk, a few days before the death. LINCOLN is behind DORIS, who is in an airport wheelchair. LINCOLN continually looks over his shoulder.

LINCOLN: I guess we're catching the 2 o'clock

DORIS: as usual.

LINCOLN: Where do you want to sit

DORIS: I'm tired...in that place

LINCOLN: you want to go to the other side?

DORIS: the nook place.

LINCOLN: near the stand in the corner, where

DORIS: No...I'm tired of there.

LINCOLN: Okay

DORIS: I don't like...no way!...

LINCOLN: you mean the--

DORIS: blue chairs...

[pause]

DORIS: time?

LINCOLN: He's wearing two watches and checks both twelve.

DORIS: Closing her eyes and then opening them··· I feel a little...

That's strange.

LINCOLN: What.

DORIS: When I close my eyes...

It's exactly the same as when they're open.

EXCERPT 12 PART TWO SCENE TWELVE

Video: Surveillance Sequence Six

Sound: "tinkle pulse" loop with bass and cymbal added, ambient surveillance booth noise.

LCD panel: Panel C activated: clear

JEAN CLAUDE:

Day 174, trip 167
February 23rd
Time at destination 4:17 am.
Location: airborne somewhere between New York and Paris.

Ms. Doris Schwarz of Warrensville, Long Island, died of a heart attack on board a Paris-bound 747 during what has been calculated to be her 167th transAtlantic flight between Paris and New York in 6 months. According to the records, on the day of her death, Mrs. Schwarz purchased a round-trip ticket, as usual, at John F. Kennedy Airport, for a Sky Air flight for herself and her grandson. Some turbulence was experienced over Newfoundland and passengers were asked to resume their seats. At 10:17pm, a flight attendant attempted, unsuccessfully, to wake Mrs. Schwarz. The death occurred between the meal service and the inflight movie.

LCD panel: Panel C deactivated: opaque

SCENE TWELVE

Trip 167. Airborne, just before Doris' death. Lincoln plays his flight simulator game, crashes, reloads, and keeps playing.

EXCERPT 8 PART TWO: SCENE T

Video *(Surveillance Sequence Two (Pulsing Stills)*

LCD panel: *Panel B activated: clear*

BILL: ············ Day 42, Trip 39 New York, September 29th
Arrived JFK on Sky Air Flight 84 from Charles DeGaulle. On time.

29.9

Same Day, Trip 40
Departed JFK on Sky Air Flight 603 bound for Paris.
55-minute weather delay due to low lying fog and poor visibility.

LCD panel: *Panel B deactivated: opaque*
Panel C activated: clear

JEAN- ············ Day 43 __, September 30th
CLAUDE: Arrived Charles DeGaulle 14 minutes early due to favorable jet stream.

Day 44, Trip 41 Paris September 31st.
Departed Charles DeGaulle on Sky Air Flight 84 bound for New York. Half-hour equipment delay due to late ar__
of connecting Flight 6009 from Johannesburg. Additional 40 minute mechanical delay caused by unspecified __
trical malfunction.

LCD panel: *Panel C deactivated: opa__*
Panel B activated: clear

BILL: ············ Same Day New York
Arrived JFK 2 hours and 4 minutes past scheduled arrival time. Further delay caused by air traffic control du__
high congestion in the air and on the ground.

Same Day, Trip 42
Departed JFK on Sky Air Flight 603 bound for Paris. On time.

LCD panel: *Panel B deactivated: opaque*
Panel C activated: clear

JEAN- ············ Day 45 Paris, October 1st
CLAUDE: Arrived Charles DeGaulle 7 hours and 14 minutes after scheduled arrival time. Flight was re-routed throu__
Frankfurt due to baggage handlers strike and consequent 4 hour airport shutdown in Paris.

Day 46, Trip 43 Paris, October 2nd
Departed Charles DeGaulle on Sky Air Flight 84 bound for New York. One hour gate hold due to heavy traffic __
destination airport.

LCD panel: *Panel C deactivated: opaque*
Panel B activated: clear

BILL: ············ Same Day, New York
Arrived JFK 1 hour and 35 minutes past scheduled arrival time. Additional delay due to strong __

Same Day, Trip 44
Departed JFK on Sky Air Flight 603 bound for Paris.
57-minute delay due to increased airport security. Extra precautions were exercised due to string of an__
__ threats.

SCENE FIVE

Surveillance sequence three. Jean-Claude provides voice-over about movement between time zones and the impact of rapid travel on the human body.

SCENE SIX Airport Lounge. Trip 78. Doris and Lincoln settle in, Doris changes clothes.

SCENE SEVEN Surveillance sequence four. Trip 139. Bill and Jean-Claude review accumulated facts about the travels of Doris and Lincoln.

As the officers recounted the log of arrivals and departures, the staged screen displayed black-and-white footage of security cameras, tracking Doris and Lincoln's mundane movements in the lounge spaces and security systems of the airport: Doris heaved a piece of luggage off a conveyor belt; Lincoln looked sheepishly at a bank of telephones; he played his flight simulator video games; she sprayed and wiped seat covers in the airport lounge before settling in; both tossed and turned as they tried to sleep in armchairs, resting limbs in awkward positions and splaying bodies over two chairs at once. Throughout these scenes, Dobson mixed an ambient background hum and a barely perceptible rhythmic loop, creating a sonic sense of anticipation that paradoxically did not build. The repetitive soundscape rendered every action strangely equivalent in a journey whose time and space markers were radically out of joint. "You know what I miss?," said Doris. "I miss the dark. Know what I hate, I hate the sun," she complained, feeling the weight of jet lag—that is, the weight of inhabiting an environment whose spatial signs are out of sync with the body's experience of progression in time. A TSA agent continued his inventory of accumulated actions:

278 trans-Atlantic flights

One million—eleven thousand—six hundred—twenty five miles flown

418 meals, 278 bags of peanuts, and 1,280 beverages consumed in flight

278 crossings at US Customs and Passport Control

276 crossings at French Customs and Passport Control

7 movies viewed an average of 22 times each

278 toiletry kits collected

1,168 time zones traversed

1,668 hours or 70 days lost.... flying east

3,336 hours lived twice.... flying west

CLOSINGS

As tales that were most interesting for being all "middle," concluding them was an ambiguous act. In the case of Crowhurst/Dearborn, the tale concluded when Roger's mediated voice and image abruptly concluded. Whether accidentally or purposely, the broadcast system lost track of Dearborn's signal, ending the scene with a fuzz of sound and image along with a radio operator calling "Roger? Roger?," highlighting the double entendre between his name and the affirmative code ("Roger that") for ending a radio conversation. In the case of Krasnoff/Doris, the tale's built-in ending was the demise of the grandmother whose bodily system gave in to extreme jet lag. The final scenes dramatized that ending, showing her deterioration and including a security officer's retroactive report of her death. The actual ending of the act and the show, however, backtracked in time to suggest that the flying would continue. Employing a sophisticated wire-frame animation, the digital airplane rotated dramatically from a frontal to a side view to a rear view, placing Lincoln and his failing grandmother in seats that eventually faced the screen at the back of the stage. This time, the screen displayed the video screen that was visible to Lincoln as he continued to play his pilot video games. "I'm losing control," he said as he is turned safely on his physically secure seat, pretending that the lurching screen in front of him—and us—was an actual one:

LINCOLN: [Excitedly] Okay, we're going down. [in his airline pilot's voice] This is Blue Sky 732. I am no longer in control of my aircraft. I repeat, I am no longer in control of the aircraft, and we are as I speak careening downward, farther and farther down…. I just want to say thank you to everybody who made these flights possible … damn…. Ladies and gentlemen, I'm very sorry but … I'm stalling out again, I'm stalling out, we're going down. Dammit. [he makes a last few efforts on the keyboard] Okay, I'm dead.

JET LAG earned significant praise and a multicity tour to a range of distinguished venues, producing more jet lag for the artists who performed it. Toward the end of the whirlwind, Builders artists took stock of the multiple cities that they had visited (and varieties of experiences endured and enjoyed): "Århus, Rotterdam, Nantes, Créteil, Budapest, … Copenhagen, Strasbourg, Munich, … Montreal." MASS MoCA and The Kitchen were even in their own country.

In preparation for its tour, collaborators debated several versions of how to represent their contributions in the program. A show that had challenged theatrical parameters also challenged its traditional systems for dividing and crediting labor. Elizabeth Diller asked to claim credit for the original idea (which as an architect made Marianne Weems wonder if that made her into Diller's technical fabricator). They compromised by giving "Original idea by Diller + Scofidio" but placing "Directed by Marianne Weems" on the same line, effectively joining architectural systems and theatrical systems for crediting the prime mover of a piece of art.

The significance of a collaboration across theatrical and architectural forms was not lost on reviewers, and it is interesting to compare the responses of different art sectors. The art curator and performance art critic RoseLee Goldberg wrote about JET LAG in the context of a Diller + Scofidio retrospective that effectively gave JET LAG the status of an installation art piece.[18] Another Scandinavian critic labeled this theatrical play a "multi-media performance installation," which echoed the mixed-media pursuits of its makers.[19] Architectural critics also placed JET LAG in relationship to prior D+S works and used analytic perspectives indebted to an architectural frame. *New York Times* architecture critic Herbert Muschamp spoke of JET LAG as an "ephemeral" work that had already "vanished into memory," which was not quite the case (it toured beyond New York). Compared to the solidity of the architecture that he was used to reviewing, however, the piece was strikingly evanescent. The fact that the piece was about "duration" made the theatrical medium even more apt.[20]

Theater reviewers like Jonathan Romney of *The Guardian* also captured the formal experimentation of the endeavor, albeit from the worldview of a conventionally time-based medium: "Crowhurst went nowhere, but still managed to persuade the world that he was moving in a straight line; Krasnoff, endless in motion, was locked into a private loop of stasis…. The physical and mental dislocation suffered by its protagonists as they cross (or fail to cross) time zones corresponds to the gap between real-time acting and life filtered through the media."[21]

As a production that toured in 1998 and 1999, JET LAG was destined to endure the hopes and anxieties of a millennial shift. Weems and Jessica Chalmers found themselves in several interviews where they were asked to defend The Builders' aesthetic of the "future."[22] Chalmers wondered aloud about why there "is a perception that JET LAG is somehow new in theater." Weems agreed: "The question has been posed so often that I began to suspect it had been sold to the press that way by the presenters, though I didn't see it marketed as such."[23] For some, such an aspiration was utopian, but for many theater makers and theater critics, JET LAG invoked a dystopian fear that theater, like human life, was being transformed into a digital specter of its former self. "Some viewers may feel that life jackets for the soul and seat belts for the imagination are needed to survive 'Jet Lag,' at the Kitchen," wrote one *New York Times* theater critic.[24] His review ultimately was positive about the production, but he read its message as menacing: "For despite its thrilling, sometimes overwhelming presence, the technology of 'Jet Lag' is simply our world. The boy knows it, plays with it and survives. The adults try to manipulate it and cannot. This production is like a single profound meditation on the muted caution of the philosopher Ortega y Gassett 70 years ago about what even then he saw as the miraculous technology of the modern city: 'the world is civilized; its inhabitant is not.'"[25] Others stepped in to adjudicate ("For them, the media is clearly the partner of theatre and not the enemy") but still knew that the threatening image of "enemy" forces would not easily dissipate.[26]

JET LAG finished touring in 2000, making room for The Builders to begin work on a new show. They were invited to remount this production a decade later, creating the opportunity to look back on whether the future had come. The response to the production at Montclair State University (Montclair, New Jersey) did not worry quite so much about the threat of futurity. Instead, it voiced the fear of anachronicity—whether it "is, perhaps inevitably, going to seem like a period piece."[27] Reviewers' responses suggested that anxiety about the future was in fact passé. Additionally, the fact that other technologies were now new changed the perception of JET LAG's characters' sensible relation to the world: "Today when someone wants to escape the world or create a fake life, they probably do so online. The distracted characters in 'Jet Lag' use technology to isolate themselves, but they also physically go places, even if where those may be is something of a mystery. The kind of loneliness portrayed here seems different from that in an age of social networking."[28] Relative to the space of social networking, JET LAG's time and space distortions now seemed physically intimate and not dystopicly drained of embodied connection as they had a decade earlier. Because the future was never The Builders' pursuit in the first place, the remounting arguably allowed audiences to concentrate on the sociopolitics of perception instead. Are we able, in fact, to sustain ourselves and our connections to others in a landscape where time and space are strangely expanded and radically compressed in the same moment? The fact that yesterday's principles of disconnection could become today's vehicles for reconnection suggests that we can and do, even if it means adjusting our sense of where the lag (… the … lag) might be.

Grandson (Jess Barbagallo)
and grandmother (Moe
Angelos) on escalator with
flight attendant (Kristen Sieh).

0157594   SITI

779841658Ø

TOUR CODE   AGENT CODE
2ITF2713118   A33743780

PLACE OF ISSUE   ISO CODE   DATE OF ISSUE
NEW YORK   NY US12JUNØØ

FARE BASIS/TICKET DESIGNATOR   FCI   SERV CARR. ID
AA ITX/F2713118   7   ØØ11/

CLASS DATE   TIME   STATUS   NOT VALID BEFORE   NOT VALID AFTER
X   Ø2JUL935A OK   Ø2JULØ2JUL

ISSUING AGENT ID
X/ 9Q4Ø*HA

REISSUE PENALTY APPLIES

/M 712474 /FCJFK VS LHR

BT   ITX/F2713118 TL BT

ØXY3.ØØXA3.ØØXFJFK3

ENDNOTES

Artist's Voice: Elizabeth Diller, architect/co-creator

From the start of the collaboration with Marianne and The Builders, there were no issues around what the role of an architect or a designer was. We were all collaborators. We were each using our skills in the strongest way—the craft of theater directing, the craft of space making—and we were impacting each other's work in ways that are so fuzzy that they are hard to detect. Whereas we were good at the third dimension, Marianne was skilled at working in the fourth dimension—the time dimension.

One thing I remember is that we were interested in the evolution of these characters who were always in motion, either in the air or in airport space. We felt that these characters behaved differently from normal people: they washed differently, they ate different kinds of food, they spoke differently. So we ended up writing little bits of dialogue for the characters to say. That's what was so great about the collaboration: we didn't know the boundaries of what we did know how to do and what we didn't know how to do. We crashed in certain ways and found that we were able to contribute in bigger ways than we originally had thought we would do.

When we brought on dbox we began evolving other kinds of media play with the stage. Between the staging and the media, Crowhursts' documentary and his real life experience, there became two parallel paths in truth and fiction. And through all this time, we were evolving the content, the story, along with the video and with the whole team.

Our culture puts a high value on the live and places the mediated as negative. In JET LAG, the characters functioned between the live and the mediated. The sets were both live and three-dimensional: time went forward and backward and could slow down or stand still. In this way, JET LAG helped us deliver some key threads in our ongoing investigations into artifice and authenticity. The piece doesn't feel dated. These characters are products of the late twentieth century. I'm really proud of the piece and remember it as a great collaboration.

Guest Voice: Louise Jeffreys, director of arts, Barbican Centre, London

JET LAG came to the Barbican in 2000. The piece explored two extraordinary lives and deaths—small tragedies of the modern world that were inextricably bound up with twentieth-century technology and were told using the selfsame media.

These are unique stories, but we nonetheless see ourselves in the characters' thwarted hopes and ambitions, which are made even more poignant by our knowledge that they are based on real lives and true stories. Our desire for success and our fear of failure, our reluctance to admit defeat, our determination and passion, our wish to protect those we love, our frailty in the face of overwhelming natural and technological forces: these feelings are at the core of human souls, and JET LAG made them manifest.

I remember Jeff Webster as Crowhust/Dearborn, the doomed yachtsman who was dwarfed in a tiny boat, adrift on an epic-scale stage. The scale and danger of his ill-prepared endeavor were made visible against the giant waves projected behind him. The loss of his dreams and his descent into a tortured psychological state were heart-wrenchingly played out in contrast to his heroic video diary. I found myself split in two—wanting to believe the reports of success despite the evidence of failure. Theater has long been dominated by the word, but Marianne gives the image equal status. Reading these pieces in a script would provide only part of the story. The images stay in my mind as I think back.

Grandmother Sarah/Doris was a very modern fugitive embarking on another doomed journey in which time and space are distorted. In this world in limbo, 167 transatlantic flights can feel as if they are a better option than facing the loss of a loved one in a custody battle. Video images of airport lounges and CCTV footage are manipulated to resemble a modern labyrinth, a descent into hell.

JET LAG exposed the complex relationships between our hearts, our minds, and the technologies of our times. Technology was at the core of each story and was the means by which the story was brought to us. I can still see the images clearly in my mind as I write and can feel the two tragic stories that they visualized.

Guest Voice: RoseLee Goldberg, founder and director of Performa

Current fascination with the body and the machine inevitably carries disturbing overtones of a world manipulated by artificial intelligence, which are eerily captured by JET LAG. For the artists, the issue is not the supposed conflict between live and mediated (whether electronic or mechanical) and the implied moral superiority of one over the other. Rather their approach embodies a full acceptance of a hybrid world that gives equal balance to both. The performers are also conscious of the duets they play with their recorded images; they perform for the camera as much as for the audience, becoming active participants in structuring all that the audience sees. JET LAG probed the psychological depths of the phenomenon of liveness. This was achieved by distinguishing foreground and background as separate stages for live and mediated action, emphasizing the fragility and corporeality of the former over the artifice and luminosity of the latter. At times, a computer image seemed to loom over the stage, while at others live performers were brought into close range. These shifts, between foreground and background, between flesh and celluloid, accentuated the emotional undertow of both stories and, at the same time, made the audience aware of the multiple registers of information present in the production. This strategy also showed the live performers engage the viewer's attention and hold on to it in real time in ways that moving images produced by projectors and computers cannot. On a stage rigged with technological paraphernalia—cameras, monitors, microphones, lights, screens, and computers—the live performer was a radical, even shocking presence. The result was not the triumph of the live, but a new, synthesized form that was half-live and half-mediated.[29]

People

JET LAG (1998)

Directed by Marianne Weems
Created by Diller + Scofidio and The Builders Association
Produced by Renata Petroni with The Builders Association

Design and video concept by Diller + Scofidio
Written by Jessica Chalmers
Video designer: Christopher Kondek
Sound designer: Dan Dobson
Lighting designed by: Jennifer Tipton

Performed by
Ann Carlson
Tim Cummings
Dominique Dibbell
Kevin Hurley
Heaven Phillips
Dale Soules
Jeff Webster

Computer animation by James Gibbs/dbox, Eric Schuldenfrei
Costume designer: Ellen McCartney
Video codesigner/video system designer/operator: Peter Norrman
Video system operator/camera operator/flight attendant: Amber Lasciak

Design associate: Lyn Rice
Lighting associate: Susan Hamburger
Production manager: Martin Stevenson
Assistant director: Shelley Lasica
Stage manager: Natalia de Campos
Assistant for computer animation: Eric Schuldenfrei
Assistant costume designer: Wren Crosley
Set construction: Adam Kovacevic, Lauren Kolks

JET LAG (2010 Remount)

Directed by Marianne Weems
Created by The Builders Association and Diller Scofidio + Renfro
Design, story, and video concept by Diller Scofidio + Renfro

Video designer: Christopher Kondek
Sound designer: Dan Dobson
Lighting designed by Jennifer Tipton
Writer: Jessica Chalmers
Company dramaturg: James Gibbs

Performed by

Maureen Angelos
Jess Barbagallo
Nick Bonnar
David Pence
Kristen Sieh
Joseph Silovsky

Three-dimensional design and animation by dbox

Costume design: Ellen McCartney

Video codesigner/operator: Austin Switser

Video associate: Jared Mezzocchi

Lighting associates: Tyler Micoleau, Laura Mroczkowski

Production manager: Neal Wilkinson

Technical director: Josh Higgason

Costume coordinator: Andreea Mincic

Production stage manager: Megan Schwarz Dickert

Managing director: Erica Laird

Venues

1998–2000   The Kitchen, New York, NY

Kulturhus Århus, Århus, Denmark

Lantaren/Venster, Rotterdam, The Netherlands

Kaaitheater, Brussels, Belgium

Maison des Arts /Créteil, Paris, France

Fin-de-Siècle, Nantes, France

Trafo House, Budapest, Hungary

KIT's Sommerscene 99, Copenhagen, Denmark

Le Maillon, Strasbourg, France

Spiel-Art Festival at the Marstall Theater, Munich, Germany

On the Boards, Seattle, WA

The Barbican Centre, London, UK

Massachusetts Museum of Contemporary Art, North Adams, MA, May 1999
(American premiere)

2010   Peak Performances at Montclair State University, Montclair, NJ, September 23–October 3

Afterparty

Company tally for JET LAG tours from 1998 to 2001 listing performances, hotel, flights, per diem, injuries, sexual encounters, drugs, and illnesses.

SOME SOURCE MATERIALS FOR THE PRODUCTION

Books

Hall, Nicholas, and Ron Tomalin. *The Strange Last Voyage of Donald Crowhurst.* New York: Stein and Day, 1970.

Illman, Paul E. *The Pilot's Radio Communications Handbook.* Tab Practical Flying Series. New York: McGraw-Hill, 1994.

Slocum, Captain Joshua. *Sailing Alone around the World.* New York: Dover, 1956.

Sobel, Dana. *Longitude: The True Story of a Long Genius Who Solved the Greatest Scientific Problem of His Time.* New York: Penguin Books, 1996.

Articles

"Britons Sail Ketch around the World, 312 Days Nonstop." *New York Times*, April 23, 1969, 1.

"Crowhurst: Only a Name in His Own Home Town." *Sunday Times*, July 28, 1969.

Dawe, Tony. "Lone Yachtsman Rescued after Quitting Race." *New York Times*, November 25, 1968.

Eszterhas, Joseph. "A Grandmother's 'Crime' Was Love." *Plain Dealer*, September 1, 1971.

"Flying Granny Grounded by Heart Attack." *London Times*, September 1, 1971.

"Flying Granny to Be Taken Home." *New York Times*, September 3, 1971.

Friedberg, Anne. "Virilio's Screen: The Work of Metaphor in the Age of Technological Convergence." *Journal of Visual Culture* 3 (August 2004): 183–193.

"Headliners." *New York Times*, September 2, 1971.

"Home from Amsterdam." *Plain Dealer*, September 6, 1971.

"La Vielle Dame et L'enfant." *Le Monde*, September 3, 1971.

"Missing Spares 'Vital to Crowhurst Voyage.'" *Sunday Times*, July 28, 1969.

"Mystery of Lone Sailor's Records." *Sunday Times*, July 29, 1969.

"Robin Gives Up His £5,000." *Sunday Times*, n.d.

"The Sea Lover." *Time*, August 8, 1969.

"Search for Yachtsman Ends." *New York Times*, July 12, 1969, 2.

Shaw, Terri. "Transatlantic Traveler Dies in Hotel." *Washington Post*, September 1, 1971.

"Theories at Odds on Lost Sea Racer." *New York Times*, July 13, 1969, 11.

Virilio, Paul. "The Third Interval: A Critical Transition." *Re-thinking Technologies*. Minneapolis: University of Minnesota Press, 1993.

"Yachtsman Retires." *New York Times*, November 20, 1968.

4 XTRAVAGANZA

OLD MEDIA AND NEW THEATER

Performer Jeff Webster opens the show.

OPENINGS

Before everyone in the audience had taken a seat, the director walked onto the stage in front of a closed curtain. He was all business: "All right, now, everybody. Listen to me. This is how we're gonna make a show." His voice reverberated in sync with the recorded voice of another director barking the same lines: "We'll work five weeks, and we're gonna open on scheduled time. You're gonna work and sweat and work some more." The two voices kept a fast, vaguely syncopated pace as their instructions continued. The director cocked his head back and forth in herky-jerky movements, as if the tape had been speeded up: "You're gonna work days, and you're gonna work nights, and you're gonna work between time, when you think you need it. You're gonna dance until your feet fall off. It's going to be the toughest five weeks that you ever lived through. Now, anybody who doesn't think he's gonna like it had better quit right now. What do I hear? Nobody?" He barely paused for an answer; the other voice on tape did not wait either: "Good! Then that's settled. Let's get started."

XTRAVAGANZA was an encounter with a world where putting on a show meant business and where being in show business meant managing many media at once. By compiling fragments from the history of American popular theater, it showed the deep entanglements of new intermedia performance in the old genealogies of extravagant spectacle. Although they were heartened by the international success of JET LAG, Weems and her collaborators where unnerved by the futuristic terms in which their intermedia work was cast. "It just drove me insane that people thought that multimedia was a new thing," Weems recalled.[1] Her frustrations sent her and a team of researchers to a theatrical archive, where they found the 1933 film *42nd Street*, a cinematic celebration of theatrical labors. The character of the director in that film provided the opening text for XTRAVAGANZA. It was the proverbial pep talk of the theatrical taskmaster who knows that his cast's love of the art (and hope for celebrity) will help him extract those extra hours of work. Builders actor Jeff Webster played the director, matching his voice to *42nd Street*'s Julian Marsh, who seemed both to ghost and propel Webster's articulations in the present. Marsh thus was reembodied in the present by an actor who seemed to be motored by the past enactment of Marsh, whose pace was speedy and urgent and seemed bent on doing everything possible to get a show on the road.

R&D

When audience members opened their programs for XTRAVAGANZA, they read a director's note that was unusually explicit:

XTRAVAGANZA looks back at theatrical forms which preceded much of what is now called multimedia performance. Extravaganzas of the mid-19th and early 20th centuries were large-scale presentations which mixed live performance, music, dance, and later film in a variety show which was based on the visually spectacular nature of each "act." Multimedia is not something which emerged with the experiments of the 1960s or even the advent of television, but with the epic pageants of Steele MacKaye, the technical wizardry of "The Electricity Fairy" Loie Fuller, the lavish stage-scapes of Florenz Ziegfeld, and the spectacularization of cinema which accompanied Busby Berkeley's move from stage to screen.

XTRAVAGANZA's argument was clear, and its mission—to act as an historical corrective to the perception of "new media"—meant that this project required a significant amount of research and development. In many ways, the seeds of XTRAVAGANZA were sewn during the production processes surrounding IMPERIAL MOTEL (FAUST) and JUMP CUT (FAUST). Energized by the work of scholars such as Jonathan Crary, Tom Gunning, and Charles Musser, The Builders' FAUST was an homage to the prehistory of cinema and to its postproduction labor processes. Having been tagged as the "future" of new media theater with JET LAG, The Builders returned to "new" media's past by recalling traditions of screen practice that mixed "projected image," "audio complement," and a "showman" who managed the display.[2]

XTRAVAGANZA reminded contemporary audiences that the pleasure of watching technical feats had a theatrical history that was linked to the aesthetics of the world fairs, music halls, and penny

Film still from *The Gold Diggers of 1935*, directed by Busby Berkeley. Underwood & Underwood/Corbis.

Promotional image for XTRAVAGANZA.

arcades. Recalling Gunning's "cinema of attractions," new media theater was continuous with the history of popular theater. Whether the technical feats were called "magic lanterns," "animated photographs," or "moving pictures," audiences came to watch the nonintegrated, unsutured assembly of screen, sound, and embodied performer. These early intermedia combinations featured the latest photographic and audio technologies, setting an historical precedent for what "multimedia" might later become. The twentieth-century history of both realistic cinema and drama might have repressed their dependence on a technical apparatus, but intermedia performance remembered a history of technological variety. Creating an intermedia performance thus did not simply add new media to drama or add new media to cinema. It involved remembering the intermedial history and intermedial apparatus already contained in both forms.

If the connection between old and new intermedia performance had been implicit in IMPERIAL MOTEL (FAUST) and JUMP CUT (FAUST), it was explicit in XTRAVAGANZA. Working with Norman Frisch as a dramaturg, Weems and her researchers gathered documents, criticism, and secondary literature from a variety of archives, including the Library of Congress, to show how popular theater has been a venue for cross-media experimentation. In addition to researching early cinematic history, Weems read biographies of Busby Berkeley (1895–1976), Loie Fuller (1862–1928), D. W. Griffith (1875–1948), James "Wild Bill" Hickok (1837–1876), Steele MacKaye (1842–1894), Florenz Ziegfeld (1867–1932), Adolf Zukor (1873–1976), and many others who did not end up in the final script. They examined research on Thomas Edison (1847–1931), traveled to his first film studio (the Black Maria in Edison, New Jersey), and immersed themselves in nineteenth-century cultural history, comparing the implications of popular forms such as vaudeville, burlesque, musical revues, nickelodeons, peep shows, and show palaces. They learned about how patents and the practice of ticketing at performances that displayed new inventions structured the business of show business.

As research for XTRAVAGANZA expanded, Weems and Frisch identified four major figures to focus on—Berkeley, Fuller, MacKaye, and Ziegfeld. They began to recast these genius figures from theatrical history as individuals who collaboratively mixed the media of their time. As Weems quoted in her journal: "When discussing the influence of Berkeley's stage work on his films, it is less accurate to see him as an isolated theatrical innovator than as the inheritor of already flourishing stage and popular entertainment traditions—those of the musical, the extravaganza, the big production number, the spectacular revue, and various 'aggregate' forms of entertainment."[3] Multimedia is not a new thing now, and Weems learned that that it was not a new thing then either.

Showing the contemporary relevance of the historical extravaganza meant venturing outside of the proscenium stage, both in the past and in the present. In looking around for contemporaneous analogies to past aggregate forms, Weems and her collaborators found a contemporaneous high-tech fairground in the spectacle of the 1990s rave dance club scene. In the 1890s, the vaudeville stage was a prime place to experiment with a live display of the technology of that time period, and in the 1990s, the mixing and sampling apparatus of the club became a site for similar behaviors. Research for this hypothesis took many forms, both participatory and discursive. Members of the company had spent enough time in clubs in the United States and Europe to be familiar with how the fundamental components of screen practice—projected image, audio accompaniment, and embodied showman— were being recombined in the club format. A Builders staff member, Mark Uhl, who was an aficionado of the New York club scene encouraged them to visit different sites and reported on what he saw and heard from night to night. They also arranged an interview with club dancer Bravo LaFortune, who agreed to consult and be part of the cast.

Weems also read the work of cultural critics who studied club culture in the "age of sampledelia" and who considered the implications of an aesthetic where mixing had revised notions of authorship.

Weems underlined relevant quotes from Lady Miss Kier, Edward Rothstein, Greg Tate, and Simon Reynolds, who said: "House [music] makes the producer, not the singer, the star.... Operating as a cottage factory, churning out a high turnover of tracks, the house producer replaces the artist's signature with the industrialist's trademark. Closer to an architect, the house auteur is absent from his own creation; house tracks are less like artworks in the expressive sense, than vehicles, rhythmic engines that take the dancer on a ride."[4] The Builders' process of postproduction had transformed a Gordon Matta-Clark house into a live studio and later propelled the unmaking and remaking of early Faust films. The club, the VJ, the DJ, and the house producer offered new postproduction analogies. The club's practices of mixing offered a new sense of pleasure and innovation in the experience of live editing, a performance of technology that would inspire the aesthetic of The Builders Association's extravaganza.

By September 2000, Weems had read around twenty-five books on nineteenth-century and fin de siècle popular culture, consulted dozens of early scripts, and watched hundreds of short early films. The R&D for XTRAVAGANZA was extensive, and as scripting began, Weems realized that she needed a principle of exclusion. She sent a first version of the script to a friend for feedback, saying that she knew it was "too long," asking if it was "didactic," and worrying that there might be "too many ideas." The first version of the original script might well have played for three hours. As a joke to herself, Weems ended the script with a quote from Steele MacKaye: "That is what I have wanted to say and I apologize for having said it at such length, but I felt that it was necessary." Eventually, the script was trimmed but the quote remained, a historical reminder of the joys, hazards, and unwieldy ambition of producing an extravaganza.

OPERATING SYSTEMS

As a new extravaganza that honored the old, XTRAVAGANZA required both traditional and contemporary theatrical operating systems. The international success of JET LAG brought a new kind of attention to the company in the field of digital design and placed it in dialogue with organizations

Virtual chorus line with performers
Moe Angelos and Aimée Guillot.

like V2 in Rotterdam. That connection enabled Builders founding member and sound designer Dan Dobson and video designer Peter Norrman to experiment with new technologies as part of a residency at Studio for Electro-Instrumental Music (STEIM) in Amsterdam. For three weeks, Dobson and Norrman had access to the interactive technologies that were housed at the STEIM studios, with the ultimate goal of contributing what they learned to The Builders' XTRAVAGANZA. The residency was instrumental in expanding their knowledge of live video technologies. Two software tools were of interest to them—Image/ine and BigEye, which were developed at STEIM. Image/ine was an early real-time visual manipulation softwares that predated others such as NATO.0+55+3d and Isadora. BigEye was a software for real-time tracking of video events. Both enabled new experimentation with live video, in the VJ/DJ world, and in the theater. They returned to rehearsal in New York City with new tools that vastly broadened the possibilities. As Norrman reflected: "Lots of people were experimenting with this new form, mainly in the techno music and digital arts scene, but I believe we were quite early in using it for both conceptual and thematic purposes in performance—I mean as part of the live mixing and de-construction of imagery as a story device, as well as for technical fluidity." [5]

As a Builders sound composer, Dobson had already worked with digitized sound, but this was the first time that video and sound could be manipulated as data: "It changed our thinking about what composition could be."[6] The visuals for JET LAG were prerecorded, essentially creating a performance experience in which all actors and artists kept pace with a video recording whose trajectory and timing had been decided in advance. In XTRAVAGANZA, the video, sound, and visual material were available to be accessed on the spot by a digital operator. Like the DJ or house producer, the operator could respond to the actors and they to him, changing the mix from night to night.

XTRAVAGANZA mimicked and extended a club scene's ethos of continuous postproduction, but it was complicated further by the playful incorporation of a range of other media techniques. In conducting further research on the "cinema of attractions," Weems unearthed a poignant image of early sound-effects artists working backstage before a table of horns, bells, hammers, broken glass, and drums to provide "audio accompaniment" to the rest of the show. Much as he had for previous shows, Dobson assembled a digitized loop of sound effects to be triggered as the show unfolded, recalling the living infrastructure of earlier spectacles. In an homage to early sound-effects artists, he and other technical designers (such as new collaborator Joseph Silovsky) staged this longer sound-effects history by placing triggers onstage for the actors to manipulate. At different times throughout the show, characters activated these triggers on cue, punctuating the scene with the sound of a gun being fired, the whinny of a horse, a train whistle, or the applause of a distant audience as the story required. As in previous performances of technology, the pleasure of experiencing that trigger was augmented by allowing the audience to witness its operating system.

Mechanical innovations joined electrical and digital innovations throughout the show as well. Such a conjunction of the mechanical and digital was necessary for MASTER BUILDER, specifically the hinges and levers that allowed the house to split and its component parts to collapse on cue. This time the digital aesthetic interacted with an industrial aesthetic to tell the history of show business. As an experienced engineer, technical director, and artist, Silovsky proved to be the collaborator that Weems needed. In his shop in the Williamsburg neighborhood of Brooklyn, Silovsky designed and built new contraptions on spec. His "video skirt," worn by performer Jeff Webster, held a projection of the dancing legs of a talented dancer from the 1930s. This image was posed against Webster's motionless torso. In a canny send-up of the industrial aesthetic of the Rockettes, Silovsky created a rolling apparatus of high-kicking wooden legs that could be manipulated by actors as a detached, virtuosic prosthetic. Its combination of clunky uniformity and industrial precision made it the perfect counterpoint to XTRAVAGANZA's digital fusion. It also continued The Builders' history of providing artists with opportunities to make what Eve Sussman called "sculpture for theater."

Working on a show about show biz meant matching a high-tech apparatus to an equally complex low-tech apparatus. Each actor ultimately had his or her long list of props and accessories to manage, ensuring that each could transform into a digitally and industrially reimagined version of Loie Fuller, Steele MacKaye, or Florenz Ziegfeld. Aimée Guillot (who played half of a sister act) and Heaven Phillips (who played Loie Fuller), for instance, had to keep track of an extensive costume list. When they toured from one international venue to another—New York, Frankfurt, Strasbourg, Brussels—The Builders used a traditional properties log to help them keep track of the "IN" and "OUT" of garments

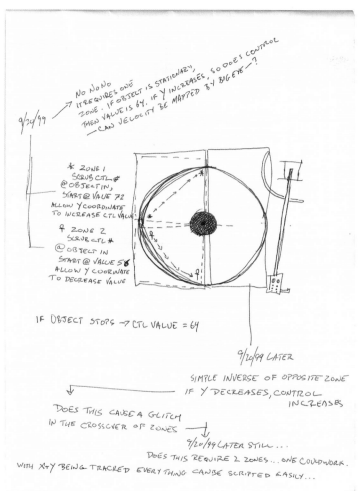

9/20/99

NO NONO
IT REQUIRES ONE ZONE. IF OBJECT IS STATIONARY, THEN VALUE IS 64. IF Y INCREASES, SO DOES CONTROL
— CAN VELOCITY BE MAPPED BY BIGEYE—?

* ZONE 1
SCRUB CTL #
@ OBJECT IN,
START @ VALUE 72
ALLOW Y COORDINATE
TO INCREASE CTL VALUE

＃ ZONE 2
SCRUB CTL #
@ OBJECT IN
START @ VALUE 58
ALLOW Y COORDINATE
TO DECREASE VALUE

IF OBJECT STOPS → CTL VALUE = 64

9/20/99 LATER

SIMPLE INVERSE OF OPPOSITE ZONE
IF Y DECREASES, CONTROL
INCREASES

DOES THIS CAUSE A GLITCH
IN THE CROSSOVER OF ZONES →

9/20/99 LATER STILL...
DOES THIS REQUIRE 2 ZONES... ONE COULD WORK.
WITH X+Y BEING TRACKED EVERYTHING CANBE SCRIPTED EASILY...

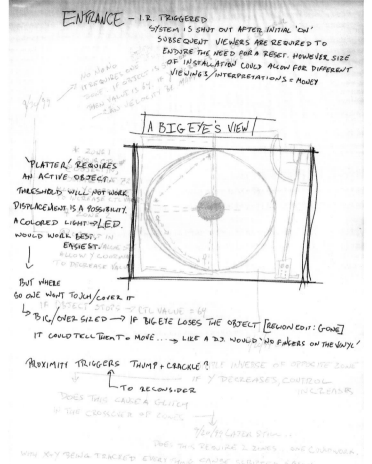

ENTRANCE — I.R. TRIGGERED
SYSTEM IS SHUT OUT AFTER INITIAL 'ON'
SUBSEQUENT VIEWERS ARE REQUIRED TO
ENDURE THE NEED FOR A RESET. HOWEVER SIZE
OF INSTALLATION COULD ALLOW FOR DIFFERENT
VIEWINGS/INTERPRETATIONS = MONEY

A BIGEYE'S VIEW

'PLATTER' REQUIRES
AN ACTIVE OBJECT.
THRESHOLD WILL NOT WORK.
DISPLACEMENT IS A POSSIBILITY.
A COLORED LIGHT → L.E.D.
WOULD WORK BEST.
EASIEST.

BUT WHERE
SO ONE WONT TOUCH/COVER IT
→ BIG/OVER SIZED → IF BIGEYE LOSES THE OBJECT [REGION EDIT: GONE]
IT COULD TELL THEM TO MOVE... → LIKE A D.J. WOULD 'NO FINGERS ON THE VINYL'

PROXIMITY TRIGGERS THUMP + CRACKLE?
→ TO RECONSIDER

Dan Dobson design note during a residency at the Studio for Electro-Instrumental Music (STEIM), Amsterdam, 1999.

Foley artists at work.

like "White Vinyl Top, Wh. Sequin Skirt, Wh. Heels, Platinum Wig, Grey Bungee Pants, White socks, Black Mary Janes, Loie Fuller wings (w/ 2 fish, poles), Wh. Loie Fuller Dress, Blue Hoop Skirt, Blue Feather Head Ruff." XTRAVAGANZA's massive costume and properties logs were testament to how much of the show's materials could not be uploaded onto a hard drive: "Rifle, Target, Whistle, Coconuts, 6 Fans, 16 Flags, Extra Feathers, Makeup Box...."

XTRAVAGANZA's mix of operating systems exposed the fragility of the old and new binary in narratives of media and technology. Its aesthetic both relied on and challenged the supporting apparatuses of theatrical infrastructure, something made further apparent by the ever-lengthening tech rider that was developed in anticipation of an international tour. The "tech rider" is a traditional mechanism for managing the load-in and presentation of theatrical shows on tour. In the context of The Builders Association, the tech rider exemplifies the worlds of "old" and "new" as domains that need each other to exist. XTRAVAGANZA's technical rider specified the traditional infrastructures of theater making: "playing area should be no less than 12 m wide × 12 m deep × 6.5 m floor to grid. Stage platform may be needed depending on seating rake." "Floor should be smooth & level." "Upstage wall must be black." More specifications were put in place to accommodate the viewing positions and to power the operating systems of a large intermedia show: "Seating rake should be no less than 10 degrees," "Load-in door must be a minimum of 2 m wide," "1 high-quality stereo reverberation unit," "8 channels of 1/3 octave graphic E.Q.," a "16 channel snake from the stage to each the FOH mix positions." Venues had to have rigging and grids in place to propel the technology to its proper height: "Producing venue will provide all rigging hardware necessary to fly speakers." The success of this new media show still depended on industrial theatrical technologies. New media machinery still had to be rigged, snaked, and flown by the living and laboring infrastructures of the theater. After lifting a large piece of equipment up four flights of stairs, hired freelance director Richard Maxwell quipped: "it's like we're loading in Pink Floyd, without the money." The history of the spectacle is also a history of the labor behind it. That labor story was both told and lived in XTRAVAGANZA.

STORYBOARD

Creating a storyboard for a tale of such extravagant proportions was challenging. After working with many writers during The Builders Association's previous four shows, Weems gave herself the task of textual assemblage, eventually composing a script culled from primary materials that were found with help from Frisch and her research assistants. She was given the unusual credit of "Direction and Textual Compilation" in the production's program. After watching countless films on the lives of chorus girls, Wild West shows, and Busby Berkeley's choreographed geometries, Weems decided to focus on nonfictional materials as the prime mover of the show. "Use specific people—Fuller, Berkeley, Ziegfeld, MacKaye," she wrote enthusiastically in her journal: "Americans who had a vision of what theater (multimedia) could be, but were somehow short-circuited (and now recuperated in relation to our theater). Find text that communicates their vision. Start w/ their vision then devolve into bills, illness, etc. End with some realization of their vision. An apotheosis."[7]

Even with the focus on central characters, the biographical materials of their lives could be taken in several directions. Weems retraced the highly cathartic plots of the Depression-era show-biz films and decided to use their rise-and-fall plot structure to retell the stories of these four "Americans who had a vision" and had endured a downfall of some sort. Weems plotted the "Text Connections" in her journal notes: "The bio stories are the 'backstage drama'—replace the characters' stories w/ the real stories. Seamy underside of the life of an 'entertainer.' Debts, struggle for $ and to 'rise,' constant travel (trains, cars, planes), maniacal dedication to work, strange companions, long protracted illness and decline while attempting to continue to work, death." The invitation to trans-historical identification was strong.

The storyboard structure ended up interweaving the rise and fall narratives of a few figures. The play started with biographical material that revealed the entwined histories of the central characters: Loie Fuller, Steele MacKaye, and Florenz Ziegfeld all launched their careers in the enormous productions of William F. "Buffalo Bill" Cody's (1846–1917) Wild West shows. These live events featured virtuosic performances that were mixed with the spectacles such as "Indians" and "cowboys" riding on horseback, engaging in gunfire, and performing cattle round-ups. In his shows, which were staged outdoors and indoors at venues such as Madison Square Garden in New York, Cody laid the groundwork for a particularly American take on the extravaganza.

XTRAVAGANZA also traced the archetypal story line of *The Broadway Melody* (also known as *The Broadway Melody 1929*; directed by Harry Beaumont)—two ingenues in a vaudeville sister act, Queenie (known for her beauty) and Hank (known for her business acumen), who come to New York to make their fortunes on Broadway. In XTRAVAGANZA, Queenie was played by Aimée Guillot, and Hank was played by Five Lesbian Brothers company member Moe Angelos, who was making her Builders debut. The script plucked the hopeful dialogue of naïve would-be starlets, with Hank offering pep talks that celebrated Queenie's "looks and my ability." This duo served as structural reminders of melodrama's rise and fall, mapping the cliché of their hopes and dreams to those of American visionaries.

The scout William F. "Buffalo Bill" Cody.

As each figure in XTRAVAGANZA branched out into his or her performance history, the storyboard tracked their respective laboratory periods and initial brushes with international fame. Jeff Webster quoted a telegram memo sent by Steele MacKaye to apply for space at the Chicago World's Fair of 1893 to feature his latest theatrical invention: "My Spectatorium will seat 12,000 people comfortably, the walls will be 8 stories in height with 25 telescopic, collapsible, and moving stages. The performance will be a revelation in the art of combining light and music with stage accessories on a gigantic scale." Florenz Ziegfeld, played by Peter Jacobs, followed MacKaye's telegram with one of his own, proposing to "exhibit my latest discovery, Sandow, the monarch of muscle STOP.... Sandow demonstrates his extraordinary command over this entire muscular system by making his muscles dance STOP." Heaven Phillips came on to play Loie Fuller, demonstrating the dance of the Electricity Fairy, and reminding audiences of how this female performer mixed science and art to an uncommon degree: "I design all of my own stage lighting, and have acquired a team of electricians which I oversee personally. The electric apparatus is so arranged that one signal effects magical changes." MacKaye delivered a monologue based in the language found in his patent petitions. The text, reciting the terms of the "Cloud Creator ... Patent Number 490.487" or the "Illumiscope," showed how much the theater served as a laboratory for imagining new possibilities: "I have devised appliances for imitating the tints of light which color the landscape." The recital of the patents also demonstrated how much the emerging patent process could be used as a "commercial weapon,"[8] in Charles Musser's phrase, providing a mechanism to install the unrealized idea as individual possession.

Life became more complicated for all of these figures when economic times changed. Market crashes changed the landscape for blockbuster shows. In the market crash of 1893, a broken Steele MacKaye wrote to his wife, "Business is the villain in the play of life, and money is very hard to get. The whole country is on the verge of bankruptcy, and men here will not invest."

June 4th

My dear Wife,

I am being taken away by friends to Lake Geneva in an almost dying condition.

Business is the villain in the play of life, and money is very hard to get. The whole country is on the verge of bankruptcy, and men here will not invest. This great conception of mine is within about one month of completion, but rumors of financial trouble for the Spectatorium have begun to float about.... Work on the building has come to a sudden stop.... The Great Chorus of 334 people has found itself out of employment.... the Spectatorium is being sold for old junk for the sum of $2,250.

Since we parted, I have been far down into the Valley, and learned a good deal concerning the darkness of its depths. I am still hoping that I may yet recover sufficiently to do a little more work in the world. I am desperately in need of some kind of nourishment which my stomach can digest. I am desperately lonely, in worriment and weariness indescribable. I'll be back with you in sixty days.

Steele

Later, a bankrupt Florenz Ziegfeld addressed a letter to his business manager after the market crash of 1929: "Well, Dan, they carried me out. I hated to go and leave so many problems in your hands.... The Shuberts own the Ziegfeld name now, and any use of the copyrighted materials must not be under the names Ziegfeld or Ziegfeld Follies."

Moments like these were juxtaposed in the text with scripted dialogue involving Queenie and Hank where the economic moral was transparent. In an interchange with a "big director" (*42nd Street*'s Julian Marsh), they were told, "The whole things is colossal. I'm going to give you my check for $5,000," even as his partner says on the side, "Don't cash it yet." As the dialogue goes on, Queenie and Hank eventually realize that the director's promises are not backed by actual cash. His last line resonated on several fronts: "That's always the way it is. I got the show, I got the music, I got the theater, I got the cast—and it's the old, old story. Money! No money at all!" That economic story had as many contemporary implications as did the intermedial story that The Builders were trying to tell. "There is a didacticism," admitted Weems: "We tried to have fun with it, but part of the story is that you can never make an extravaganza with a non-profit art budget."[9]

REHEARSAL/ASSEMBLY

The term *extravaganza* was used first in eighteenth-century Italy and eventually throughout Europe to refer to popular stylized stage setups of battleships and forests. In using that reference as well as later forms as inspiration in rehearsal, The Builders devised a process for assembling many media while simultaneously keeping visible its component parts. "Non-integration is essential to the musical genre which is based on shifting dialectic between integrative and non-integrative elements," Weems quoted in her journal: "Superabundances, variety, heterogeneity, and blatant spectacle." IMPERIAL MOTEL (FAUST) and JUMP CUT (FAUST) drew inspiration from early theatrical conventions that displayed the wonders of new photo and audio technology, and XTRAVAGANZA's rehearsal became a site for sharing the pleasures and tricks of new technologies. This process was never progressive or consistent. The development of the operating systems and the storyboard happened together in a laboratory where scripts and technology mutually revised each other. Like other Builders casts before them, XTRAVAGANZA's actors became habituated to a process of acting with technology as intimately as they acted with each other.

Rehearsal also ended up being a mixing and sampling process. Each day was another attempt to get bodies, primary materials, projected images, and sound accompaniment to interact in a new combination. Much of this effort lay in finding, within primary material, an internal hook that could be exploited, manipulated, and sampled for a contemporary aesthetic. After Jeff Webster opened the show as Steele MacKaye, for instance, he began to narrate his decision to join the Wild West shows. MacKaye's narration was supplemented with projections of Wild West documentary footage with Webster bluescreened inside the film as its central impresario. Dan Dobson sampled the Wild West sounds of rodeos and staged Native American rituals into a stylized beat that would be familiar to a contemporary club crowd.

Weems and Norrman had been captivated by train footage, at one point thinking that an image of a train would close and end the show: "Start w/ train going West—'flashback' through scenes of artistic life—end again with train." The train did not become the opening image for the show, but it recurred throughout to suggest moments of transition. Norrman and Dobson sampled and repeated the sights and sounds of its whistles and its engines. The sampled train was at once the marker of the passage of time, the celebration of American engineering, and a nod to early cinema, where trains in motion had been both structure and support for showing off the capacities of early film camera techniques.

Performer Aimée Guillot.

The use of new screen practices animated other parts of the dialogue. Notably, all scenes played by the "sister act" occurred in a manufactured studio setting. On a small set on stage left, actors Angelos and Guillot interacted with others playing producers and stars with a bluescreen in the background. Historical chorine films played simultaneously in the center of the stage. The cinematographic trick occurred when a video operator onstage composited Angelos and Guillot onto the background of the historical film. In a nod to a long history of cinematographic chicanery, the pleasure lay in watching the black-and-white antics of historical figures that also were played by flesh and blood actors simultaneously. In a later scene, The Builders used bluescreen tricks to comment on gender and power within the show business industry. Re-performing dialogue from early chorine films, Aimée as Queenie struggled to conform to the expectations of an overbearing film director who began to say her lines for her: "No, not like that. Like this: 'It was grand of you to come.'" Queenie finally achieved the desired reading but only when The Builders operators dubbed the director's voice over Aimée's. Audience members laughed when they heard Queenie say her line in the falsetto of the male director's voice, but it also underscored the narcissistic structure of the scene in which a male director hopes to see his own projections reflected back to him.

In general, however, the performing "acts" were places where the operating systems of live editing "mixed" both a club aesthetic and historical data to produce a new media extravaganza. Using the vaudeville convention of serial acts, narrative moments in the story were interspersed with dance and sound spectacles that largely were absent of dialogue. Motifs and images from history were isolated and inserted into a contemporary intertextual landscape, repeating the past to bring forward unorthodox connections to the present. Ziegfeld's early attempts to bring Sandow the Muscleman to MacKaye's Spectatorium returned as documentary footage on the XTRAVAGANZA stage. This time, however, the footage of a disrobed Sandow rhythmically flexing his muscles was accompanied by the seductive rhythms of contemporary club music. Sandow's display was effectively queered for the present, positing him unexpectedly as a precursor to the b-boy.

Frederick Childe Hassam, *The MacKaye Spectatorium*, 1893.

MacKaye's innovative moving double stage for the new Madison Square Theater, New York, 1880.

As an early theater innovator, Loie Fuller created performances that were easy to transition to contemporary club dances. Her flag and Electricity Fairy dances were early forays into what later generations might call psychedelic. Fuller's electrical laboratory found myriad ways to perform the new technologies of her time: her capes spiraled inside colored rays of projected lighting, flags waved at different angles to refract luminescent rays, and lit snowflakes appeared to fall from the sky. In The Builders' reinterpretation, these historical dances were newly imagined with a different cast and club music, inserting New York's virtuosic club dancer Bravo LaFortune into the mix. But the flag dance also was open to new interpretations through juxtaposition with other references, especially when

178

Loie Fuller, 1901.

Contemporary version of Loie Fuller's "electricity fairy" dance.

a cast of flag-waving Builders were juxtaposed with the flag-waving formations in Busby Berkeley's films.

The aesthetic of mixing was political in its range of referents and its occasional disregard for the implications of those referents. The impulse to connect, sample, and juxtapose based on the formal properties of sound and image showed up the modernist roots of the process, even if it took modernism into unintended directions. For Simon Reynolds, sampledelia means thinking less about content, text, and narrative than about the ambient atmosphere that is created: "As instrumental music, techno is closer to the plastic arts or architecture than literature, in that it involves the creation of an imaginary environment or kinesthetic terrain…. Devoid of text, dance music and ambient are better understood through metaphors of the visual arts: 'the soundscape,' a 'soundtrack for an imaginary movie,' 'audio-sculpture.'"[10]

For Weems, this kinesthetic terrain was a new version of a long tradition of aggregated, intermedia performance. This principle of assembly meant releasing from the impulse to order content narratively. "Spectacularizes the camera," Weems wrote of early and later technotheater: "camera itself is liberated from the demands of narrativity in order to assert its own presence as an element of autonomous display—of spectacle. Realistic consistency is violated for the sake of producing cinematic effect—trick cuts, reverse motion, patterns visible only from certain camera angles, etc."[11] Just as the screen practices of nineteenth-century popular theaters always joined a "showman" to its experiments in image and sound, the presence of the DJ or house operator was central to the aesthetic of the club and the aesthetic of XTRAVAGANZA. The potential for making operators into showmen appeared throughout rehearsal. "Don't separate performers from designers," Weems wrote to herself in her journal: "both have to perform both functions, if the performance of the technology is really going to be foregrounded."[12] Designers Peter Norrman and Dan Dobson thus took their places on the stage with fellow performers who addressed them throughout as "Dan" or "Peter," asking for cues as the show needed. The decision to mix the operating system explicitly into the aesthetic of the performance might have been Brechtian to some eyes, but it was vaudeville to others. And perhaps to a few, those operators recalled the explicit presence, spontaneous mixing, and skilled virtuosity of a DJ. In preparing Loie Fuller's flag dance, the technical crew came onto the stage with wires and cables, eventually dropping them to whirl a flag in unison and with pulsing precision. Techies could be b-boys, too.

Mechanical legs operated by performers, designed by Joe Silovsky.

If the performance of technology was about the display of new technologies, it was also very much about displaying technology's unrecognized capacities. Audiences that experienced electricity in their daily lives were turned on to new uses of the electrical. Although the technological revised the site of performance, the stage reciprocally propelled the imagining of new technological tricks. This sense of mutual construction resonated with the sense of contemporary media theorists of how the dance club stage and allied performance venues reimagined contemporary technology in the 1990s. "It's about finding out what a new piece of equipment facilitates that wasn't previously possible or even thinkable," said Simon Reynolds: "This involves locating and exploiting potentials in the new machines that the manufacturers never intended.... It's about inventing a new kind of posthuman virtuosity."[13] In many ways, Busby Berkeley's move from stage to screen came from his realization of how the capacities of the camera could document goings-on onstage and also splice and recombine its images into new geometries. "It's unlimited what you can do for the camera," said Moe Angelos's character, Hank, just before XTRAVAGANZA embarked on its own camera tricks, choreographing a dance that was shot from above and projected in symmetrical units in Busby-like patterns on the screen.

Using the stage as a vehicle for imagining the alternate capacities of technology produced an intriguing kind of encounter. Its viewing strategies were multifocal and dynamic, encouraging spectators to vacillate among the screen, the body, and the operating system to decide where the spectacle might be. Many moments called as much attention to the mediating powers of performers as to the mediating powers of technology. Peter Jacobs and Heaven Phillips engaged in a mediated tap dance together. In this iteration, however, their feet remained largely unmoved while the sound of tap pumped through the speakers, encouraging a purely auditory appreciation and eliciting pleasure because of the withdrawal rather than the abundance of visual spectacle. The embodied performers of the Kaleidoscope dance were heightened and potentially overwhelmed by their Busby Berkeley re-patterning on the screen, but other moments called for different spectatorial calibrations. The ability of many Builders actors to replicate the distinctively nasal speech of early cinematic acting—with its trills, barks, and counterintuitive runs up and down a vocal register—were themselves technical feats.

When Bravo LaFortune did his own dance with the syncopated and unexpected asymmetries of his club dancing, he too was caught by a camera from above and redivided on screen. For some audience members, however, Bravo's own low-tech, embodied virtuosity upstaged by far the technologies; after all, even Busby Berkeley's patterns could not compete with a legend.

CLOSINGS

If JET LAG was the piece that consolidated The Builders Association's reputation as a "new media" theater company, then XTRAVAGANZA was the piece where The Builders tried to expand the implications of the attribution. Reviews that celebrated their work criticized them in almost exactly the same terms, lamenting or reveling in their collusion with a "future" of new technology that left the tradition of theater behind. In relation to this performance, Alisa Solomon summarized the pro-theatrical, anti-technology discourse earlier quoted: "Live performance is dying, lamenters have been saying for a century at least. Strangled by the more alluring glitz of ever expanding technology. First it was radio, then the motion picture, then TV, and now the 'digital age' that have been blamed for mesmerizing audiences and drawing them away from the finer forms of the drama, thus depriving spectators of the communal, even mystical, powers of theatrical presence. In this alarmed discourse, technology is always the enemy of the theater, an all-consuming colonizer of the superior art form."[14] With XTRAVAGANZA, The Builders sought to recall the technological incorporation and cross-medium redefinition that constitutes the global history of theater. For Solomon and many other reviewers, XTRAVAGANZA was a reminder that popular theater had enabled the new in new media for centuries.

Although XTRAVAGANZA drew a connection between old and new extravaganzas through a shared history of technology, The Builders' operating systems also exposed an uncanny connection between old and new in the history of theatrical economics. Even as they were devising narratives of the rise and fall of American visionaries, the company faced its own economic hurdles. The always precarious situation of nonprofit theater became more precarious when Weems learned that The Builders' managing director had been embezzling money from the company, using funds to pay for a drug habit that also was part of his nightly club experience. The moment replicated all too closely the stories of artists taken in by conniving producers, the standard plot of many Broadway stage films.

While "melodrama" might have been the appropriate word for the embezzlement scandal, "tragedy" was the word that surrounded the events of their international tour. XTRAVAGANZA's premiere in Chicago was slated for September 12, 2001, an opening date that would unravel when the World Trade Center was bombed on September 11. Their four-day premiere at the Athenaeum Theater presented by Performing Arts Chicago was reduced to two, with artists and technicians gathering in Chicago bars in the intervening days not to rehearse but to reflect together about the politics of their position and to establish the whereabouts of close friends in New York. In a long and heartfelt company meeting, Weems gave members of the company the option to return to New York City rather than perform. Joe Silovsky suggested that "the show must go on," however, and all members agreed to remain in Chicago for the performances. *Chicago Tribune* critic Richard Christiansen's review of XTRAVAGANZA joined a reflection on the themes of the show with a reflection on "the tumult of the past week." The subtitle for the review responded to The Builders but also to the era of New York's World Trade Center: "gone too soon." After driving shared cars from Chicago to New York, The Builders encountered a changed Manhattan and a still smoldering downtown.

When The Builders eventually performed XTRAVAGANZA in New York, it was not at the originally intended venue, as the program notes at St. Ann's Warehouse explained: "We were supposed to have landed at the Winter Garden at the World Financial Center this past February. We are very grateful to Arts at St. Ann's for opening their doors to these performances, and we are delighted that everyone at the World Financial Center Arts & Events program will resume their presentations in the Winter Garden this fall." Their next show was already in the beginning stages of research and development, but the geopolitics of the moment made its argument all the more urgent. When The Builders turned from XTRAVAGANZA to ALLADEEN, it was with a sense of the dependence of new technologies on history and the dependence of new technologies on the political and economic asymmetries of globalization.

ENDNOTES

Artist's Voice: Moe Angelos, performer/co-creator

When I entered into the rehearsal process with XTRAVAGANZA, a script of sorts existed. This document was small but powerful, clocking in at around twenty pages, if I recall correctly. It was more of a storyboard than a script in the truest sense, as it contained snippets of scenes and some monologues, but there was quite a bit of open territory with headings that said things like

INTERLUDE 7: Loie takes the train to Paris.

Then it would go right on to the next scene, with no further elaboration. But that's where the fun part came in. All those unadorned headings were landmarks for what movement the show had to make, and constructing those is what we did in rehearsal. Marianne, with much help from Shelley Lasica, assistant director, and David Neumann, choreographer, and the great Team Video, Peter Norrman and Jeff Morey, dramaturg Norman Frisch, Dan Dobson's soundscape, and Joe Silovsky's technical wizardry, all pitched in for the cause, and together we'd create segments that were not always directly related to those before and after but were all joining forces to tell the same few stories, although not in a conventional narrative drive, over the longer haul of the show.

I struggled mightily at first to follow the "story" of XTRAVAGANZA. There were two problems with my approach, one being that I was looking for some traditional narrative hook to drag my sorry self through the show, and this hook was going to require some work to find, and I am essentially lazy. Second, I was looking for said hook in the wrong haystack, in the more conventional performer haystack of some sort of connection with my fellow performers, formed because of what emotional journey we were passing through onstage.

The great lesson I learned doing that show was that Marianne was telling these stories through a visual language in conjunction with the more traditional theatrics of scenes of dialogue between characters that further a plot. The pictures, the video, the media were also telling the story. This is patently obvious to anyone who has seen a Builders' show, but it is anything but clear if you are one of the humans running around in that show. From inside, it is not possible to see the totality of the stage picture. Therefore, I could not follow the "story" of the show, as layered, complex, and nonlinear as that was.

But the stories were there. Some sections of the show were little scenes telling a familiar American tale of a small-town hayseed who moves to New York with a pair of tap shoes and a dream to be on Broadway. In our research we watched many of these kinds of films—*42nd Street*, *The Broadway Melody*, all the Gold Digger films. We even watched some Judy Garland and Mickey Rooney films, and though these were from a later era, they perpetuated that make-it-in-show-biz-against-all-odds theme. We took stock characters from these stories and boiled them down to four or five—the fresh-faced talented ingenue, the romantic lead, the wisecracking no-nonsense gal with moxie, the irascible alcoholic producer/director, the high-maintenance star. Taking scenes or snippets from those films as a jumping-off point we cobbled together a number of scenes from the different movies, which all followed more or less the same arc. This comprised one story track for the show.

These stories were fragmented and intertwined with the show biz patter scenes, set against visual backdrops of either archival images from the works of these masters or Marianne's latter-day reenactments of those works. That is how the stories were told.

It is curious for me to think about it now but at the time, I sometimes had little idea of what was being conveyed to the audience from inside the performance of the show. It was only somewhere deep into the tour of XTRAVAGANZA that I figured out to once in a while step outside of the playing space and go look from the audience to see what picture was being made. This still happens to me, a decade later. Now we usually use a wide shot, live-feed of the whole stage that is incorporated into the video mix. Sometimes when I can see a monitor, I can see more or less what the audience sees to get more of the total picture, and thus the total story.

Artist's Voice: Norman Frisch, dramaturg

XTRAVAGANZA presented itself in the year 2000 as a dramaturg's dream—an opportunity to collaborate with The Builders on a project that rolled together many of the ensemble's ongoing theatrical and cultural preoccupations at that time with a handful of my own. The show's intent from the outset was to mirror our current historical moment of the expanding digitalization of theater with an era a century earlier that had first witnessed the electrification of stage performance and the emergence of cinema. And it was constructed around a framework of source materials drawn from the biographies and oeuvres of four pioneering theater artists of the early twentieth century.

Dancer Loie Fuller, stage designer Steele MacKaye, impresario Florenz Ziegfeld, and director Busby Berkeley all contributed enormously to the development of technologies that would define the theater of the twentieth century. XTRAVANGZA followed their stories chronologically from the pre-Edison entertainments of Buffalo Bill and his traveling Wild West shows through several decades of rapid innovation in theater technologies, culminating finally in the migration of electrified spectacle in the 1920s away from the Broadway stage and west onto the Hollywood screen. In doing so, it chronicled America's historical appetite for novel modes of entertainment and its age-old penchant for celebrating and then discarding its true creative geniuses.

In each of those four remarkable lives, early years of struggle and artistic ambition were followed by heydays of great celebrity and success giving way to final years marked by penury and despair. This pattern of creative trajectory—from brilliant youth to bitter old age—holds a lifelong fascination for me, and not since XTRAVAGANZA have I had an opportunity to explore it in as complex and fulfilling a manner.

XTRAVAGANZA was definitely a "show" of the "Hey, kids! Let's put on a show!" variety. Counterpointing the historical source materials was a layering of character tropes, imagery, and texts lifted from early American film musicals, and from these The Builders constructed their own miniature, digitalized version of a Follies-styled spectacle.

I recall it now—fifteen years later—as a performance that was great fun to play and great fun to watch, and certainly, we felt ourselves mirroring the giddy exuberance of the show's central characters, both historical and fictional. But what returns to me most often now, as a sixty-year-old, are thoughts of those great, forward-thinking artists in broken old age—how unable they were to foresee the legacy of their own achievements or realize how cherished their memories would become to us.

I am not a person who is very hopeful personally, but I am hopeful historically—and I think this cultural optimism is what drew me then and draws me still to the work of this company.

People

Direction and text compilation by Marianne Weems

Sound design by Dan Dobson

Video design by Peter Norrman

Lighting designed by Jennifer Tipton

Set design by John Cleater

Dramaturg: Norman Frisch

Performed by

Moe Angelos

Aimée Guillot

Peter Jacobs

Brahms "Bravo" LaFortune

Heaven Phillips

Jeff Webster

Costumes by Wren Crosley

Choreography by David Neumann and Shelley Lasica (flag dance instruction by George Jagatic)

Technical direction by Joseph Silovsky

Video associate: Jeff Morey

Sound associates: Perchik Miller, Robert McLean

Lighting associate: Erik Bruce

Assistant directors: Shelley Lasica, Amantha May

Managing director and presentation producer: Mark Uhl

Produced by Renata Petroni and The Builders Association

Company manager: Monique Curnen

Historical research provided by Norman Frisch, Peter Campbell, Julie Dubiner, Jenny Schwartz, Sally Sommer, Tamsen Wolff, and Tom Zummer

Translation services by Abigael Sanders

"Broadway Rose" vocal composition and arrangement by Heaven Phillips

Video screen design and engineering by Diller + Scofidio

Stage manager: Natalia de Campos

Program design by Erica Bjerning

Dance coach: Andrea Kleine

Special thanks to Ann Carlson, Charles Goddertz, Christopher Kondek, Christian Marclay, Victor Morales, and STEIM

Venues

October–November 2000 Kaaitheater, Brussels

Rotterdam Schouwburg, Rotterdam, the Netherlands

La Maillon, Strasbourg, France

Mousonturm, Frankfurt, Germany

Le Volcan, Le Havre, France

2001 Guggenheim Museum, New York, NY

Whitney Museum of American Art, New York, NY

Presented by Performing Arts Chicago at the Athenaeum Theater, Chicago, IL

2002 St. Ann's Warehouse, New York, NY

Afterparty

Jeff Webster dancing with a "video skirt."

SOME SOURCE MATERIALS FOR THE PRODUCTION

Books

Adorno, Theodor W. *The Curves of the Needle.* Cambridge, MA: MIT Press, 1927.

Allen, Robert Clyde. *Horrible Prettiness: Burlesque and American Culture.* Chapel Hill: University of North Carolina Press, 1991.

Altick, Richard D. *The Shows of London.* Cambridge, MA: Belknap Press, 1978.

Attali, Jacques. *Noise: The Political Economy of Music.* Minneapolis: University of Minnesota Press, 1985.

Barrios, Richard. *A Song in the Dark: The Birth of the Musical Film.* New York: Oxford University Press, 1995.

Bourdieu, Pierre, and Richard Nice. *Distinction: A Social Critique of the Judgment of Taste.* Cambridge, MA: Harvard University Press, 2002.

Clarke, Norman. *The Mighty Hippodrome.* South Brunswick, NJ: Barnes, 1968.

Committee on Broadband Last Mile Technology, Computer Science and Technology Board, National Research Council. *Broadband: Bringing Home the Bits.* Washington, DC: National Academies Press, 2002.

Current, Richard Nelson, and Marcia Ewing Current. *Loie Fuller: Goddess of Light.* Boston: Northeastern University Press, 1997.

de Certeau, Michel. *The Practice of Everyday Life.* Berkeley: University of California Press, 1984.

Frith, Simon, and Andrew Goodwin. *On Record: Rock, Pop and the Written Word.* New York: Pantheon Books, 1990.

Gaines, Donna. *Teenage Wasteland: Suburbia's Dead End Kids.* New York: Pantheon Books, 1991.

Griffiths, Paul. *A Guide to Electronic Music.* New York: Thames and Hudson, 1979.

Hebdige, Dick. *Subculture: The Meaning of Style.* London: Routledge, 2002.

Hove, Arthur, and Tino Balio, eds. *Gold Diggers of 1933.* Madison: University of Wisconsin Press, 1980.

Inouye, Alan S., Marjory S. Blumenthal, and William J. Mitchell, eds., Committee on Information
    Technology and Creativity, National Research Council. *Beyond Productivity: Information,
    Technology, Innovation, and Creativity.* Washington, DC: National Academies Press, 2003.

Kroker, Arthur. *The Possessed Individual: Technology and the French Postmodern.* New York: St.
    Martin's Press, 1992.

Kroker, Arthur, and Michael A. Weinstein. *Data Trash: The Theory of the Virtual Class.* New York: St.
    Martin's Press, 1994.

Leppert, Richard D., and Susan McClary. *Music and Society: The Politics of Composition, Performance
    and Reception.* New York: Cambridge University Press, 1987.

Martin, Nicholas Ivor. *The Da Capo Opera Manual.* New York: Da Capo Press, 1997.

McClary, Susan. *Feminine Endings: Music, Gender and Sexuality.* Minneapolis: University of Minnesota
    Press, 1991.

Oettermann, Stephan. *The Panorama: A History of a Mass Medium.* New York: Zone Books, 1997.

Primavera 2003: Exhibition of Young Australian Artists. Museum of Contemporary Art, Sydney,
    Australia, 2003.

Rhodes, Richard. *Visions of Technology: A Century of Vital Debate about Machines, Systems, and the
    Human World.* New York: Simon and Schuster, 1999.

Rose, Cynthia. *Design after Dark: The Story of Dancefloor Style.* London: Thames and Hudson, 1991.

Ross, Andrew, and Tricia Rose, eds. *Microphone Friends: Youth Music and Youth Culture.* New York:
    Routledge, 1994.

Rovin, Jeff. *The Fabulous Fantasy Films.* South Brunswick, NJ: Barnes, 1977.

Rubin, Martin. *Showstoppers: Busby Berkeley and the Tradition of Spectacle.* New York: Columbia
    University Press, 1993.

Rush, Michael. *New Media in Late Twentieth-Century Art.* New York: Thames and Hudson, 1999.

Sicko, Dan. *Techno Rebels: The Renegades of Electronic Funk.* New York: Billboard Books, 1999.

Tamm, Eric. *Brian Eno: His Music and the Vertical Color of Sound.* New York: Da Capo Press, 1995.

Thomas, Tony, Jim Terry, Busby Berkeley, and Ruby Keeler. *The Busby Berkeley Book.* Greenwich, CT: New York Graphic Society, 1973.

Thornton, Sarah. *Club Cultures: Music, Media and Subcultural Capital.* Cambridge, UK: Polity Press, 1995.

Walser, Robert. *Running with the Devil: Power, Gender and Madness in Heavy Metal Music.* Hanover: University Press of New England, 1993.

Ziegfeld, Richard, and Paulette Ziegfeld. *The Ziegfeld Touch: The Life and Times of Florenz Ziegfeld Jr.* New York: Abrams, 1993.

Scripts Consulted (from the Library of Congress's "Playscripts")

Allen, Searl. "Ten Minutes of Rapid Fire Talk Entitled Prattling Pals." 1908.

Crawford, Miley Pleasanton. "The Lone Hand Four Aces." 1915.

Hoadley, Harold. "Bill Ryan, the Stagehand." 1914.

Hoffman, Aaron. "A Vaudeville Cocktail: Something New under the Sun—A Monologue." Part 4, 1914.

Kiralfy, Imre. "Columbus and the Discovery of America." 1890.

McCree, Junie. "Disturbing the Peace: A Satire on Unnecessary Noises." 1915.

Moliere, Anais Redin. "An Amateur Snap Shot, or, Photographic Blunders: A One Act Farce." 1900.

Pastor, Tony. "The Monkey and the Dude, or, The Monkey and the Masher: An Original Song / The Property of Tony Pastor." 1884.

Films

Babes in Arms. Directed by Busby Berkeley. Los Angeles: Metro-Goldwyn-Mayer, 1939.

Carmen Jones. Directed by Otto Preminger. Los Angeles: Twentieth Century Fox, 1954.

Gold Diggers of 1935. Directed by Busby Berkeley. Los Angeles: Warner Bros., 1935.

High Society. Directed by Charles Walters. Los Angeles: Metro-Goldwyn-Mayer, 1956.

The Movies Begin. Vol. 3, *Experimentation and Discovery.* Kino Video, 2002. "How It Feels to Be Run Over" (1900), "Exploration of a Motor Car" (1900), "The Other Side of the Hedge" (1903), "That Fatal

Sneeze" (1907), "Visit to Peek Frean and Co.'s Biscuit Works" (1908), "A Day In the Life of a Coal Miner" (1910).

Pathé Freres (1905–06): "Histoire d'un Crime," "Ali Baba," "Rêve et Realité," "Revolution en Russie," "Alladin et la Lamp Merveilleuse," "Le Cherd Embolle," "Magic Bricks (Chinese Box Tricks)," "Denar's It's Scotch," "Ladies Shoes," "Dream of a Rarebit Fiend."

The Perfumed Handkerchief: A Chinese Opera . Directed by Yang Jie. West Long Beach, NJ: Kultur, 1981.

Show Business. Directed by Edwin L. Marin. Los Angeles: RKO Radio Pictures, 1944.

The Spirit Moves: A History of Black Social Dance on Film, 1900–1986. Directed by Mura Dehn. Dallas, TX: Dancetime Publications, 1987.

Tales of Hoffman. Directed by Michael Powell and Emeric Pressburger. The Archers and Vega Film Productions, 1951.

That's Entertainment! Treasures from the Vault. Directed by Gene Kelly and Bud Friedgen. 1976.

2001, a Space Odyssey. Directed by Stanley Kubrick. Los Angeles: Metro-Goldwyn-Mayer and Stanley Kubrick Productions, 1968.

Performer Tanya Selvaratnam in front of a digital London videoscape.

Global Souls are seen as belonging to a kind of migratory tribe, able to see things more clearly than those imprisoned in local concerns can, yet losing their identity often as they fall between the cracks. A Global Soul is a ventriloquist, an impersonator, or an undercover agent: the question that most haunts him is "Who are you today?"

Pico Iyer, *The Global Soul: Jet Lag, Shopping Malls, and the Search for Home*[1]

OPENINGS

Seated in rows before a proscenium stage, it suddenly seems as if we are here to watch a video … or maybe a video game. Kaleidoscopic digital squares zoom in and around a video screen, forming grids that constantly change, their internal patterns lining up to form new symmetrical patterns. The images dance to the steady beat of techno music, accelerate, and refigure into new arrangements of luminous, multicolored eye candy. More blocks slide in and fit together with a satisfying synthetic click. They gradually begin to form a two-dimensional busy city street. As the techno beat continues, the iconography of LED advertising—stores, signs, billboards, buses, and taxis—passes through the screened proscenium. In their pixilated luster, the digitized screens of global consumer culture advertise international clothing chains, telecommunication conglomerates, and athletic equipment. Under the banner of Virgin Atlantic, a small grid of squares appears in rows like thumbnail images on a computer screen, forming shelf after shelf of compact discs for sale. The synthesized whooshes, plops, and kerchunks mimic the soundscape of a high-end website search. Suddenly, a mailbox, a phone booth, and a fire hydrant digitally slide onto the set—not by means of a gurney, a trap, a sliding stage, or a run crew but by the transit systems of a software program as electronically mediated objects. Digitally rendered human silhouettes begin to appear and move through the mise-en-scène. By the same means, a vendor's food cart drops from the sky with a synthesized crash.

One human character, however, walks onto the stage supported by the embodied medium of a live actor (performer Tanya Selvaratnam), and, in so doing, clears a three-dimensional set space in front of the video screen's two-dimensionality. She speaks into a telephone headset using a friendly tone and a not fully locatable cosmopolitan accent: "I love karaoke. It's like magic. You can be anything you want. You just have to find the right song." She confirms a rendezvous in Las Vegas at the newly refurbished Aladdin Hotel and ends the connection to make another call. Her solicitous tone changes to a demanding one as she speaks with a car rental operator named Monica. She bristles at what she decides is a slow and unclear response to her request for a rental reservation: "Don't you speak English? Where are you from?" She blames Monica for the fact that a rental car cannot be found quickly: "Well, this is obviously going to take longer than I thought. I'll have to call you back." She immediately takes another call from a friend in Hong Kong, speaking in Mandarin about their travel plans with Anglophone references to "Las Vegas" and "package deal" interspersed. On a fourth call, she tells her boyfriend that she is in a "permanent state of jet lag" and then apologizes for the noise of a bus that has stopped next to her. The digitized bus "exits," and the conversation continues.

This opening scene from ALLADEEN represented in miniature the unfettered space of possibility that is afforded by global travel and global technologies. Its imagery and soundscape mimicked that of the web, including the "choice," "presence," "movement," and "possibility" that Tara McPherson argues "structure a sense of causality ... structuring a mobilized liveness which we come to feel we invoke and impact, in the instant, in the click, reload."[2] The ALLADEEN set dramatized the freedom of movement that is felt in an uploadable world. We have come to feel that this "volitional mobility"[3] is a condition of contemporary existence, and ALLADEEN dramatized the fragile frictions of wires, cables, broadband, planes, cars, buses, and laborers on which that apparently friction-free world relies.

Stills from a music video created for ALLADEEN filmed in New York, London, and Bangalore by Peter Norrman and Ali Zaidi, 2003.

R&D

"I am the slave of the lamp" is intoned by the genie who magically appears after Aladdin rubs a glistening golden oil lamp, and the genie continues: "and I and other slaves are here to do thy bidding."[4] Marianne Weems met with folklore scholar Marina Warner after reading her scholarly treatment of the legend and dozens of other analyses and retellings of the Aladdin myth. By 1998, The Builders Association's JET LAG was touring, and the company was feeling not only bodily fragilities but also the cross-cultural politics of global travel. As The Builders moved across international cities, they encountered new languages and new cityscapes and were struck by the homogenizing rhetoric of global connections. "The world" was increasingly presented as a cosmopolitan jewel that offers exotic lands and a wealth of products to cosmopolitan consumers.

Weems had been talking with Keith Khan of the London-based group motiroti about doing a project ever since she saw *Moti Roti, Puttli Chunni*, a spectacular, partially parodic, but always "loving recreation" of Bollywood's characters, stock narratives, and imagery.[5] Khan, Ali Zaidi, and other motiroti collaborators had a long-standing interest in a certain element of postcolonial subjectivity that they called "self-orientalization."[6] For Weems, Khan, Zaidi, Norman Frisch, and other collaborators, the Aladdin tale had enormous resonance. In Warner's terms, it "flagrantly flourishes the panoply of orientalism," bringing "the horizons of empire into one huge glorious tableau."[7] As such, his tale seemed a metaphor for contemporary global consumer subjectivity, traversing vast scales and accessing impossible riches with a touch and a wish. The lamp was Aladdin's magical hand-held technology, but the mouse and the cell phone are now the new luminous objects—or potential "genies" that promise fantastic fulfillment.

If both society and the theater are dependent on the labor of builders, then ALLADEEN offered an expanded exploration of who those builders were in the twenty-first century. The global management of labor was one of the central themes of ALLADEEN, especially at a time when a rise in "information" and "affective labor" drives the development of service economies. When The Builders began research in 2001 for this piece on the call-center industry, European and North American citizens were

beginning to recognize the role played by offshore labor, including call-service workers, in a global economy. Companies found that they could cheaply hire educated Indian workers to field calls for technical support, international travel, catalog shopping, and other forms of telephonic personal service. The newspaper story that triggered the idea for ALLADEEN appeared in the *New York Times* on March 21, 2001: "Hi, I'm in Bangalore (but I Can't Say So)."[8] The article dramatized acts of international mimicry that supported global transactions: "Ms. Suman's fluent English and broad vowels would pass muster in the stands at Wrigley Field. In case her callers ask personal questions, Ms. Suman has conjured up a fictional American life, with parents Bob and Ann, brother Mark, and a made-up business degree from the University of Illinois: 'We watch a lot of *Friends* and *Ally McBeal* to learn the right phrases.'"[9] The article described the rise of the offshore customer service industry and quoted successful company founders who proclaimed: "India is on its way to being the back office for the world." Weems collected more articles about the offshoring of service industries, exploring how jobs migrated from the United States to India and how a twenty-four-hour industry depended on a labor force in a range of time zones.

The Builders Association had already begun a longer conversation on the precarious place of humans within technological systems that purported to collapse global temporalities. In part, these discussions came about in response to The Builders' experiences as artists on an international presenting circuit. After MASTER BUILDER, their subsequent shows received attention and backing from artistic directors and theater festivals outside their native United States. The maintenance of the company and of the lives of its artists depended on a willingness to move from theater festival to arts festival in European, Asian, and North American cities. "We were in airports all the time," remembers Weems.[10] The corporeal effect of international travel was something that they regularly felt in their own lives as what performer Moe Angelos called "migrant cultural workers."[11] JET LAG was one production where they explored the perceptual effects of global travel on global souls. ALLADEEN took such issues in another direction, making explicit the global traveler's dependence on laborers who rarely were able to move themselves.

OPERATING SYSTEMS

With the tale of Aladdin and the site of the call-center industry as central themes, Weems, Khan, Zaidi, and other collaborators embarked on their own transnational process of research. They used a grant from the British Arts Council to travel to Bangalore and Hyderabad and to interview call-center trainers, trainees, and operators about their lives, their hopes, and their techniques of cross-cultural acting. They visited Customer Communications Group at Customer.com, a company whose "multi-channel, outsourced solutions deliver twice the quality of other alternatives at a lower cost."[12] In videotaped interviews, a trainer spoke directly into the camera about her attempts to "hire people without any mother tongue influences…. if there are any dialectical or mother tongue influences, we do our best to neutralize it." Another South Asian trainee described his attempts to "get the accent … come what may" and took satisfaction in his ability to mimic regional variations across the United States, offering a convincing Texan accent as an example. The artists created an extensive archive of videotaped interviews with workers that described life in a call center and beyond. Interviews included stories of career success and humorous critiques of customer behavior and vacillated between wondrous impressions of US society and critical accounts of American myopia and self-importance. The artists saw the call-center operators as both genies and Aladdins who were looking for ways to make global magic work in their own lives.

The Builders' investigation of these operating systems also focused on space, particularly the juxtaposition of a colorful world of transnational possibility next to the monochromatic uniformity of the call center's corporate campuses. In office after office, operators sat in cubicles or at standardized desks spaced evenly apart. Aware that the same office landscape could be found in Bangalore, London, Paris, Atlanta, or Hong Kong, Peter Norrman from The Builders and Ali Zaidi from motiroti documented workplaces filled with fluorescent lights and collected other images of office culture. Particularly compelling was the image of office chairs and computer screens spaced evenly along a long desk underneath a bright LED screen announcing retail and stock transactions in cities around the world. The juxtaposition of local conformity (below) and global variety (on top) became a central trope in ALLADEEN's stage image.

1970 typical office environment.

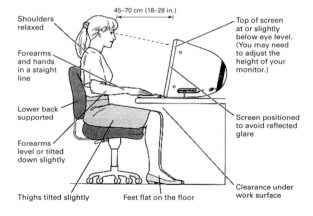

Shoulders relaxed

45–70 cm (18–28 in.)

Top of screen at or slightly below eye level. (You may need to adjust the height of your monitor.)

Forearms and hands in a staight line

Lower back supported

Forearms level or tilted down slightly

Screen positioned to avoid reflected glare

Thighs tilted slightly

Feet flat on the floor

Clearance under work surface

The ideal typing position.

In ALLADEEN as in JET LAG, theatrical bodies dynamized the flatness of architectural rendering while the CAD-ification of the mise-en-scène rendered the theater space static. In so doing, it exemplified what Hans-Thies Lehmann calls a postdramatic turn away from normative action and toward states—the creation of an encounter that approached the condition of viewing a "static painting" that simultaneously wanted to move.[13] This kind of aesthetic reflection on movement and stasis was paralleled in the social theories on globalization that Weems was reading. She underlined this passage in an interview with Pico Iyer, the author of *The Global Soul: Jet Lag, Shopping Malls, and the Search for Home*:

I begin deliberately with those dizzying surfaces and passageways—movement, an inundation of data, which I think reflects how the world is today—and you have to fight your way through it to get to the stillness and the settledness and the space that begins to open up in those last two chapters. The first chapters make you almost jet-lagged, there's so much information that you can't tell right from left, east from west. In part, the book is about the passage from speed to slowness and surface to depth. To me, that's the big challenge in the global era. The need for stillness, for seceding from that world, is greater than ever.[14]

As a former dramaturg with The Wooster Group, Weems was familiar with the formal concerns around nonnarrative stasis in postdramatic theater. After JET LAG and with ALLADEEN, Weems found that such formal questions could be joined to social content, especially in a globalizing landscape that was confounding perceptions of speed and slowness, proximity and distance. ALLADEEN was thus an attempt to expose the mundane territory and vulnerable bodies at the center of a world that promised friction-free connections and high velocity travel:

Some customers are very positive. They say, "Oh, wow, I'm talking to someone in India." There's also a difference in reactions after September 11th. There is some perception that this is a foreign country, and there is a change that's happened. And for the layman on the street that's completely understandable. Some people are impressed that we're so far away, and they are very positive. Some people say, "Why should your company be in some place where I can't get service?"

When you get a graveyard shift, you wake up at different times, you sleep at different times, your whole system gets totally warped. And once you're in that warped system, it's OK. Other than that, it's a great job. It's a super place to be.

Call-center workers in Bangalore. Real name: Anshuman Deb (ERO name: Andy Ramos), Real name: Alex Sangma (ERO name: Alex), Real name: Sanila Menon (ERO name: Sandy), Real name: Karthik Venkatraman (ERO name: Jeff Gordon).

I had this guy who had a fetish for toes. He asked me what kind of varnish I had on, and "What color is it?" I all could say was, "Can I help you with a reservation?" ... He went on about his fetish. So I had to release the call. I said, "Thank you for calling Ramada."

There is a company which changes your name so you'll have a more American-sounding name. For instance, Karthik Venkatraman is difficult to pronounce, so they'll Anglicize ... something as simple as possible. Some companies do it because they want the customer to think the call is being taken somewhere in the US rather than Bangalore. There are some companies who won't lie but won't give you the whole truth. If you ask them, "Where are you calling from?," they'll say, "We're headquartered at so-and-so-place in Texas."

Ultimately, in creating a piece about the call-center industry, The Builders Association sought to demystify a form of labor that, at the time, went largely unregistered by the consumers who depended on it. Such a theatrical act of exposure partook of a longer genealogy in Brechtian political theater. As a company that made visible their own operating systems in previous productions, The Builders positioned themselves in relation to a Brechtian aesthetic.

But ALLADEEN also challenged the legacies of a Marxist worldview that positioned such systems and people as "the real" or "authentic" base behind or beneath superstructural illusion. Call-center labor was already saturated with the stuff of illusion, and its operating systems were not detachable from the interpersonal encounters that it created. As such, this site exemplified shifts in post-Marxist theories of the social. For example, Ernest Laclau and Chantal Mouffe—the thinkers whose work prompted the coining of the term *post-Marxist*—argue against any social model that gives structural primacy to any single dimension of a social system, including the laborer or the economic. The two critique a variety of social theorists (including Louis Althusser) who, they argue, consistently fall back on such a model by seeing the social as determined "in the last instance by the economy": "If society has a last instance which determines its laws of motion" (they worry about Althusser's paradigm), "then the relations between the overdetermined instances and the last instance must be conceived in terms of simple, one-directional determination by the latter."[15] Laclau and Mouffe reject the notion that social formation is unidirectionally determined by a fixed realm of necessity or an immovable conception of "the base": "There is no single underlying principle fixing—and hence constituting—the whole field of differences."[16] Any conception of the "last instance," whether imagined temporally in terms of finality or spatially as an undermounted operation, short-circuits our ability to plot relational exchange and contradiction across multiple registers of the social.

Although Brecht did not accept a fixed vision of society's supporting apparatus, his theater labored under a determining vision of labor. Theater's exterior processes backstage bore an analogy to the real, authenticating realm of necessity that theoretically was both hidden from and necessary to the operations of illusion. As Hans-Thies Lehmann and others have noted, "the question of a political theatre changes radically under the conditions of the contemporary information society," which means that this model of labor was one site of radical change.[17] A twenty-first-century post-Brechtian postdramatic theater thus would have to resist representations of the labor that presumed its status as the authenticating "real." If a post-Marxist vision is, in part, about antagonizing the values and reality effects given to certain "underlying principles," then a post-Brechtian postdramatic theater has to imagine the realm of material necessity, of labor, or of the operating system as something other than foundational or as determining "in the last instance."[18] Such a theater could never imagine itself outside or uncorrupted by the social structures that it tried to question.

STORYBOARD

As noted in earlier chapters, The Builders had been moving away from a model of theater-making that was based in the "deconstruction" of canonical dramatic literature. As in JET LAG, they found themselves more interested in crafting stories and new writing from other sources. Because the process of "writing" did not follow the tradition of playwright as primary author, they sought writers like Martha Baer who felt comfortable supplying what Weems increasingly called "textual material," samplings of words and dialogue that could be reassembled and dispersed along with the bodies and technologies of rehearsal. Baer proved to be a critical player in forging an imaginative link between the tale of Aladdin and the social politics of new technology represented by the industry. A former V-Girl, Baer became a managing editor at *Wired* magazine in 1996 and was a published novelist. As a creative and analytic writer responsible for tracking the emerging fields of digital technology, she proved to be a perfect collaborator. As a critic, Baer brought a deep and skeptical knowledge of new technologies. As a dramatic writer, she could provide text that became the basis of an alternative and ever-changing script. Together, the company began to imagine the digital reinvention of Aladdin's lamp and his dialogue with the genie.

Drawing from the extended development process that was used in JET LAG, The Builders held storyboard sessions that were primarily about establishing a structure that juxtaposed narrative elements with bodies, images, and technological effects in different combinations. The deconstruction of canonical plays was a signature technique of postdramatic theater, but The Builders still needed to generate new texts to have something to deconstruct and remake—and they needed Baer to maintain flexibility when building and unbuilding dramatic writing. Weems began by schematizing the distinct stages of the Aladdin narrative, and then she and the cast devised call-center-based improvisations and scenes that loosely matched the central themes of each stage. For example, the episode in which Aladdin is lured by the genie to a mysterious desert site became fodder for a call-center scene in which an operator received a call from a client who needed directions for driving from Los Angeles to Las Vegas.

Performer Tanya Selvaratnam as Phoebe, a call-center pseudonym that was drawn from the cast of the television show *Friends*, received a disoriented call from performer Heaven Phillips, who was driving from Los Angeles to Las Vegas. Phoebe brought up Google Maps on her computer and offered vague directions: "You follow this street, the 15 in Los Angeles, and if you take it all the way, you are going to hit this desert…. Now you can't miss it because there is nothing else there." As she spoke, maps, translations, and popular references moved across the large video screen. The exchange between the remotely located call-center operator and the clueless driver calling for directions thus produced an uncanny meditation on geographic space. An operator in India read a map with a bird's-eye view, offering directions to a driver in the United States who was viewing the landscape from the ground. The screens promised cross-global informational exchanges while a transnational workforce rushed to keep up with the promise. The stagescape was a constantly changing composition of images, sounds, and embodied actors whose actions seem to trigger each other in a percolating network of screens, speech, and gesture, repositioning referents for the real and the illusory, the client and the customer, the remote and the proximate.

Excerpt from "The Story of 'Ala al-Din (Aladdin) and the Magic Lamp"
[In which the magician takes 'Ala al-Din on a long walk and conjures the appearance of the cave.]

... They advanced farther and farther into the countryside, and the cunning magician ... took an opportunity to enter one of the gardens.... Thus the African magician led 'Ala al-Din imperceptibly far beyond the gardens and crossed the open country until they almost reached the mountains.

'Ala al-Din ... said ... , "Uncle, where are we going? We have left the gardens very far behind us, and I see nothing but mountains. If we go much farther, I don't know whether I will have enough strength to return to the city." The fake uncle replied, "Take courage, nephew. I want to show you a garden that surpasses all the ones you have seen. It is not far off, just a step from here...."

The magician led him much farther, telling him many entertaining stories, to make the way seem less tedious and the fatigue more bearable.

At last they came to a place between two mountains....

He said to him ['Ala al-Din], ... "You should now know that under the stone there is hidden treasure that is destined for you and which will make you one day richer than the greatest king in the world. Indeed, there is no one in the world, save you, who is permitted to touch this stone and to lift it, in order to enter."[19]

Excerpt from the script for ALLADEEN: Part 2 (Bangalore Call Center), Scene 6

Phoebe: OntheRoad Customer Guidance. This is Phoebe. How may I help you?
Las Vegas Lady: Yeah. I just rented a car from you guys? And I'm trying to get from LA to LV, and I was just wondering if you could give me some directions?
Phoebe: You're trying to get to Louisiana, ma'am?
Las Vegas Lady: No, no. I'm in Los Angeles trying to get to Las Vegas, and I lost the who-zee-what-sis—you know, the thingamajiggy with the directions on it that you guys gave me.... And I've just gotta tell someone.... I just won a gazillion smackaroonies in the lottery, and I'm gonna blow the whole wad....

Phoebe: I think there is something wrong with the connection. Can you hold on please?

Las Vegas Lady: Um? Sure?

(HOLD MUZAK)

Phoebe to Rizwan (in Indian accent): What is a Smackarooni?

Rizwan: Pasta. Spaghetti.

Phoebe: No, SMAC-a-rooni. Not mac-a-roni.

(On screen: Phoebe Googles "smacarooni." We see the suggested alternative spellings appear…. Phoebe gives up and resumes the phone call.)

Phoebe: Hello, ma'am. I'm back again.

Las Vegas Lady: You know, I am utterly confused as to where I'm going, and I'm feeling a little lost in space out here to tell you the truth—

Phoebe: *Lost in Space!* That was a great show….

(Video: Bollywood images of a romantic, Technicolor desert fade-in and alternate with a GPS map of Los Angeles.)

Las Vegas Lady: What?

Phoebe: Do you remember Angela Cartwright?

Las Vegas Lady: Yes, I do, but—

Phoebe: She was the daughter on *Lost in Space*!

Las Vegas Lady: … have you got the directions?

Phoebe: I'm just pulling it up, m'am. The computers are quite slow today.

Las Vegas lady: Oh.

Phoebe: Angela Cartwright. I always used to sing along with her.

Las Vegas Lady: You're so cute. Where are you from?

Phoebe: I'm from the global calling center, ma'am.

Las Vegas Lady: No, but where are you?

Phoebe: Oh, here, I've got the directions….

Las Vegas Lady: Oh, good.

Phoebe: If you follow this street, the 15, in Los Angeles, and you follow it all the way … the big street … The 15 …

Las Vegas Lady: Uh huh.

Phoebe: You're going to hit this desert.

Las Vegas Lady: Uh huh.

Phoebe: And if you go through this desert—there's nothing else there so you can't miss it—you go all the way through this big desert, and at the end of it is Las Vegas.

Las Vegas Lady: OK—15 to Vegas.

Phoebe: That's right. Thanks for calling OntheRoad Customer Guidance. Have a nice day.

The Builders built a storyboard based on other juxtapositions between the Aladdin story and call-center scenarios. In a later portion of the narrative, Aladdin is transformed into an entirely new figure by virtue of the lamp's magical powers. In rehearsals for ALLADEEN, The Builders used that moment to stage a triumph for Joey (played by Rizwan Mirza), a call-center operator who achieves career success. The ancient Aladdin tale thus continued to offer resources for dramatizing the hopes and fantasies of private success in a neoliberal economy. It offered Weems, Baer, and the cast an opportunity to extrapolate and twist elements of its basic structure to generate new scenarios. As Weems wrote in her journal: "Good structure of linking stories (like the Thousand and One Nights). The stories don't link narratively; it's just one person asking another about their story, again and again. The structure is the endless pattern."

Using a variety of improvisation and scripting techniques, they created characters who struggled to keep "the mother tongue" at bay and to engage clients with their new knowledge of American popular culture. As an operator with the Western name Rachel, performer Jasmine Simhalan made reservations by spelling out names with references to American popular culture ("H as in Harry Potter, J as in J-Lo") and attempted to be geographically responsive when talking to a client located in San Jose ("Oh, chilly today, sir?"). However, her efforts at familiarity risked a misfire when she continued, "Terrible about that elephant," improvising while reading a newsfeed of an animal rights case as she worked. "What?" asked the caller. "The elephant who was abused," she anxiously responded. "Oh, ... oh, perhaps you did not read about it yet," she said, embarrassed by her overloaded knowledge of geotrivia.

Scene in a karaoke bar.

"Multitrack by Nature": An interview with writer Martha Baer
by Charlotte Stoudt, a dramaturg for ALLADEEN

Q What are the first three words you think of when someone says "Aladdin"?

A Lamp, jinn, pantaloons.

Q From the vantage point of *Wired* magazine, what gets your attention in terms of the way technology is changing our lives, our assumptions about what is possible?

A Well, I'm an editor at *Wired*, and being an editor is all about storytelling. That doesn't change no matter what the subject matter. You can have the inside exclusive on the coolest technology, but if the storytelling is weak, it doesn't mean anything.

Q It's difficult to dramatize the paradoxes of time, space, and identity that the Bangalore call-center operators represent. How did you approach this script? What questions have you been considering?

A Well, I'm still very much in the middle of writing, but let's take the telephone right off the bat. It's a tool that holds so many contradictions between identity and distance. But what's fascinating is that the telephone is an aging technology, not an emerging one. It's not postmodern, and what I noticed about the call operators' style of selling over the phone is that it's archaic—the ancient hard sell. It makes me think of Lily Tomlin with a headset or the obsession with generating leads in *Glengarry Glen Ross*.

Q By definition, capitalism eats its young. So what will replace the call center?

A Telephony as we think of it is undergoing total transformation. Once you shift the telephone from analog to digital, you can integrate so many other electronic functions. In the old model, a line gets a call: it's point to point—a single exchange via voice. With digital telephony, you can interfere with the voice, manipulate, store it, catalyze other events, bring up other kinds of data. The new model of telephone might work like this: some technology searches for a phone number associated with, say, the use of sporting goods—via records of past purchases made over the phone. It dials that number and gets a female voice, which tells the technology to let the potential customer know that the company has new swimsuits. Then it will figure out the kind of price range that's appropriate. And so on. And all of this will take place within the customer's mobile existence—not merely in front of the computer, as with Internet shopping. In the end, it's pretty much about selling things, isn't it?

REHEARSAL/ASSEMBLY

Performance was thus fundamental to the mystification process within the call-center industry—and performance was thus fundamental to The Builders Association's act of demystification as well. As noted above, ALLADEEN provided an opportunity to reconsider how twenty-first-century humans imagine their relation to larger systems of support, labor, and human welfare.[20] To some, a globalizing world of digital connection has done away with terrestrial systems of labor and support. Rather than the under-mounted "base" of industrial labor imagined in vertical Marxist (and often Brechtian) visions of social organizations, humans are now connected electronically and even wirelessly in laterally networked relationships. With the loose ties of a network replacing hierarchical social systems, people are presumably freer to move: we can make connections and drop them, transfer money without seeing cash, and initiate new collaborations without meeting collaborators in real time.

In such a changing context, theorists of globalization also speculate that concepts of work have changed as well. The hypermaterial labor of a Marxist base has been replaced by the mobilization of what Michael Hardt and Antonio Negri call "immaterial labor." Whether taking shape in the exchange of information or in the "affective" offering of compassion, care, excitement, and hospitality, such "immaterial forms" are central to a growing service economy.[21] Overall, then, the digitally networked world of immaterial work presents itself as a kind of frictionless space where economic exchange seems to bypass the gravitational and referential pulls of economic power and labor seems no longer to leave any material trace of its enactment.

Importantly, such images of a friction-free world have been complicated and qualified by those who think about how they actually work. Saskia Sassen argues that the global marketplace remains "embedded" in the material infrastructures of cities and citizens who animate them. "Emphasizing place in a complex global economy," she says, "is one way to address what I see as the need to destabilize the accepted dominant narratives and explanations of globalization."[22] For Sassen, global exchange, no matter how electronically "diffused" and "dispersed," will always require its "territorial moment."[23] Similarly, Hardt and Negri argue that a so-called immaterial sphere still depends on material labor whether or not we notice it: "Immaterial labor almost always mixes with material forms of labor: health care workers, for example, perform affective, cognitive and linguistic tasks together with material ones, such as cleaning bedpans and changing bandages. The labor involved in all immaterial production, we should emphasize, remains material—it involves our bodies and brains as all labor does. What is immaterial is its product."[24]

For theater artists—and Builders artists, in particular—this kind of simultaneity had an intriguing ring. Long before the era of globalization, the laborers of the theater engaged in all kinds of material production to create an immaterial product. Mobilizing the resources of bodies, space, and props from the object world, theater artists have been in the business of creating affective spaces of "ease, well-being, satisfaction, excitement, or passion" that have left little material trace. Because of this long-standing conjunction where performance can stand in both for the encumbering realm of material making as well as the ephemeral realm of motion and affect, ALLADEEN could be a prime place to investigate the paradoxes of globalized connection. Lehmann invokes this media scene in his meditations on the politics of the postdramatic theater:

The basic structure of perception mediated by media is such that there is no experience of connection among the individual images received but above all no connection between the receiving and sending of signs; there is no experience of a relation between address and answer. Theatre can respond to this only with a politics of perception, which could at the same time be called an aesthetic of responsibility (or response-ability). Instead of the deceptively comforting duality of here and there, inside and outside, it can move the mutual implication of actors and spectators in the theatrical production of images into the center and thus make visible the broken thread between personal experience and perception. Such an experience would not only be aesthetic but therein at the same time ethico-political.[25]

In many ways, ALLADEEN was an exploration of globalization's material embedding. That embedded material appeared in the bodies of operators who wear the headsets that facilitate global communication. It appeared in the monochrome office parks that have been inserted into cities throughout the globe to facilitate a global service industry. Joining fiber optic lines that turned "another continent into our 'back office,'" these laboring bodies and laboring spheres are part of a local and material system that underpins a globalized experience of delocalization. And a theater that linked these wires and these bodies seemed a prime set to underscore the politics of global connection.

As The Builders Association and motiroti artists learned in interviews, performance-based techniques of vocal training and rehearsal trained service workers to neutralize their biographical locality, creating a seamless service context whose human territorial specificity went unregistered by its clients. The artists thus set about identifying what it felt like to be trying to make others feel good. They began to make lists of typical scenarios of economic and emotional management where customers try to "get help for an inexplicably complex problem" or "seek the wrong product" or "try to get something for free." They then made lists of "What the operators do (response strategies): try to help, try to make the customer happy, placate, falsely compliment, end the call, deflect, bring caller back to the business of the call, offer alternative solutions, offer bargain discounts."[26] From there, the two ensembles improvised scenarios of affective labor, casting themselves as individuals who were responsible for maintaining "emotions of ease, hospitality, excitement, and frustration."[27] Showing call-center training systems thus would reveal the affective process by which the mystification of service occurred. It used the hyperbolic capacities of theatrical performance to underscore the unregistered capacities of everyday performance, exposing the new base that supported global citizenship—more precisely, the lateralized, mimetic, and dynamic set of social interactions that sustain global personhood.

Combining their improvised rehearsals with videotaped footage of interviews and training classes from their trip to Bangalore, Weems, Khan, and Zaidi assembled data that exposed this affective training ground. After displaying the interview on the neutralization of "the mother tongue," Weems decided to combine documentary footage of actual training with its embodied reenactment by Builders actors. In one documentary scene, a white American-accented male trainer stands next to a trainee who is trying to pronounce American state capitals. In the video and onstage, the trainer and trainer-actor stop the student and student-actor as they refine syllables and consonants for "Santa Fe, New

Bangalore operator training scene. Recorded in Bangalore,
recreated onstage.

Mexico … Santa Fe … Albany, New York, Albany, New York, … try this, Albany, … Albany, New York."
As they moved down the list of American geographical landmarks, the trainer and trainer-actor both
told the student not to rush and offered encouragement by saying there was "great energy … a lot of
juices there … a lot of juice."

The footage showed the unequal ground on which a circuit of global mimicry rests. South Asian
citizens received cross-cultural training in American pronunciation and American popular culture,
delocalizing the Indian site of the call center to address global citizens who wanted to hear the
language and accent tones of the highly local site of the United States. The dramatized call center
thus tried to create a system of tech support whose service was not interrupted by the jarring tones of
another's local context—and to minimize the psychic awareness of global dependency that comes when
a privileged client asks, "Where are you from?"

The lessons also showed trainers using the skills of the acting teacher to generate a degree of
comfort and confidence in racial mimicry ("great energy"). That conjunction made their reenactment
all the more striking. In the final production, the recorded scenes of training—in American capitals, in
American sports, in American television shows—were displayed on screens next to their reenactment
by the live actors. The actors took on the personas of those who take on a persona as videotaped
documentations showed laborers who also take on a persona when they do their job. ALLADEEN's
staged mediascape offered a distributed network whose "original" performance was projected and
deflected.

The process of assemblage continued, and the collaborators located images—collections of
scenarios, parts of scripts, video documentation from Bangalore, and digitized images of corporate
offices, Aladdin recreations, and contemporary consumer culture—in their bodies and their desktops.
As with many other production processes, this rehearsal process could not wait for its technology to
arrive during tech week. Neal Wilkinson, Dan Dobson, Allen Hahn and other collaborators installed,
mounted, and flew screens, projectors, lights, and speakers throughout the playing space. The
entire ensemble worked up new characters in the same moment that they worked up techniques

for projecting them. They crafted new text in the same moment that they experimented with the placement of text on running LED screen. They plotted transformative shifts in the narrative in the same moment that they tried out blue screens, Mylar screens, and other technological tricks of magical transformation.

Director's program note

'Ala al-Din immediately mounted his horse.... Although he had never been on horseback before, he rode with such grace that the most experienced horseman would not have taken him for a novice.... Those who knew him when he played in the streets as a grown-up urchin did not recognize him, and even those who had seen him recently hardly knew him, so much were his features altered, by virtue of the lamp.

From *The Arabian Nights II: Sinbad and Other Popular Stories*[28]

The story of Aladdin's journey from urchin to king appears nowhere in the Arabic and Persian manuscripts from which the tales of *The Thousand and One Nights* are drawn. Scholars suspect that Aladdin may have first appeared as a French addition around three hundred years ago. Yet in spite of his questionable lineage, Aladdin survives today as one of the most widely recognized fairytale heroes, from Beijing to Burbank. The poor boy whose many wishes are granted by a genie is the subject of silent and talking film spectacles, British pantos, ice spectaculars, computer games, and theme park rides. We have taken this as the focus of our own new trilogy—stage performance, website, and music video—transporting Aladdin into the era of global telecommunications and virtual identities.

The fantasies that lie at the heart of Aladdin's story are instantaneous wish fulfillment, endless wealth, and total personal transformation—fantasies that remain fiercely compelling today. In the call centers of Bangalore, India, we found a setting in which such transformations are being constantly and routinely enacted—culturally, socially, and economically—on both ends of the fiberoptic phone lines.

ALLADEEN is a lens through which we view the realm of contemporary technology and its dissonant mixing of the local with the global. The territory we survey is the social imagination in an age of corporate colonialism. Through it runs a river of cultural images, with its sources in distant times and lands far, far away.

Marianne Weems, director

Call center onstage: performers Tanya Selvaratnam, Rizwan Mirza, Jasmine Simhalan.

CLOSINGS

As the production of ALLADEEN and commitments to present it fell into place, The Builders wanted to find a way to join the cross-cultural politics of their own lives as what Moe Angelos called "migrant cultural workers" with the cross-cultural politics of the show. This had been a research-intensive production, and many elements of their research were not going to be able to be represented directly. They also felt acutely the alienating global politics of touring cities where they had little time to make local connections. They turned to a different form of technology to address the gap by creating a public website for ALLADEEN—http://www.alladeen.com.[29] On the website, they uploaded research on the Aladdin tale, stories, documentation, and statistics from the call-center industry for prospective audience members to explore, thereby extending the digital space of the theatrical far beyond the proscenium of the hosting venue. They also created an interactive portion of the website where they asked participants to post wishes for others to see—and perhaps for a genie one day to answer. As individuals posted humorous hopes for a side of fries and poignant ones such as hoping for sick relative to heal or for a dead parent to come back to life, the simple wish structure created a provisional site for connecting the local specificity of individual biographies with a theater piece that had embarked about a global tour. These wishes were threaded back into the production on a nightly basis, running across the LED boards in a karaoke bar where the performers enacted yet another layer of performance.

ALLADEEN was one the most politicized shows The Builders had made to date, so its reception becomes a place where recurring questions of the theatrical role of new technology interact with volatile questions of technology's social and postcolonial effects. As noted in previous chapters, The Builders' mix of theatrical screenscapes is often celebrated and critiqued in the same terms, which welcome or worry about the transformation of the theatrical realm by new technologies. Some reviews of ALLADEEN worried about reification, wondering if The Builders Association was producing eye candy that distracted from the potent social message of call-center politics. Jennifer Parker-Starbuck, for instance, worried that "the humour and gorgeous visual production mask an underlying critique of what it means to live as the workers or how it feels ... to serve, American interests."[30] For her, "the gloss of the production, in effect, re-performs the central act of capitalism, the forced erasure of visible labor in the production of the commodity. While the playbill lists all of those involved in the production ... the technological wizardry stands out not for the human production of it, but for its own slickness as commodifiable/commodified theater."[31] From the perspective of Weems and other company members who were scrambling to raise funds as a nonprofit theater, the notion that they were re-performing "the central act of capitalism" was unexpected. But this kind of reading might be the occupational hazard of any post-Brechtian theater that performs our enmeshment within the technologies that it exposes. In the same review where Parker-Starbuck expresses this concern, she also voices a recognition of her own embeddedness:

During much of the piece, I thought back to many of the recent calls I had received and wondered if I had perceived an Indian accent, or whether the caller had tried to relate to the weather in New York, or say something about the sightseeing possibilities? Later, I learned that many other audience members were processing similar thoughts.[32]

This moment provoked in Parker-Starbuck and apparently in other audience members a momentary self-consciousness of their systemic interdependence in the midst of an apparently independent interaction—receiving a phone call. It was a moment when the apparent autonomy of global technology turned out to be embedded in a system of global dependency. As such, it seems an exemplary instance of Lehmann's political hopes for the postdramatic: it repurposed the theater to "make visible the broken thread between personal experience and perception."[33]

Some of these concerns about The Builders Association's theatrical reuse of technology have come from those who feel that wireless phones, broadband networks, and digital screens flatten the theater and render theater a frictionless pool of visual pleasure. But what if we invert the gesture and decide also to see theater as form that re-encumbers wireless, broadband, and digital images with the frictions of performance? From this perspective, ALLADEEN is not only a digital intervention in the space of theater but also a theatrical intervention in the space of the digital. Consider, for instance, Margo Jefferson's sense of the set of ALLADEEN as "like a giant computer that supplies verbal information and visual distraction."[34] As a giant computer with a "set" underneath, the naturalized worlds of computers, digital images, and web searches are fitfully stalled by the social labor required to "support" the goings-on of the screen. If Tara McPherson is right in suggesting that contemporary experience of the web screen is that of "volitional mobility," then the contingent lives and terrestrial specificity of a call center shows the precarity of our sense of volition.[35] Staging technology here has visual, temporal, and social dimensions, defamiliarizing the visual, temporal, and social habituations that go unregistered in the course of depending on it. Staging technology means experiencing it at a different temporality than the one to which we have become habituated when the technology (usually) works. It means seeing the technology within a larger system that is usually foreclosed and disavowed in the moment of its use.

Finally, it seems significant that The Builders Association took on the questions of the call-center industry in a theatrical space whose genealogies are located in time and space contingencies that are not simply pre-digital but arguably pre-industrial. They juxtapose an apparently unfettered, although occasionally pixilated world of electronic connection with the highly fettered space of the theater, where the actor onstage and the operator in her cubicle were obligated to show up at a certain time. To think about digital connection in postdramatic theater is to juxtapose the apparently noncontingent world of the digital with the avowedly contingent dimensions of performance, all to expose the supporting actions that produce the experience of seamlessness.

As it turns out, the digital world cannot do without the analog any more than immaterial economies can do without the materiality of servicing bodies. In ALLADEEN—as in other work by The Builders—the show juxtaposed the apparent autonomy of globalizing technology and the inconvenient heteronomy of the theater. ALLADEEN showed the bodily and aural cultural training that is required to sustain a call center in Bangalore. Its scenes juxtaposed the travel plans of the most entitled global

Anonymous wishes from the ALLADEEN
website used in the music video.

Director: Ali Zaidi; videographer: Peter Norrman.

citizens with the occupational obstacles of those
who are less so. It juxtaposed the screens and
sounds of global connections with the bodies
of workers whose headphones support digital
connection. Through this particular conjunction
of performance and technology, ALLADEEN
asked audiences to ask themselves to what
degree inconvenience can be "off-shored."

ENDNOTES

Artist's Voice: Keith Khan, co-creator and designer

Having seen JET LAG at the Barbican Theatre in London, I was inspired to see the unique union of contemporary themes and visual media in The Builders' work. I thought it was fantastic. I hadn't seen theater like it and engineered to meet Marianne via a mutual friend, Norman Frisch, the dramaturg. I discovered that when she was in the UK with The Wooster Group in 1991, Marianne had brought her company to visit the show that Ali Zaidi and I named our company, motiroti, after. The whole company had come on a joint outing. I had directed and Ali designed that show—*Moti Roti, Puttli Chunni* (1993) (thick bread, thin veils), but it was truly a collaboration of both our inspirations. It was a pastiche of Bollywood films played out in real time on stage counterpointed with a gritty real UK Asian experience on 16 millimeter film. Marianne was clearly the mistress of theatrical mystery where it meets contemporary dilemmas, and I was a UK designer putting on large-scale popular spectacles. In addition, motiroti, with Ali Zaidi, made intriguing arts events about cultural enquiry and diverse communities place in the world. It was so exciting to find someone who was as concerned simultaneously with contemporary and popular culture as well as with high theatrical technical that I thought that I'd found a soulmate.

That is where the gestation of ALLADEEN began and continued on a two-year creative partnership between the three protagonists—Ali, born in India and raised in Pakistan; Marianne from Seattle, Washington, to the lower East Side of New York; and myself, from Trinidadian heritage but a true blue Brit by education and attitude. The huge, valuable, and giving supporting cast—from Penny Andrews and Kim Whitener through to Norman Frisch—all made massive contributions to the realization of the venture, as did the final cast, crew, producers, coproducers, and funders who helped us on this colossal venture.

The project that we discussed would be about wish fulfilment, with jinns, magicians, and some UK cultural tropes from this old tradition. It became apparent that in basing the show within this unique British cultural form was singularly culturally specific and one-dimensional. Although we soon abandoned this direct treatment, the residue that remained was cultural inversion that stayed firmly in the final version of ALLADEEN. Cultural

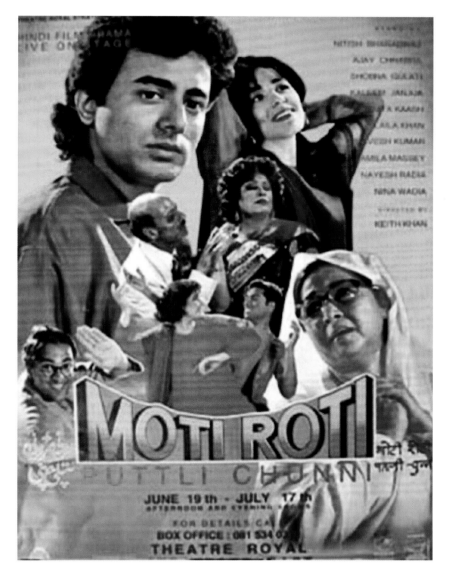

Motiroti poster for the premiere of *Moti Roti, Puttli Chunni*, 1993.

questioning had long been a strong factor in the work that Ali Zaidi and I had worked on with our company motiroti. Marianne transformed it when she brought in the article "I'm in Bangalore (but I Can't Say So)."

Much of the thinking that Ali's and my earlier projects explored was pushed to an extreme in ALLADEEN. Early motiroti projects intertwined audience, expectation, class, and race in sophisticated ways. Our earlier work explored many of these themes while focusing on an Asian (Indian) audience base—contemplating the value of different cultural forces that inform first-, second-, and third-generation subcontinental influences in accessible ways and using design and performative techniques to explore this. ALLADEEN was a synthesis of many of these influences and pushed it further because we had to bear in mind that the piece would always be culturally dislocated. Popular cultures—whether Bollywood, Hollywood, karaoke, or digital dance games—became constant points of reference that we would come back to. We edited out many direct "orientalist" images from films to keep the reference in the digital sphere, where culture is transmogrified by media. In one of the final production periods of ALLADEEN, Ali and I were based in a downtown New York sublet, and I also managed to put into play a massive parade for the Commonwealth to celebrate the queen's golden jubilee. The ALLADEEN work undoubtedly influenced the style and thinking of this major UK royal event—a parade that featured four thousand performers.

We also saw the Bangalore of the raj—which was a long-lost colonial empire with a guest-only policy, men-only bar areas, and Indian "rest rooms" that genuinely had beds for postprandial siestas. We played drunken snooker on vast billiard tables. We also ate the most tasteless food that Indians had inherited from the British, like cucumber sandwiches with the crusts cut off. And we saw the third side of India—gaudy south Indian temples adorned with hundreds of deities and huge palaces with space for pachyderms to bathe. The interplay between these class-divided spaces was palpable, and as foreigners we had access in a way that many locals were did not.

Ali, Marianne, and I spent many long hours debating how cultural synthesis and brokerage were the central themes of the project. India has its own strong cultural values and amazing film industry, which Ali is directly attached to. His father had been the second director a classic film, *Mughal-e-Azam*. We loved this hybridity of a culturally forceful country. We loved the digressional aspect of storytelling. Like *One Thousand and One Nights*, every story took a journey to another story and another story. Ali was the expert of this. We discussed how contemporary India felt and how much of British Asian culture could sometimes be more simplistic and singular than this enormous collision of cultures that modern India is. We really played with the mobility of cultural traditions—how contemporary people are forced to act on multiple identities in real time, online, with their friends and family. Much of the emphasis was on this state of flux and this duality. It was fascinating for us, therefore, to play with these fixed identities that are standardized in the two nations' popular film cultures—America's portrayal of Arabic, Oriental, and Indian people in Hollywood and the equally fossilized portrayal of Americans in Indian films as blond or villainous.

Halfway through the creative process, 9/11 occurred, and this sophisticated hybrid image became more polarized. In addition, American media started to publish more stories about the loss of jobs in the United States to India. Both events validated the creation of a relevant global project created somewhere between India, America, and the UK.

Guest Voice: Pico Iyer, essayist, novelist, and author of *The Global Soul: Jet Lag, Shopping Malls, and the Search for Home*

It's every writer's dream—partly because it happens so rarely—to learn that you're not alone at your desk, working on some solipsistic madness, but that artists elsewhere, in even more complex and exciting fields, are working on the same page as you. Or, even better, expanding and illuminating that page until it feels as if they might be staging and crafting your innermost thoughts, as well as your hopes.

I knew very little about The Builders Association when I received a letter from Marianne Weems, at the dawn of the new millennium, saying that she was beginning to hatch a project called ALLADEEN, reflecting on call centers in Bangalore. So far ahead of the curve was she, in fact, that I, 100 percent Indian by blood, had never heard of these centers until Marianne mentioned them in the context of her project.

"Anything you might like to do," she said, as I recall, about crossing cultures and crossed purposes, about shifting identities and lives lost in translation, about the power of storytelling in our mediated world or the loss of voice, would be fine. The work was designed to enact and exemplify the sense of networks and parallel lives that it was exploring. I wasn't used to hearing about projects so exhilaratingly contemporary. It was as if ideas were being plucked out of the globe's dreams and intuitions instead of its headlines. And when I wrote a little vignette about walking through the night in Bangkok, finding the transformations of *The Arabian Nights* taking on new currency and strangeness in the world of displacement, I knew somehow that Marianne would see exactly how it might echo and reflect the dissolves and emergences she was describing in cross-media form.

That was only the beginning, though. Very quickly I realized that The Builders Association had been writing and drafting my life, in effect. The company had already put on JET LAG, and that material was so real to me that I drew hugely from it in writing about movement and dislocation in my next book. Everything Marianne and her colleagues did seem to be probing, pushing, flickering around the new distances and dreamlike connections that had been my life and my lifelong subject. In that sense our formal collaboration was only a realization—a proof— of an invisible conspiracy that had been simmering for years. If I were to describe what I try to explore on the page, I would probably just produce a list of Builders Association's titles—JET LAG, INVISIBLE CITIES, CONTINUOUS

CITY, HOUSE/DIVIDED. But when I approach these themes, it's just dry words on a page. As soon as The Builders Association touches them, they become suggestive images, overlapping screens, echoing voices, haunting fables.

Metamorphosis has meanings and implications in the postmodern world that Ovid could never have imagined, but it is no less winged and magical an experience now than it was among the ancients. Working with The Builders Association on ALLADEEN taught me what Ovid might feel like in a multimedia world and how collaboration itself gains fresh shape and excitement when you find others who can see how transsexuals in Bangkok might shed light on and even be partners to self-styled Brads and Jennifers in modern Bangalore.

People

Directed by Marianne Weems
Conceived by Keith Khan, Marianne Weems, and Ali Zaidi

Design: Keith Khan, Ali Zaidi
Video design: Christopher Kondek
Sound design and original music composition: Dan Dobson
Lighting designed by: Jennifer Tipton
Text: Martha Baer (with additional material created by the company)
Dramaturg: Norman Frisch
New York producer: Kim Whitener
U.K. producer: Penny Andrews

Performed by

Rizwan Mirza
David Pence
Heaven Phillips
Tanya Selvaratnam
Jasmine Simhalan
Jeff Webster

Production manager: Neal Wilkinson
Technical director: Joseph Silovsky
Associate lighting designer: Allen Hahn
Video systems design: Peter Flaherty
Video associate: Jeff Morey
3D animation design: James Gibbs/dbox, Eric Schuldenfrei

Website (www.alladeen.com):

Directed by Ali Zaidi

Conceived by Keith Khan, Marianne Weems, and Ali Zaidi

Music video directed and produced by Ali Zaidi

Additional video by Peter Norrman

Sound and music by Dan Dobson

Original music by Shrikanth Sriram (Shri)

The following artists have all contributed to the development of ALLADEEN:

Additional text: Pico Iyer, and Josh Marsden

Assistant director: Lear deBessonet

Second assistant director: Alec Duffy

Observer: Stewart Laing

Production managers: Nick Schwartz-Hall,

Rigger: Billy Burns

Performers: Monique Curnen, Navtej Johar

Costume supervisor: James Deanes

Stage managers: Natalia de Campos, Anna Kiraly

Production assistants: Heather Delaney, Kimon Keramidas, Mireya Lucio, Andrew Schneider, Alyssa
    Sheldon, Kate Stannard

Sound assistants: Eleanor Dubinsky, Rob Laakso, Alison Brummer Edith Blackman, Liz Tyler Brody,
    Kelly Hannon, Patrick Dugan, Jason Marin, Eva Pinney, Aaron Mason, Rie Ono, Meredith Salvago

In Bangalore:

Video: Ali Zaidi, Peter Norrman

Research and production: Jyoti Makhija

Technical production, hire, and crew: Mike Isaac and Frame of Mind

Call-center personnel:

Supervisors: Samita Nag Ghosh, Prakash Gurbaxani, S. Nagarajan, Romola Nath, Manoj Pachisia, Ravindra Ranganthan (Ravi)

Trainers: Sonal Bhimani, John Howard, Sharu Jose, Sunayna Murthy, Shermeen Shuaib

Operators/Electronic Relationship Officers (EROs): Ateef Abdullah, Aarti Angelo, Riaz Basha, Maggie Bernerdette, Anshuman Deb, Manoj M. Desouza, Rebekkah Shonali Edward, Dexter Fernandes, Meher Hussain, Jimmy Joseph, Vivek Leonard, Sanila Menon, Rohit Raghav, M. K. Raghavendra, Natasha Sabharwal, Alex Sangma, Samson S. S., Rohit Thimmiah, Preeti Thomas, Karthik Venkatraman, Mathew Vergis

Invaluable assistance in India:

Dr. B. K. Chandrashekar (former Minister for Information Technology, Government of Karnataka, India), Dr. Rathi Jafer (Manager, Arts, Culture & English Studies, British Council, India), Nasreen Munni Kabir (film consultant), National Film Archive of India

Special thanks to the following for their wisdom and assistance:

Alison Bean, Maggie Bernerdette, Karla Barnacle Best, Paula Brown, Ann Carlson, Jessica Chalmers, Sally Cowling, Nadia Derrar, Dexter Fernandes, Sarah Frankland, Sarah Hickson, Greg Hilty, John Howard, Pico Iyer, John Kieffer, Vivek Leonard, Dean Moss, Renata Petroni, Kate Schelter, Mary Ellen Strom, Sue Timothy, Noreen Tomassi, Jessica Wanamaker, Philippa Wehle, and Anthony Willsea

Special thanks for CD artwork in the Virgin animation sequence:

Bjork, Mark Jones, Jim Merlis, Scott Rodger, Royksopp, The Strokes, Blak Twang, Wall of Sound

Company portraits from the ALLADEEN website, 2003.

Venues

2003   Wexner Center for the Arts, Columbus, OH

Museum of Contemporary Art, Chicago, IL

Walker Art Center, Minneapolis, MN

Singapore Arts Festival, Singapore,

Barbican BITE:03, London, UK

La Ferme du Buisson, Noisiel, France

Romaeuropa Festival '03, Rome, Italy

Warwick Arts Center, Warwick, UK

Contact Theater, Manchester, UK

Tramway, Glasgow, UK

Brooklyn Academy of Music Next Wave Festival '03, New York, NY

2004   REDCAT, Los Angeles, CA

On the Boards, Seattle, WA

Bogotà International Theater Festival, Bogotà, Colombia

Hopkins Center, Dartmouth, NH

Bergen International Theater Festival, Bergen, Norway

Bonn Biennale, Bonn, Germany

Melbourne International Arts Festival, Melbourne, Australia

Belfast Festival, Belfast, Northern Ireland

2005   Highlights Festival, Usine C, Montreal, Canada

Krannert Center for the Performing Arts, University of Illinois, Urbana, IL

John F. Kennedy Center, Washington, DC

Generation	The Man	The Woman	Famous people of the generation
GI Silent	John F. Kennedy Cary Grant	Katharine Hepburn, Marilyn Monroe	Walt Disney, Ronald Reagan, George Bush, Bill Cosby, Woody Allen, Martin Luther King, Jr.
Boom	Paul McCartney	Raquel Welch	Bill Gates, Al Gore, Steven Spielberg, Hillary and Bill Clinton, O. J. Simpson, Oprah
	Brad Pitt	Julia Roberts	Eddie Murphy, Michael Jordan, Michael Dell, Tom Cruise, Jodie Foster, Cindy Crawford
Millennial	Bart Simpson	Sandra Bullock, Sheryl Crowe	Britney Spears, Prince Harry, Anna Kournikova, Leann Rimes, Aaron Carter, Dooney Waters, Jessica McClure

U.S. information chart to be used by call-center operators in training.

Afterparty

SOME SOURCE MATERIALS FOR THE PRODUCTION

Books

as-Ashqar, Umar Sulaiman. *The World of the Jinn and Devils*. Translated by Sh. Jamaal Zarabozo. Boulder, CO: Al-Basheer Co., 1998.

Barnouw, Erik, and Subrahmanyam Krishnaswamy. *Indian Film*. New York: Oxford University Press, 1980.

Burton, Richard F., trans. *The Book of the Thousand Nights and a Night: A Plain and Literal Translation of the Arabian Nights Entertainments*. 1885. New York: Modern Library, 1997.

Chideya, Farai. *The Color of Our Future*. New York: William Morrow, 1999.

Desai, Anita. *Fasting, Feasting*. New York: Mariner Books, 2000.

Glennon, William. *Aladdin*. Woodstock, IL: Dramatic Publishing Co., 1965.

Haddawy, Husain, trans. *The Arabian Nights II: Sindbad and Other Popular Stories*. New York: Norton, 1995.

Iyer, Pico. *The Global Soul: Jet Lag, Shopping Malls and the Search for Home*. New York: Knopf/Vintage, 2000.

Kunzru, Hari. *The Impressionist*. New York: Dutton, 2002.

Kunzru, Hari. *Transmission*. New York: Dutton, 2004.

Lahiri, Jhumpa. *Interpreter of Maladies*. Boston, MA: Houghton Mifflin, 1999.

Neary, Jack. *Aladdin and the Wonderful Lamp: Based on the Arabian Nights Tale*. Boston, MA: Baker's Plays, 1993.

Norris, James. *Aladdin and the Wonderful Lamp*. Anchorage Press Plays, 1940.

Patel, Jayant. *Seeking Home: An Immigrants Realization*. New York: J. Patel, 1991.

Said, Edward W. *Orientalism*. New York: Vintage, 1979.

Senna, Dani. *Caucasia.* New York: Riverhead Books, 1998.

Spivak, Gayatri Chakravorty. *A Critique of Postcolonial Reason: Toward a History of the Vanishi*
     Present. Cambridge, MA: Harvard University Press, 1999.

Suri, Manil. *The Death of Vishnu: A Novel.* New York: Perennial, 2002.

Films

The Adventures of Prince Achmed. Directed by Lotte Reiniger. Berlin: Comenius Film GmbH, 1926.

A-Lad-in His Lamp. Directed by Robert McKimson. Los Angeles: Warner Bros. Pictures, The Vitaphone
     Corporation, 1948.

Aladdin and His Lamp. Directed by Lew Landers. Los Angeles: Walter Wanger Productions, 1951.

Aladdin and the Wonderful Lamp. Directed by Chester M. Franklin and Sidney Franklin. Los Angeles:
     Fox Film Corporation, 1917.

Aladin et la lampe merveilleuse. Directed by Jean Image. Paris: Films Jean Image, 1970.

Aladin ou la lampe merveilleuse. Directed by George Méliès. 1906.

Ali Baba and the Forty Thieves. Directed by Arthur Lubin. Los Angeles: Universal Pictures, 1944.

Ali Baba Goes to Town. Directed by David Butler. Los Angeles: Twentieth Century Fox, 1937.

Arabian Nights. Directed by Steve Barron. Los Angeles and London: ABC and BBC, 2000.

Arabian Nights. Directed by John Rawlins. Los Angeles: Walter Wanger Productions for Universal
     Pictures, 1942.

Dil to Pagal Hai. Directed by Yash Chopra. Yash Raj Films, 1997.

Gopal Krishna. Directed by Vishnupant Govind Damle and Sheikh Fattelal. Prabhat Film Company,
     1938.

The Magic Carpet. Directed by Lew Landers. Los Angeles: Columbia Pictures, 1951.

Le Meraviglie di Aladino (Wonders of Aladdin). Directed by Mario Bava and Henry Levin. Los Angeles:
     Metro-Goldwyn-Mayer, 1961.

Mughal-e-Azam. Directed by K. Asif. 1960.

Directed by George Blair. 1957.

. Directed by Ray Harryhausen. Los Angeles: Columbia Pictures Corporation,
ns, 1958.

Ted Tetzlaff. Los Angeles: RKO Pictures, 1955.

ted by Radhakant. 1963.

ted by Raoul Walsh. Los Angeles: Douglas Fairbanks Pictures, United

ted by Jack Kinney. Los Angeles: Columbia Pictures, 1959.

s. Directed by Alfred E. Green. Los Angeles: Columbia Pictures, 1945.

6 SUPER VISION

SURVEILLING THE AUDIENCE

SUPER VISION production image reproduced in *Wired*.

R VISION, one woman takes the stage, apparently without technology. There
d voices, and no live feeds. She (performer Tanya Selvaratnam) might be the
members to turn off their technology (cell phones and recording devices)
rs in case of emergency. Instead, she says this:

to SUPER VISION. We want to thank you all for joining us here in Los Angeles,
huttle and Barbie. As we begin tonight's performance here at The Roy and Edna
want to ask a few questions about what we are doing here. When I say we,
not just those of us on stage. We start by asking, "Who's here?," and so all of you have
answered. All of you have answered with your credit cards, which can tell us more about you than your
neighbor can. The consumer-profiling company Claritas, whose clients include everyone from Coca-Cola to
the US government, maintains an extensive array of consumer data. Claritas (which is Latin for "brightness")
tracks what you buy, where you go, and what you watch. And so you're watching SUPER VISION....

The woman on stage is actually not technology-free but is very much empowered by technology:

By downloading the zip codes of you, our valued audience members, into Claritas's central database, we
know more about you and can respond to your needs and desires. According to Claritas, 57 percent of you
are Bohemian Mixers. You are under fifty-five, rent your homes, and have advanced graduate degrees. You
buy Latin music, watch soccer, and are most likely to drive an Audi. Another 38 percent of you are comprised
of today's Young Digerati; you are between the ages of twenty-five and forty-four and also have advanced
graduate degrees; you are racially diverse, and you enjoy snow-boarding and watching the Independent
Film Channel. If you have a car, it is most likely to be a Prius.

labor

Over a decade earlier, a carpenter had opened the show of MASTER BUILDER, cheerfully displaying the tools of his trade and telling the audience how they worked. The prologue to SUPER VISION returned to that conceit, but by 2005, both the tools and the trades were different. As the prologue performer continued, different clusters of audience members giggled and guffawed in succession. They might have been responding with the shock of recognition ("That's me") or the urge to disidentify ("Obviously that's someone other than me"), but the moment dramatized the odd interpretive capacity of data management. With its systems of categorization and its unseemly power of inference, data-management techniques produced consumer profiles that appeared both ludicrous and stunningly on the mark. Hedy Weiss of the *Chicago Sun-Times* called it "a giant gotcha moment."[1]

The giggles and guffaws might have registered another level of ambivalence as audience members wondered whether the analysis was "for real" and were unsettled to realize that it was. The apparently benign act of paying for a ticket had unleashed what many apparently benign acts unleashed at the start of the twenty-first century—a large network of processes that synthesized, collated, and analyzed individual data. Such perfectly legal processes of data extraction and data inference were used by every theater that presented SUPER VISION. The Builders requested and received the (general) zip codes of that evening's ticket buyers, analyzed them using Claritas, and reported their findings to the audience. The data were used to write a new prologue for each locale but also could be used to encourage future attendance and to devise future amenities. In Seattle, "residents of the 98103 zip code ('Bohemian Mixers') are likely to earn $30,000 less per year than their seatmates from 98112 ('Money and Brains') but are more likely to go to the gym."[2] In Minneapolis, those from zip code 55403 "may make as much as $50,000 a year more than the 'Multicultural Mosaics' sitting next to them who live in 55104."[3] In San Francisco, "If you live in 94110, you're branded with the 'Multiculti Mosaic' label. Those in 94117 are 'Money and Brains.'"[4] Just as the carpenter's tools supported the apparatus of MASTER BUILDER, Claritas's tools occupied, however unnervingly, a similar position in SUPER VISION. The uses of personal data were the central theme of SUPER VISION and integral to the theatrical apparatus of audience development on which SUPER VISION's presenters relied. There was, in fact, no exit.

R&D

ALLADEEN showed how strategies of mimicry and constructed identity motored a global labor industry, but SUPER VISION pushed questions of digital identity in a different direction. Call-center operators had access to data that personalized their client interactions, and such data resources were part of a large, complex, and expanding network of digital data that was accessible by private and public sectors and by corporate and individual agents alike. Weems and a research assistant began to collect articles about data networks, exploring them as sites of collection and information but also as sites that used information management to develop new processes of surveillance and manipulation. In the United Kingdom, new online medical records both enabled responsive medical treatment and provoked new concerns about privacy of patients.[5] Legal scholar Daniel J. Solove's book *The Digital Person: Technology and Privacy in the Information Age*, contextualizes the increase in surveillance systems after the September 11, 2001, attacks in the United States, including the rise of "background-check" companies in the private sector as well as increased "private sector to government" information flows.[6] He elaborates on the rise of a surveillance discourse, noting the potential for the "Orwellian dangers" of knowledge to corrupt democratic rights. He distinguishes these concerns from "the Kafka-esque dangers" of digital data expansion, describing their capacity to install "the harms routinely arising in bureaucratic settings: decisions without adequate accountability, dangerous pockets of unfettered discretion, and choices based on short-term goals without consideration of long-term consequences or the larger social effects."[7] A data-driven world thus has encouraged access and transparency but also created new forms of corruption, abuse, and opacity. The great good of transparency has brought new questions about what kind of information is rightfully public. In the end, the world of informatics does not necessarily lead to informed action.

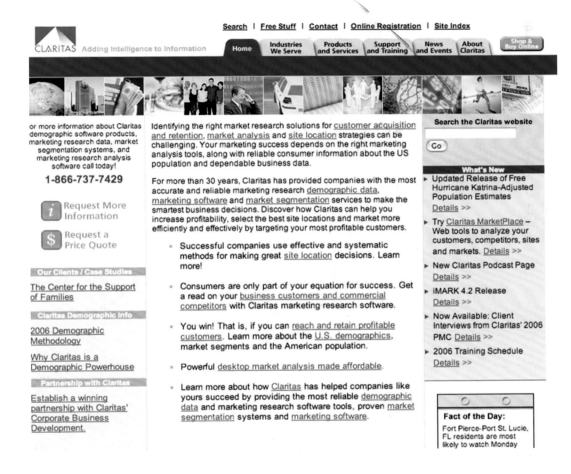

Research for SUPER VISION: "Claritas combines demographic, consumer behavior, and geographic data to help marketers identify, understand and reach their customers and prospects." Courtesy of Nielsen, 2004.

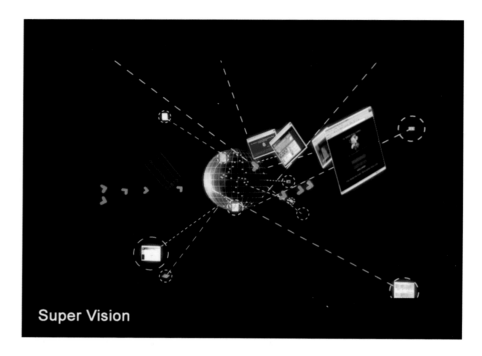

Super Vision

Early dbox portrait of personal data.

But it was not necessarily accurate to call such data networks new. Christian Parenti's *The Soft Cage: Surveillance in America from Slave Passes to the War on Terror* offers a historical take on the "soft cage" and its many early iterations. In her copy of the book, Weems underlined and bracketed Parenti's tales of architectural systems, biosystems, and regulation systems that tracked humans to information about them. Particularly compelling was the story of the Tappan brothers, who in the early 1800s tracked and recorded the trustworthiness of different traders who transported goods "on credit." The Tappans questioned traders about their business in ever-expanding "ledgers" that

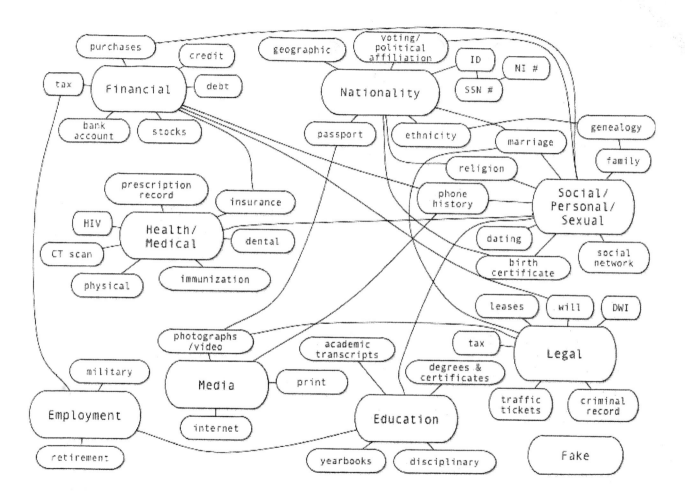

Map of a databody.

became early versions of what we now would call "risk analysis files."[8] Other merchants sought access to the Tappan brothers' valuable information and were willing to pay a fee for it. A credit reporting company was thus born, and the industry of credit tracking created more methods of human data surveillance.

The rise of data surveillance and digital data networks also created new opportunities for credit and data fraud. In the first years of the twenty-first century—before the popularization of the term *big data*—newspaper articles were examining the implications of these new data capacities. Weems collected relevant stories for a research and development packet for designers and actors. Articles described a kind of "dumpster diving" at hospitals for the records of deceased people whose data continued to live. Potential thieves secured access to such data and lived new lives based on birth records and passport documents that no longer had a physically human referent.

John E. McGrath's book *Loving Big Brother: Performance, Privacy, and Surveillance Space* was the first place that Weems encountered the phrase "data bodies," a term that became central to the production: "Our data bodies carry stains that are perhaps harder to clean than mud or sin—the marks of past late payments or motoring offences. They pursue us, confronting us as we apply for mortgages or visas, transactions or new tattoo."[9] McGrath invokes sociologist Liz Stanley's suggestions that we are in a constant state of producing such data selves and live under the constant pressure of a potential "audit": "These audit selves are habitually invented to fit the expectations of the particular auditing body—immigration authorities, prospective employers, insurance companies."[10] Once again, the process of creating new audit selves simultaneously created tempting new processes of manipulation, including debt leverages and credit swaps whose referents and collateral were increasingly unclear. Many other groups—governmental, commercial, medical, social, familial—were implicated in such processes.

Weems reached out to James Gibbs and his collaborators Charles d'Autremont and Matthew Bannister at dbox, prior collaborators on JET LAG and ALLADEEN who agreed to be central artistic collaborators in this new project. To give data a visual presence, dbox took inspiration from a number of different sources, including Edward Tufte's data visualization work, Kurt Gödel, M. C. Escher, Johann Sebastian Bach, Douglas Hofstadter's book on human cognition, Thinkmap's Virtual Thesaurus, and bird imagery. Gibbs recalled their fascination with "this theory that if all bird calls could be translated, they would essentially just be saying 'I am here.'"

Anticipating the social reach of the bird metaphor, SUPER VISION's development process coincided with the emergence of the social networking platform Twitter. Members of The Builders Association, including Gibbs, Weems, and Angelos, were among some of Twitter's first users as it became a public platform: "like, users number six and seven."[11] Members of the company gradually realized that every time they relayed a "tweet," browsed the Internet, or purchased something with a credit card, they were making another point of entry into the datasphere and further asserting their presence. As these fleeting and apparently unrelated pieces of information accumulated, a portrait or "data body" of the user began to form for the group. The challenge for dbox was to put these abstract data organisms onto the theater stage.

With the concept of the "data body" animating their conversations, The Builders and dbox began to imagine how to represent a "data body" onstage. Furthermore, what could the stage offer to a data-body discourse that was both fascinated and horrified by an immaterial figure that seemed to have many material implications? In the previous decade, new media artist Julia Scher threw down the gauntlet to position the arts as a domain of both data exploration and data activism: "In our everyday lives—when controllers and machines intentionally archive, file away, and ultimately define our experience, where surveillance registers all and selects accordingly, thereby reconstructing a body in private, out of view, furthering a strategy of domination—we live in a reality where resignation is the greatest weapon for any control system, any mechanism of suppression."[12] N. Katherine Hayles's groundbreaking exploration of the posthuman, first published in 1999, cautions against an unqualified digital embrace but argues that dystopic horror was itself based on possessive conceptions of self that needed to be questioned. Hayles notes that in many dystopic narratives, "As long as the human subject is envisioned as an autonomous self with unambiguous boundaries, the human-computer interface can only be parsed as a division between the solidity of real life on one side and the illusion of virtual reality on the other, thus obscuring the far-reaching changes initiated

by the development of virtual technologies. Only if one thinks of the subject as an autonomous will independent of the environment is one likely to experience the panic performed by Norbert Wiener's Cybernetics and Bernard Wolfe's Limbo."[13]

Michel Foucault's study of panoptic surveillance had shown how much the perception of one's autonomous individuality actually propelled rather than resisted wider networks of surveillance.[14] Furthermore, Jacques Derrida had already posited that the idea of a "solid real," unmediated by representation, was in fact an epiphenomenon of representation itself.[15] The perception of an unmediated real was an effect of mediation. Instead of the solid and virtual or presence and absence oppositions that structured traditional metaphysical thinking, Hayles offered a different analytic framework that emphasized the dialectical relationship between pattern and randomness. "*Pattern tends to overwhelm presence*," she wrote in italics, "*leading to a construction of immateriality that depends not on spirituality or even consciousness but only on information*."[16] If a conceptual organizing shift then from "presence and absence to pattern and randomness" organized contemporary cultural production, quite crucially that sense of "pattern" was interdependent and "interpenetrated with randomness and its implicit challenge to physicality."[17] In Hayles's complex world, oppositions between the material and the virtual selves could no longer hold. Moreover, the rise of new technologies could provide a vehicle for exposing the interdependence of selves and the fiction of autonomous will. In Hayles's words, "When the human is seen as part of a distributed system, the full expression of human capability can be seen precisely to *depend* on the splice rather than being imperiled by it."[18] As a media theater company that critiqued new technologies while simultaneously exploring our saturation with them, The Builders Association used the metaphor of the interdependent data body to structure SUPER VISION's aesthetic, even as it also tested the capacity of actors, designers, and audience members to take responsibility for the splice.

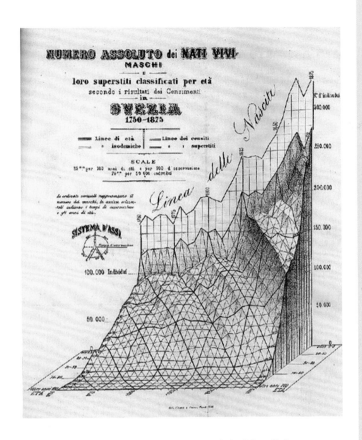

Italian statistician Luigi Perozzo's model of Swedish census data, 1880.

OPERATING SYSTEMS

When The Builders Association developed JET LAG with what was then the two-person team Diller + Scofidio, the architectural group dbox had actualized all of Elizabeth Diller and Ricardo Scofidio's designs. dbox attracted people who were trained in architecture but for whom the building of a physical building was less interesting than the act of imagining virtual spaces. As a testing ground for every new spatial software, dbox ran a for-profit business that was at the forefront of digital rendering in the field of commercial real estate. But dbox also had nonprofit, aesthetically oriented pursuits as well. After forming relationships with James Gibbs and Matthew Bannister, Charles d'Autremont and other dbox affiliates, they set to work on imagining data's relation to bodies, space, and spectatorship. Just as their previous shows had placed a backgrounded operating system into the theatrical foreground, this new collaboration

Performer Rizwan Mirza in a concept image created by dbox.

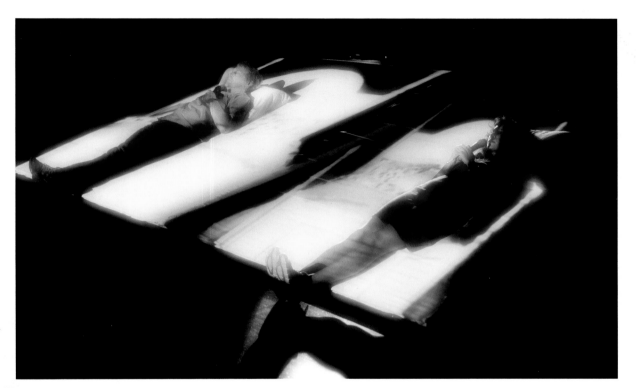

repositioned Gibbs from the domain of sophisticated visual and technical design to a central position as an artistic collaborator.

From there, The Builders Association worked to secure other partners who could assist in conceiving the operating systems of a data-based performance project. Keyhole, Inc., founded in 2001, was a pioneering software development company that specialized in geospatial data visualization applications before it was acquired by Google in 2004 (and became what is known as Google Maps today). The Builders proposed that Keyhole be used (and advertised) as a critical tool in the new production. Keyhole executives initially expressed interest but ultimately declined.

Weems pitched their idea to Siemens, which recently had announced a philanthropic interest in public art programs that educated citizens about science and technology. Weems's technical aspirations for this production were significant: "What I wanted to do in SUPER VISION—and what I kept saying to anybody who would listen to me—was that I wanted to enmesh the performers in the media."[19] But SUPER VISION needed expensive technology. Indeed, speculation about the expense of the show later structured viewer responses to it.[20] With an optimistic budget of $600,000, funding weighed constantly on Weems's mind, even in interviews for the *New York Times*, where she admitted, "'It's hard to make the finances work, and I don't plan on becoming any less ambitious.' Part of the problem, Weems said, is that corporations aren't particularly enthusiastic about supporting art critical of technology and globalization. 'In our shows, we try not to lecture,' she said, 'but what you see are people isolated, melancholy, in various states of fragmentation. Technology is not always creating communities that anyone would hope for. And this is a political message.'"[21]

Other collaborators did bite, however, including Tony Award–winning set designer Stewart Laing, who became a key part of the production team. Weems had met Laing ten years earlier at a Wooster Group rehearsal, and he had closely followed The Builders' work, even securing British Arts Council funds to observe the final rehearsals of ALLADEEN. For SUPER VISION, he initially imagined that the actors would play on a huge scroll that overtook the stage, referencing the older media of inscription that first recorded human data. How actors would interact with this scroll was another question.

dbox orchestrated an all-night charrette at which collaborators pictured the data body and generated gorgeous visual ideas—from an outlined figure whose shadow silhouette was filled with data text to a lone figure that was overwhelmed by a grid environment of personalized data screens. To provide these data bodies with an organic, living presence, animation sequences were rendered in 3ds Max, a software application that was used to create motion graphics and three-dimensional models. Sequences also were programmed to give the visualized data points accurate physical behaviors so that words and images would move in a recognizably lifelike way, even congregating together like a flock of birds.

A residency at Krannert Center for the Arts at the University of Illinois at Urbana-Champaign also provided The Builders with access to the motion-capture laboratory in the university's computer science department. Actors, including long-time Builders Moe Angelos, Joe Silovsky, and Tanya Selvaratnam, were outfitted with motion-tracking sensors and instructed to experiment. Another important contribution to SUPER VISION's data-body operating system came from the Wexner Center for the Arts, which provided the company with funds, space, and time to organize an in-depth residency at The Ohio State University's Advanced Computing Center for the Arts and Design (ACCAD) and its motion-capture laboratory. Builders' designers worked with and recorded students and actors with motion-capture (mo-cap) nodes affixed to their joints and limbs as they moved about the space performing pedestrian tasks. These partial mo-cap bodies became one of the bases for "picturing the data body" as the production process continued. The mo-cap nodes were representations formed by electronic codes but also carried an unmistakable sentience. The Builders Association's goal was to refuse either utopic or dystopic imaginings that polarized the digital from the real, and the mo-cap assemblages offered a visual metaphor for a data-driven human that carried all of the force and weight of the bodily association as well.

Looking back on this image motif, it is intriguing to realize that the assembly, dis-assembly, and re-assembly of nodes matched Hayles's discussion of the force of "pattern" and "randomness" in a world that avows technological interdependence. In such a symbolic world, "floating signifiers give way to flickering signifiers. Foregrounding pattern and randomness, information technologies operate within a realm in which the signifier is opened to a rich internal play of difference. In informatics, the signifier can no longer be understood as a single marker—for example, an ink mark on a page. Rather, it exists as a flexible chain of markers bound together by the arbitrary relations specified by the relevant codes."[22] So too, the characters in SUPER VISION were not represented by the apparently autonomous marker of a single performing body. Data figures were positioned within a flexible chain of systems, screens, and codes. Moving nodes formed a human representation and then suddenly

SUPER VISION rehearsal with motion capture.

dispersed like a flock of birds. Gibbs recalled that the metaphor of flocking provided a central dramaturgical and technological structure: "We mainly had the idea of cell phone conversation being phatic: 'I'm here.... Where are you?' 'I'll be home later,' etc. That led to the 'I'm here' idea as the content of the bird calls."[23] Builders were fascinated by the concept of "the dread"—the moment of silence just before the flock moves in unison. They tried to create design systems that mimicked flocking as a collectivized network of communication. Meanwhile, other human shapes formed within gridlike patterns that could suddenly fall like a stack of blocks. Importantly, these "virtual" processes of human assembly and human disassembly heightened the affective power of their "real," if posthuman, effects.

STORYBOARD

Like the scripting processes for JET LAG and ALLADEEN, SUPER VISION's storyboard process developed from improvisations of new material rather than from adaptations of historical texts. By this point in the history of The Builders Association, Weems answered interviews about her Wooster Group roots by differentiating her commitment to story: "the main difference is the concept. These pieces are accessible. The stories are there. It's not really that deconstructed."[24] Having uncovered examples of otherwise upstanding citizens who manipulated identity and credit data in elaborate Ponzi schemes (pre–Bernard Madoff), the first scenario focused on an upper-middle-class family where the husband and father (and presumed breadwinner) managed a portfolio of financial transactions that were based on his nine-year-old son's identity and Social Security number. He was thus a product of the contorted history of reporting and manipulation that descended from the Tappan brothers' early invention of the credit industry.

Weems hired screenwriters Jed Weintrob and Andrew Osborne to take a first pass at some of The Builders' scenarios, and drafting a letter of agreement was complicated given Weems's desire to treat text not as an authoritative origin but as one form of contributed material. According to the letter of agreement, "All parties understand that the text will be edited, revised, and amended during the rehearsal process and will be incorporated during rehearsal." When these writers returned their versions of the script, however, Weems found them to be "too explicit" and to be "overtelling": "We already knew what stories would be necessary inside the assembly, so deviation or expansion of those stories wasn't necessary and in fact unbalanced the whole assembly."[25] Weems continued to search for someone who knew "how to write to order."

Constance DeJong came from the conceptual art world, had been a writer for Tony Oursler, and had written the libretto for Philip Glass's opera *Satyagraha* (1979). After hiring DeJong, Weems and Gibbs went back to the improvisational drawing board, bringing in Builders actors Moe Angelos, Kyle deCamp, Rizwan Mirza, David Pence, and Tanya Selvaratnam to improvise while DeJong listened and composed scripts from the actors' exchanges. During improvisation rehearsals, Kyle deCamp and

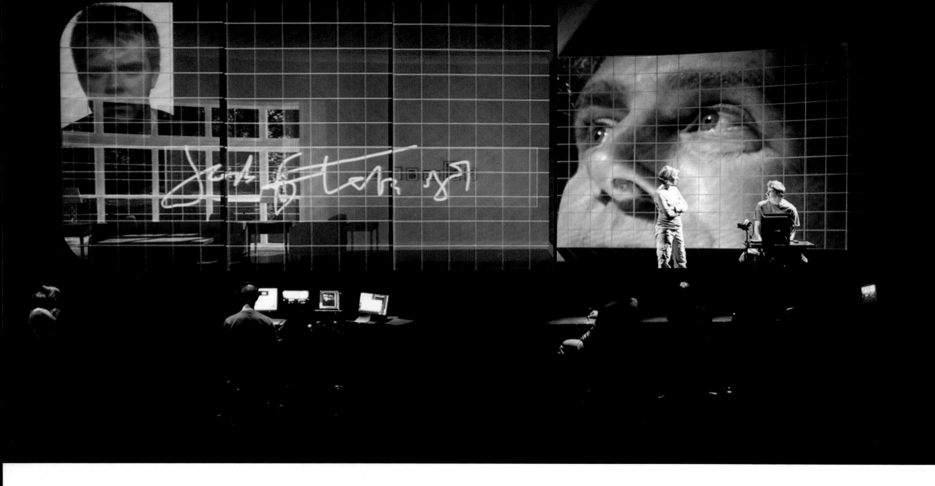

Wife (Kyle deCamp) interrogates Husband (David Pence).

Grandmother (Moe Angelos) Skypes with Granddaughter
(Tanya Selvaratnam).

David Pence improvised the Fletcher couple, whose husband has a massive secret that was both his obsession and a source of anxiety. "I never see you on Saturdays anymore," deCamp as Carol began: "it seems like this is taking so much time. What is going on?" "Listen," Pence as John responded: "it would take me twenty minutes to explain this to you, and I don't have that time." Improvisations went on, with moments of inspiration and moments of aimlessness. Weems suggested returning "to these Claritas categories" for inspiration, looking for "things that you don't realize you want."[26] In giving Carol a motivation, they needed socially identified interests that did not feel socially identifying to the upper-middle-class wife who held them, at least not until a Claritas marketer pointed out that reading *Architectural Digest* or listening to National Public Radio marked her inside a particular social category. After seeing how often deCamp's Carol had the desire to take her son, John Jr., to the park, they decided to give Carol and Johnny a mother-and-son bird-watching project with the Audubon Society, a hobby whose gazing and tracking also resonated with both the flocking metaphor and the theme of surveillance.

The group created more dialogue around the other two scenarios. Tanya Selvaratnam was cast as Jen, a young member of the digerati who lives in New York and engages in regular video chats with her aging grandmother played by Moe Angelos in Sri Lanka. Selvaratnam's Jen wants to create a digital archive of her grandmother's life but also is pulled by the technological and social distractions around her, answering telephones or texting in the middle of a conversation with her confused grandmother. "Darling, when are you coming?" the Grandmother asked. "I'm in New York, Grandma. Don't you remember?" At other times, the Grandmother began without warning to tell a story from her early adulthood. "You've never told me that story before," said Tanya's Jen, her archival interests piqued: "Grandma, I've been typing up some of your stories. Do you remember the stories you told me?" The Grandmother, however, ultimately was unable to stay focused as the granddaughter tried to remind her of her memories. As a reviewer later noted of this poignant scenario, "For all the world, [technological communication] looks like a great way to keep in touch with the oldies, but when it comes to real time, real contact, and real involvement, well, life is just too busy for Jen."[27] The exchange explored the degree to which identity remains intact when the self does not remember her own data: "There is no remote control for Alzheimer's."[28]

Issues became more politicized when conceiving the third and final scenario of the Traveler, a Ugandan businessman of Indian descent who traveled the world as part of his occupation. In what ultimately became four scenes, the Traveler was stopped by security agents at four passport control offices. Rizwan Siddiqi Mirza, who also had been in the cast of ALLADEEN, returned to play the Traveler, and Joe Silovsky played all four passport agents and also worked as The Builders Association's technical director. In each scene, the stakes of the exchange between Traveler and Agent became more heated and surreal. After the bombings of the World Trade Center on September 11, 2001, travel security systems were very much on the minds of a global population that weighed the tradeoffs of increased safety measures against curtailed civil liberties.

Most often the Traveler scenario exemplified what Daniel Solove defined as the Kafka-esque dangers of increased security—that "bureaucratic" world where "decisions" are made "without adequate accountability" and inside "dangerous pockets of unfettered discretion." "You started to use a Visa card," noted the agent who looked up the Traveler's buying patterns on his computer: "And stopped using your MasterCard? Why?" When the Traveler told the Agent that his company was responsible for his expenses, the agent asked, "But what about your personal accounts?" "That's personal!," the Traveler shouted indignantly. The explicitly racist undercurrent of traveler security was also thematized in another scene entitled "POI (Person of Interest)":

Agent: India, Morocco, Sudan, Algiers, Jordan, Turkey, Turkey.... Where's your visa for Turkey?

Traveler: Oh, that's in my other passport, my Indian passport.

Agent (starts typing quickly): So you have dual citizenship. And the visa for Turkey, that's in your other passport. Your Indian passport. Why's that?

Traveler: I use that one for vacations.

Agent: Vacations?! What's there to see in Turkey?

Traveler: Oh, it's a lovely a country; it's full of history, beautiful mosques....
(Agent looks up and then types even faster).

Agent: Mosques?

Traveler: History.

The Builders Association cast endeavored to keep the scenarios credible, even as they mixed engaging banter with what many reviewers called the "eeriness" of unexpected surveillance. Audience members' responses to the Traveler's scenes no doubt varied with their own perspectives on the politics of security. One reviewer felt that the passport officials "too often are made to look like fools, when in fact they are a crucial line of defense these days,"[29] and another felt that these scenarios were apt and scary testaments of what the world had become. The company's experience with Mirza was that he was stopped so often at national borders when they were touring ALLADEEN that the company had to build extra time into the touring itinerary. But Mirza also hoped that this portrayal resisted any impulse to position the Agent as unambiguous oppressor and the Traveler as unambiguous victim: "I wanted the character to be sympathetic but to seem a little bit shady, a little bit dodgy, at times. So the audience would say, 'Well, wait a second. I am looking at these things that seem to be mapping out a particular pattern of strange activity.' Then to bring them back to 'Oh, no, no, he's fine.' ... They have points of references from past two years—with what is happening not just in America but all over the world. We are not far from what we portray in this show."[30]

Eventually, The Builders assembled a selection of scenes for each scenario and began to think about an overall structure. After much experimentation, Weems wrote in her notes of October 24, 2004, that she wanted to "go with a *La Ronde* structure." Given that the intermedia operating systems were still to be integrated with the textual material, this choice seemed best to Constance DeJong as well: "You kind of left one story and reentered another, as opposed to having the two stories bang up against each other, which we tried. We tried a different kind of flow. What I feel about the structure now is that flow is achieved through this synchronicity of sound and image—speech drops aside, another scene comes on. That there is a continuous flow to the piece."[31] DeJong also provided other textual motifs that linked scenes together with the emerging design of the show, including a small monologue for Kyle deCamp on "the dread," the special moment before a flock of birds takes off in unison. The monologue thus contributed to a steadily accumulating array of bird motifs, including Carol Fletcher's hobby and her anxiety about her husband's secrets, a literal flock of birds, and the cluster of mo-cap nodes that dbox created to look like a mo-cap flock. These gatherings and dispersals throughout the show indexed the possibilities and perils of the posthuman data body.

The Traveler's exchanges morphed into several scenes, and the exchanges about the Fletcher family and the Grandmother's archive developed into a network of scenes and monologues that were part of a continuous flow. Most disturbingly, John Fletcher Sr.'s data schemes revolved around the use of John Fletcher Jr.'s name as a repository for fraudulent credit. "Come on, sweetie," he would say to the digital embodiment of his son, calling to a mo-cap rendering of a child: "People always told me: fate is something you just can't control. Well, I never bought that. Fate can be redesigned." In many ways, both the Fletcher scenario and the digerati granddaughter's story centered on figures who place their hopes for the future in the datasphere, whether to speculate financially in elaborate investment schemes or to retain memories of a human life.

That comfort, however, is easily undermined if such digital faith does not have an equally complex sense of its enmeshment with other kinds of material processes. As SUPER VISION's storyboard unfolded, John Fletcher Sr. found himself under threat of creditors. By the end of the story line, he borrowed the maximum amount on a number of financial lines by buying useless items for the family's home. Knowing that financial ruin was imminent, he tried to make a radical escape. Meanwhile, Jen's preoccupation with her Grandmother's archive could not overcome other kinds of distance or substitute for a different kind of care. "Did you take your pills today, Grandma?" she asked, realizing that she would not receive a clear answer: "Is there someone there who can give you a glass of water?" In fact, the plaintive exchanges between Jen and Grandmother thematized the paradoxes of digital data and the precarities of digital connection. Those themes ultimately drove the preoccupations of The Builders Association's next show, CONTINUOUS CITY.

REHEARSAL/ASSEMBLY

I would say that we—Matthew Bannister, Charles D'Autremont, and I—were all interested in narrative, which is a kind of a funny thing to be interested in if you are studying architecture.[32]

James Gibbs

After a year of research and experimentation dbox's operating systems combined with those of video designer Peter Flaherty to create a collection of design concepts that were ready to be integrated with actors and text. Dan Dobson's soundscapes were, as always, an integral part of the realization of this material. Many in the cast were confused by the metaphor of birds until Dobson added his soundtrack of electronic "chirps" and "tweets" to dbox images.

In addition to giving life to data bodies, Gibbs and dbox were also responsible for creating virtual sets for SUPER VISION which were housed inside the physical set designed by Stewart Laing. For one of the three story lines, a lifelike suburban home with a digital child was rendered using 3ds Max. The photorealistic lighting effects were accomplished using the Brazil rendering plug-in for 3ds Max, which used advanced ray-tracing capabilities to accurately portray how light propagates in a space.

Such effects were resource intensive, and a render farm had to be set up at SUPER VISION's premiere venue, St. Ann's Warehouse in Brooklyn, New York. This render farm, Gibbs explained, consisted of a dressing room at St. Ann's that was filled with "five or six dbox employees"[33] and

SUPERVISION rehearsal photo: Rizwan Mirza, 2004.

computers that could deliver the completed video sequences. These elaborate measures were necessary to accommodate any changes or edits that arose throughout the rehearsal process. As Gibbs recalled, updates to the sequences were required throughout the development and rehearsal process, and video clips had to be re-rendered to suit the architecture of each theater.

A key part of Laing's set was the "compressed" space between the large front and rear projection screens. It consisted of a small alleyway that the actors occupied for most of the show. The front screens were created from Textaline, a relatively new material at the time that allowed video to be projected while obscuring the actors. The same apparatus allowed the screen to be made transparent by lighting the actors behind it, thereby creating a changeable surface on which information appeared and disappeared around the bodies of the actors.

Technical director Joe Silovsky, set designer Stewart Laing, and production manager Neal Wilkinson ran the five projection screens of SUPER VISION along three separate

268

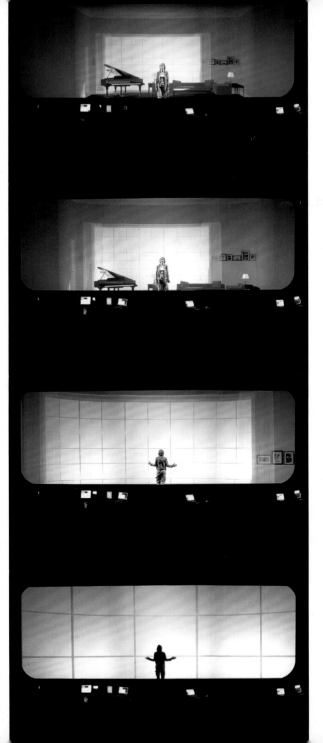

Three-dimensional rendering by dbox of the family living room.
The perspective shifts during the course of the scene. Performer
Kyle deCamp.

tracks. Each screen was roughly eleven feet wide and six feet high. To accomplish the intended transitional effects between scenes, an independent controller had to operate each screen. In this scenario screens were moved via a custom-made multidirection controller developed by Joe Silovsky. The controls had triggers and limit switches but ultimately depended on backstage technical associate Jamie McElhinney who watched the show on a monitor and controlled the screens via this custom-made system (which McElhinney and the crew named the "Jabberwocky 3000".)

To test the AutoCAD-generated sets, actors rehearsed with Peter Flaherty's video designs while dbox's digital videoscapes were gradually incorporated. Fletcher family scenes were set in the architectural interior of a designer kitchen; its double-sash windows and beveled cabinets slid into position to surround the husband and wife who stood inside it. Through those windows could be seen a digitized exterior of manicured lawns and trimmed bushes. When the whoosh and jolt sounds of simulated building ended, the chirpings of birds could be heard "outside." deCamp and Pence focused on calibrating their movements in relation to the digital space so that they could create the effect of naturally triggered interaction. deCamp, for instance, practiced moving dishes into the sink and turning on the water, supported by Dan Dobson's sound cue of water running from a spout. Rehearsal thus developed technical and intuitive connections between actors and designers. Because The Builders were working with technology that mixed video and sound live, actors were not struggling to time their dialogue and gestures to a steadily running score. Nor were designers and operators waiting backstage for signals from a stage manager. Rather, all agents of the performance participated in its unfolding through simultaneous collaboration in a shared systemic field. As Dobson described it, "They are cuing off us. We are cuing off them. Everybody is doing their thing, and it's never just press Play and walk away."[34]

Cueing happened reciprocally—the way that birds flock—but that system of exchange was also the means by which new concepts and performance techniques were generated. For Gibbs, who came from the field of architecture, this process required a new learning curve. As Gibbs recalled in an interview with Nick Kaye, "Time is not necessarily unusual for dbox because we do time-based work, animation, and movies. But working live—and working with a time that therefore has to be flexible—was fascinating for us."[35] For instance, when David Pence entered his den as John Fletcher Sr., transforming into a father who was obsessed with his master plan, the three dbox designers listened to the intensity of his voice and the degree to which it seemed to overwhelm the tones of spousal banter in the previous scene with his wife, Carol. At that moment, they created the idea that they came to call "the crush"—a moment "where his den expands and starts to destroy or crush part of the living room set." Responding to "David Pence's performance as the father—as the volume got turned up on that, the set could respond to it. So finally we have this moment where a virtual space overwhelms a physical space, but the idea emerged from the process."[36] In the process of creating intermedia performance, there was no clarity (and no perceived need for clarity) about what came first—actor, design, script, sound, or stage set. By having all of these dimensions interact during daily tech rehearsals, ideas from one domain triggered ideas in another.

While designers found themselves altering their vision in response to performers, performers also developed a collaborative sense of what it meant to be acting with a designer as a scene partner. David Pence described his intimate rapport with sound designer Dan Dobson as the two of them worked together to represent the mania of John Fletcher Sr.: "I feel Dan Dobson right here, almost at my lips. He's right inside the tip of that microphone. That's partly a manifestation of the technology, but it's also specific to the way Dan works. He isn't merely an operator up there in the dark behind the audience. He really feels like a performer to me, and there is continual give and take between us.... He is playing me, and I am reacting to him."[37]

In the Traveler's scenes with the Agent, other technical challenges required collaboration among actors and designers. Each time that the Traveler encountered the Agent, illuminated screens of his intimate data—credit card statements, travel itineraries, bank accounts—appeared above him as the agent's interrogation proceeded. Each successive encounter revealed a new data body, which was graphically represented by different garishly colored veins originating from the actor and spreading across the stage. His financial, medical, and familial information accrued in a final scene where he was

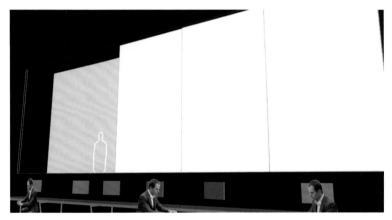

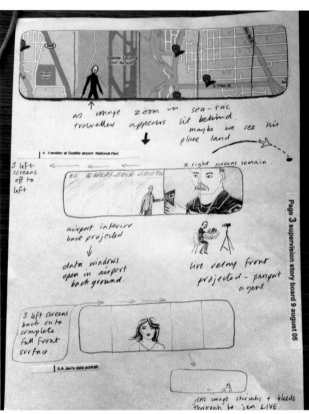

Clockwise: Set designer Stewart Laing; Stewart Laing storyboard;
design render by dbox, inc.

Sound designer Dan Dobson in rehearsal, 2010.

trailed by a stage-wide tweeting, twittering cloud of data. When the Agent encountered questionable patterns or asked a pointed question, warning lights flashed as new data appeared at another point on the screen. The technical effect of picturing the Traveler's "suspicious" data body meant that the actors playing the Traveler (Rizwan Mirza) and the Agent (Joe Silovsky) were not in standard proximity to each other. Rather, they were each positioned in direct address to the audience while surrounded by the data screens. "None of the performers ever really look at each other. Joe Silovsky and Rizwan Mirza are a perfect example of that in this show," said Weems. "What is being staged is the network."[38] This technique began in MASTER BUILDER when none of the actors inhabited a shared room. In this case, the alienated acting technique provided a form by which to advance the menace and alienation of the surveillance theme. As the Traveler, Mirza described how he found emotional inspiration in a structure that simultaneously produced desired technical effects: "I am not even looking directly at his projection because I'm standing behind the Textaline screen, so it's faded. So I am looking at a general idea of his face.... It helped me in this particular situation because the Traveler is confronting someone who doesn't really see him for who he is.... So that disconnect has helped."[39]

While the feeling of "disconnect" advanced the emotional stakes of the Traveler's theme, in other portions of the play, the challenge was to "connect" with different representations of data bodies. One of the most uncanny—and for some reviewers "creepy"—elements of the show involved the representation of John Fletcher Jr., the young boy who was appropriated by his father for credit manipulation. For Weems, the technical pursuit of SUPER VISION was "to enmesh the performers in the media," and this boy ended up being the most enmeshed of all. The first steps of the motion-capture process produced a tantalizingly sentient pattern of luminous nodes, a data body representation that haunted the entire production. The final steps of the mo-cap process, however, produced a fully rendered if completely flat depiction of a young boy who was playing and cavorting in space. dbox then interwove this mo-cap boy into the AutoCAD kitchen environment. He went through doors, ran outside, and talked to his mother. The nodes were compelling because they were partial indexes that seemed lifelike, but the uncanniness of the fully rendered mo-cap boy lay in the fact that his liveness turned out to be partial. Once again, the technical efficacy of the mo-cap body simultaneously depended on actor interaction to bring it into being. In this case, the boy's capacity to seem lifelike depended on Kyle deCamp's ability to act like a mother who felt that he was alive. "So somewhat ironically for me, it's the warmth of my performance that effectively animates him, although he appears to be an 'animation' onscreen," described deCamp: "I animate our interactions through my moment-to-moment responses, and play it differently every night. I quickly discovered where I could inflect emotion, rhythmic pauses, overlaps, and play around with the movements between his projection, the moving projection screen, and myself."[40] The boy thus becomes a fully posthuman being through a relational process that required the mediation of technology and the mediation of acting. The result was also a change in the felt capacities of the medium and the new sense of

Father (Harry Sinclair) delivers a monologue as the screen moves with his live image from stage left to stage right.

possibility that he presented. One reviewer noted that the child's data body had capacities that human bodies did not: "this phantom child is the only one who can touch his house, since most of the domestic idyll is on video, too."[41] And Kyle deCamp developed new ways to think about what it meant to act as and with a cyborg: "What a remarkably consistent little performer he is!"[42]

In debates about the relation between performance and new technology, critics and artists worry about effects on the presumably authentic or autonomous domains of the body or identity. Acting within a large network of screens and soundscapes certainly calls for different modulations by the actor. For David Pence, the combined experience is dialectical and has a different kind of safety: "I am aware of myself as a physical human being in the way any actor in a show feels himself on the stage: light on my skin, a lot of people out there, another actor to look at or talk to—maybe. Those are really the tactile realities that are just about being alive onstage. But also, I feel that I am inside that technology and being delivered through that technology. And this is a sensation I don't want to lose, because I treasure it. I feel—and again I sort of personalize it—I feel safe, as if Marianne is presenting me. It's like I'm part of a beautiful machine."[43] Although Pence's statement might sound utopic to some, it dovetails with Hayles's sense of the possibilities of informational technology for a postliberal conception of being human. For her, "the human is seen as part of a distributed system, the full expression of human capability can be seen precisely to depend on the splice rather than being imperiled by it,"[44] but Pence seemed aware of his expressive dependence. He did not feel that his autonomy as an actor was corrupted by technology but felt himself to be enabled by it. The network was an invasion of the actor's personal life, but it also was personalized by him. Data relations bring new questions about the nature of the human (and the nature of theatrical performance), and one kind of answer lies in the recognition that there can be agency in being part of a system, a network, or a pattern.

CLOSINGS

As each SUPER VISION story came to a close, audiences witnessed central characters altering their relation to the datasphere. John Fletcher Sr. tried to escape his impending audit by retreating to a remote arctic part of the world, only to find that the imaged background of his new environs was built on the same digital grid of his living room. His efforts to go "off grid" were thus countered by a visual background that put him back on it. The Grandmother and granddaughter's long-distance relationship was imperiled by memory loss and by an overreliance on technology for its suturing. In the end, technological and personal disintegration was symbolized by the diffusion of the Grandmother's image into a random fuzz of pixels. The dialectical tension between pattern and randomness structured the drama of these data bodies, a tension that was furthered in the Traveler's story. As the Agent inquired into the Traveler's health, travel, and finances and his queries became more and more pointed, the Traveler allowed himself to be enveloped in his data. In an ambiguous final image that some interpreted as "acceptance" and others as "eerie," he walked across the stage with his data falling and dispersing from his body.

As with other Builders shows, reactions to SUPER VISION mixed discomfort and fascination. A technological storyboard that focused on the borders of the human resulted in a combination of pleasure and distress that provoked the use of the word *creepy* in many reviews. For Weems, the enmeshment of performers in the medium provided a form to match the enmeshment of humans in the datasphere, an experiment that was bound to produce a range of emotions and effects. For some reviewers, SUPER VISION achieved a "certain delicacy in that intersection of glee and creepiness."[45] That sense of mixture—along with ambiguity about its perceptual and critical effects—prompted other reviewers to describe it as "a magnetic visual pull of a gigantic slow-motion video game. It's a woozy, faintly disquieting seduction, but a game-like sense of artifice lingers."[46]

But however much words such as *woozy*, *disquieting*, *slick*, or *creepy* may aptly describe a posthuman relation to the datasphere, not everyone appreciated the presence of such affects in the space of a theater. Weems's direction for the actors to "do less" as performers within a strong media environment meant that they risked backgrounding their skills in the eyes of reviewers who thought that they did not deliver "knock-out performances."[47] Others lamented the "emptiness"[48] of the characters or the sense that there was "no forward-moving dramatic progression, no real deepening of theme or development of narrative."[49] However, others noted the cool aesthetic of the piece and seemed to link it back to its conceptual goals. The characters were "less people than an assemblage of facts, making the performance as chilly as an arctic wind—which I suppose, is the point."[50] A critic writing about the performance at the Brooklyn Academy of Music felt that such a chill was the point, saying that the actors "give intentionally awkward performances, their coldness enhancing the liveliness of the design."[51]

In many ways, the differing responses to this conjunction of performance and technology reflect back on earlier questions about the relation between theatrical and visual aesthetics. The integration of theatricality's time and visuality's space—the juxtaposition of motion and stasis in a partially animated Matta-Clark house in MASTER BUILDER or in JET LAG's motion-filled environments that never went anywhere—has been a constant theme in Builders work. It also means that different viewers enter with different notions of what constitutes emptiness, fullness, stasis, and forward-moving. Occupying this ambiguous zone is part of what it meant for The Builders Association to be exploring the "frictions" of performance and new media, and SUPER VISION tried to show that such frictions might be most insidious when least dramatic. For yet another reviewer, such a proposition deviated from some of the high jinks found in other technologically informed aesthetic styles: "The pace of the screen information is always steady. Private details scroll lazily by, emphasizing that there's no escape from the computer's constant watch. By maintaining this easy pace, Weems thwarts the common practice of presenting techno-menace as an endless array of jump-cuts and jarring sounds. Her control of environment and volume gives us time to consider the characters' inexorable loss of self."[52]

Because one of the occupational hazards of SUPER VISION was its descent into a literal diatribe against the dystopic perils of a data environment, a final reviewer welcomed the constraint of abstraction and used a visual art to praise its effects:

It sounds like a *1984*-style documentary about how governments and corporations misuse the mountains of personal data they collective from private citizens. In the theater, though, *Super Vision* blossoms into something completely different, a computer-enhanced visual poem about the pitfalls and promise of life in the information age.... instead of preaching a strident sermon about how "dataveillance" threatens the right to privacy, they've transformed our fears into a fast-flowing stream of nonliteral images that stick in your mind like the swirling colors of an abstract painting.[53]

If "abstract painting" referenced the modernist sense of "flatness" that accompanied its groundbreaking compositions, the flattening of the theatrical space in SUPER VISION might have been necessary to represent the data body and encourage its sustained contemplation.

ENDNOTES

Artist's Voice: James Gibbs, co-creator, dramaturg

One of the signatures of The Builders' work is that no one element stands in isolation. The physical set is also a container or receiver of video and computer design, the tech and the actors' performances are integrated, and the words that the performers say are written in concert with the stage picture they inhabit. A student looking at the work recently described it this way: "the design is an absolutely necessary component of the show; without it, the words alone don't make sense." To create this type of work requires moving each part of the piece forward together, and this can make for a complicated process as we discover what functions together. Sometimes we wander down a dead end. Sometimes we find that two elements are becoming redundant to each other. And sometimes things click, and all the elements pull together. When this happens, we've found a moment in the show. The shows are made by finding these moments and then scoring them into a whole.

In SUPER VISION, we had the dead ends and the clicks—in abundance. In our first comprehensive workshop at the Wexner, we spent a few days in the motion-capture studio recording the performers' movements as they went about key daily activities. The idea was that points of data in a chart could be reconfigured to form human figures paired with performers onstage. We would create constellations of data and link them to the live bodies with projection. We had some other ideas about representing the data body, but this seemed most promising. A day later, we gathered in the theater with some ideas about text, a few projectors, and our brave performers. We projected on the floor. Tanya and Jeff imagined themselves as a couple in bed, discussing one of the day's digital transactions—perhaps it was a problem with the online banking? Stewart wanted to see a steeply raked stage, so some rickety plastic tables were found and canted precariously on one set of legs, and projectors were focused on these. Tanya and Jeff sat upstage for a moment and were persuaded to lie on the tables talking while the little stars of our mo-cap data danced on their bodies. Each movement threatened to topple them to the stage.

At coffee, my collaborator Matthew Bannister and I cornered Marianne to tell her we had concerns about the development. "Are you kidding?" she said, "Don't worry, we're just getting started. It's always like this." We soldiered on.

Over time, the image of data as a motion-captured constellation eventually found its moment in the show, but it became clear that it held for just a single strong moment and would not be the central visual metaphor for the data body. The body, we realized, had to remain the performer's real body, and our job was to surround that real body with the data that it generated. The image was of a physical person who was nearly obscured by their information—enclouded with it. The set became a way to make this happen. In group meetings that included Stewart, Peter, and most of the rest of the company, we worked out the set as a narrow corridor that would surround the players with projection surfaces both front and back. Concerned about locking the performers behind a projection surface for the whole show, we decided that the front screen would be made of moveable panels, which Joe found a way to automate and motorize in our longer workshop at St. Ann's Warehouse.

When we arrived at that workshop, Joe had his hands full. He was performing in the show, tinkering with the motorized screens, and had a small construction project to undertake. Also, with Neal Wilkinson, we hadn't given up on that raked stage but had elaborated on it a bit. Stewart became obsessed with an infinite empty grid of data space imagined as a kind of infinite photographers cyclorama—a space of disorientation. We followed and jumped forward with this idea as a group, picturing this as the escape at the end of the show. The Father character, snapping the tether of his data trail, would arrive in this nowhere space. This was mocked up as a model. Over long conversations, we established this consensus: we would run the entire show in our narrow projection hall, letting the data become more and more claustrophobic, focusing the house on this narrow plane. In a huge finale, wildly unexpected for the Builders, we would ditch our digital projections, dropping the screens and revealing this deep stage space, blown out with the bright lights of every rentable instrument in town, curving away unmeasurably, and inhabited, at the end, by our sole human figure, setting out in the quiet.

If you've seen SUPER VISION, you may have noticed that it doesn't end this way. Neal built the thing at St. Ann's. Joe helped by soldering the screen actuators (whatever those might be) and being called to the stage to don a wig, or try another scene, or don a moustache, and try it again. This thing was made strong so that an actor could inhabit it, and it required a lot of plywood and a lot of lumber. It was a skateboard half-pipe but built to break into modules and travel on a truck for quick reassembly. And here's the thing about performance—you never know. We had many reasons why this was a good idea, and made sense, and would work, and we had many smart people agreeing about it. When we got it built, got it painted, and rented every super-bright HMI light that we could find, we ran the show, dropped the screen, and blasted those lights. David walked, mystically, heroically, out onto that thing, and there it was—a guy, after a long journey in the maelstrom of our contemporary digital world, walking around on a big white piece of plywood, squinting a little, because, well, yes, it was pretty damn bright. Looking out at the house, trying to see past those lights for a moment, David:

"Uh ... hey guys?"
Silence. Then a click, and Marianne, on mic, very slowly:
"Kill. Me. Now."

So that was a No.

This idea had followed us through development as a kind of vestigial organ, and the thing was, we didn't need it anymore, but we didn't know that. Until we saw it. By the time we saw it, the stories were inhabiting the stage set—the projection corridor—with fullness, completely. It was done. That strip of performing space—sandwiched with front- and rear-projected data and virtual space—was a world in itself, a magic box. In the end, the pleasure of the show was finding all the variations on using that box and playing it, making the music of the show on it. We didn't need to transcend it. We needed to trust it.

Guest Voice: Saskia Sassen, scholar and author of *Globalization and Its Discontents: Essays on the New Mobility of People and Money*

The auditorium was bright and bubbly with people who had just met at the huge 2010 Zero1 Biennial in San Jose, near Silicon Valley. Lightness was the overarching atmosphere.

Then it started. A wall-to-wall screen, with visual geometries that included people, pain, laughter, familiar, and unfamiliar images. The music was deep and encompassing. The atmosphere had turned deep, dark, threatening. We were now beholden to the screen. The first human voices from the stage emerged in a sudden silence; they stood out in their littleness against the imposing screen with its visual geometries. Yes, the voices came with bodies and chairs to sit on and the many little mobilities of sitting, talking, gesturing. They were definitely not robotic—they could have been your neighbor, your college classmate. It was the littleness of the voices that struck me as the key actor at that moment. I am not sure at all others saw it like this, but that is how I experienced that moment.

Yes, this is a film/performance about digitally enhanced capacities for supervision, for tracking, for never forgetting. And yet it brings the littleness of the human voice as a destabilizer of images of power. This tension between the machine and the human is classic theme. To bring new life into it and throw out the tropes of the subject is a major accomplishment. This portrayal is intelligent, witty, moving, and it touches on a bare-bone truth that insists in being present amid the overwhelming technical powers being portrayed.

People

Conceived and created by The Builders Association and dbox

Directed by Marianne Weems

Conception by Marianne Weems, James Gibbs, Matthew Bannister, Charles d'Autremont, and Dan Dobson.

Text by Constance DeJong

Additional text by company members

Set and costume design by Stewart Laing

Lighting design by Jennifer Tipton and Allen Hahn

Virtual design by dbox

Video design by Peter Flaherty

Sound design and original music composition by Dan Dobson

Production manager: Neal Wilkinson

Technical director: Joseph Silovsky

Performed by

Moe Angelos

Kyle deCamp

Rizwan Mirza

David Pence

Owen Philip on video as John Jr.

Tanya Selvaratnam

Joseph Silovsky

Harry Sinclair

Initial story development by Jed Weintrob and Andrew Osborne

Technical manager: Jamie McElhinney

Video associate: Jeff Morey, Hal Eagar (courtesy of The Gertrude Stein Repertory Theater)

Assistant director: Kate Stannard

Many thanks to the following artists for their essential contributions toward the development of SUPER VISION:

David Pence originated the part of John Sr.

Video designer: Chris Kondek

Performers: Harry Sinclair, Jeff Webster

Demographics consultants: Moe Angelos, Kevin Slavin

Research associate: Kelly Cooper

Production assistants: Alison Currie, Ernesto Klar, Gabriele Voerhinger

Choreographer: Francesca Harper

Video assistants: Anna Henckel-Donnersmarck, Cheuk Yan "Spider" Kwok

Assistant technical director: Kimon Keramidas

Video researcher and assistant: Peter Kerlin

Prologue dramaturg and research associate: Steve Luber

Stage manager: Ela Orleans

Costume design assistant: Michelle Phillips

Project documentarist: Kate Richards

Associate assistant director: Isis Saratial Misdary

Sound assistant: Josh Schmidt

SUPER VISION was created with the support, commitment, and artistry of the entire dbox team: Mark Bannister, Mark Bodal, Keith Bomely, Scott Davison, Jonathan Doyle, Mark Gleghorn, Jessica Haas, Christa Hamilton, Uken Huang, Kim Hyunsuk, David Jaubert, Gloria Kim, Lisa Kim, Kayako Kobayashi, Tang Ku, Ai Le, Marc Lin, Alex Martin, Gina Matsui, Clark Nelson, Michele Orosz, Martin Solarte, Peter Wildman, Daniel Yao, and Phillis Yeh. Thanks especially to Ivor Ip for his ongoing involvement.

Venues

2005 Walker Art Center, Minneapolis, MN

Wexner Center for the Arts, Columbus, OH

On the Boards, Seattle, WA

Brooklyn Academy of Music Next Wave Festival 05, New York, NY

Montclair State University, Montclair, NJ

2006 Perth International Arts Festival, Perth, Australia

New Zealand International Arts Festival, Wellington, New Zealand

Liverpool European Capital of Culture, Liverpool, UK

Tramway, Glasgow, UK

ZeroOne, San Jose, CA

Yerba Buena Center for the Arts, San Francisco, CA

Krannert Center, University of Champaign, Urbana, IL

Museum of Contemporary Art, Chicago, IL

University of California, Davis, CA

RedCat, Los Angeles, CA

2007 Hopkins Center, Dartmouth College, Hanover, NH

SUPER VISION company during rehearsal at St. Ann's Warehouse, 2005.

Afterparty

Multimedia Theater Glossary

By Rizwan Mirza

Multimedia—a genre of modern theater in which former Midwest residents move to New York or Los Angeles and develop work and existential angst using technology.

The **Artistic Director**—an autonomous Opinion-a-Tron who graciously allows us, the viewers, performers and executive producers to bring The Vision to life. Also see Part-Time Baby Sitter.

The **Dramaturg**—an enigmatic figure who interjects their historical knowledge of past productions/sociological observances into the conceptual and rehearsal process thereby creating fresh, innovative resentment among the road crew.

The **Performers**—an interesting mix of actors, many with no formal training, who appear on STAGE cleverly masking their self-centered, emotionally bankrupt innards to create fresh and even more innovative resentment and disgust among the road crew.

The **Performance Space**—no not a stage, well sometimes. Always make sure to call the stage the Performance Space. But do note, in multimedia theatrical pieces there need not be a stage. This should inform you of the brilliance of the work. And lack of funding.

Relationship to the Space—a complex feeling pattern of understanding/harmonizing with the oft obvious.

Upstage/Downstage—stage positions that honestly I still don't know for sure.

Stage Left/Stage Right—when you are standing on the stage, the left side is stage left, I think.

Various Technicians—a veritable "Les Mis" like crew of goateed, wool-hatted, "cleverly" captioned tee shirted, unshaven (females included) sexually deviant beer drinking souvenir-buying geniuses.

SOME SOURCE MATERIALS FOR THE PRODUCTION

Books

Attali, Jacques. *Millennium: Winners and Losers in the Coming World Order.* New York: Times Books, 1991.

Garfinkel, Simson. *Database Nation: The Death of Privacy in the Twenty-first Century.* Sebastopol, CA: O'Reilly Media, 2000.

Keefe, Patrick Radden. *Chatter: Dispatches from the Secret World of Global Eavesdropping.* New York: Random House, 2004.

Lyon, David. *Electronic Eye: The Rise of Surveillance Society.* Minneapolis: University of Minnesota Press, 1994.

Lyon, David. *The Information Society: Issues and Illusions.* Cambridge, UK: Polity Press, 1988.

Lyon, David. *Surveillance after September 11.* Cambridge, UK: Polity Press, 2003.

Lyon, David. *Surveillance as Social Sorting: Privacy, Risk, and Digital Discrimination.* New York: Routledge, 2002.

McGrath, John. *Loving Big Brother: Performance, Privacy, and the Surveillance Space.* New York: Routledge, 2004.

Monmonier, Mark. *Spying with Maps.* Chicago: University of Chicago Press, 2002.

Parenti, Christian. *The Soft Cage: Surveillance in American from Slavery to the War on Terror.* New York: Basic Books, 2003.

Poster, Mark. *The Mode of Information.* Chicago: University of Chicago Press, 1990.

Smith, Robert Ellis. *War Stories: Accounts of Persons Victimized by Invasions of Privacy.* Providence: Privacy Journal, 2001

Virilio, Paul. *Negative Horizon.* New York: Continuum, 2003.

Zawacki, Stephen. *Love, Marriage and Green Cards.* Boca Raton, FL: Universal Publishers, 2000.

Articles

Ahmed, Ayesha. "Single and Searching a Look at Muslim Matrimonial Services." *Atlanta Magazine*, December 31, 2003.

Belson, Ken. "Saved, and Enslaved by the Cell." *New York Times*, October 14, 2004.

Berger, Ivan. "He Loves Me Not, Digitally." *New York Times*, February 2, 2004.

Cash, Erica. "Europe Zips Lips: US Sells Zips." *New York Times*, August 7, 2005.

Costello, D. "Families: The Perfect Deception—Identical Twins." *Wall Street Journal*, February 12, 1999.

"Feds Accuse Milwaukee Mother, Daughter of Scamming Lenders." *Milwaukee Journal Sentinel*, April 23, 2003.

Garfinkel, Simson. "Separating Equifax from Fiction." *Wired*, September 1995.

Hays, Constance L. "What They Know about You: Walmart, An Obsessive Monitor of Customer Behavior." *New York Times*, November 14, 2004.

Jonietz, Erika. "Total Information Overload." *Technology Review*, July–August 2003.

Koerner, Brendan I. "How to Disappear." *Wired*, July 2002.

"Lifesavers: Death Is Inevitable, But Your Digital Self Can Live Forever!" *Wired*, March 2010.

"Medical Records Move On-Line." *Orange County Register*, October 25, 2003.

Melillo, Wendy. "Private Lives?" *Adweek New York*, November 8, 1999.

Mihm, Stephen. "Dumpster-Diving for Your Identity." *New York Times Magazine*, December 21, 2003.

Morgan, Joe. "Plastic-Happy Britain Has More Credit Cards Than People." *The Times* (London), November 3, 2004.

Muoz, Lisa. "Proposed California Bill Targets People Who Steal Children's Identities." Orange County Register, March 12, 2003.

"Patient Records Go on Database: Personal Medical Information on Fifty Million People Will Be Put on a New National NHS Database Whether Those Affected Give Their Consent or Not." *The Times* (London), July 21, 2003.

Penn, Stanley, "Con Artists: Nigerians in UC Earn a Reputation for Ingenious Schemes—Though Most Are Honest, Those Who Break Laws Perpetrate Many Frauds—A Student with Forty Identities." *Wall Street Journal*, June 4, 1985.

Richtel, Matt. "The Lure of Data: Is It Addictive." *New York Times*, July 6, 2003.

Schwartz, John. "A Young Hacker Buys Options: Borrowing an Investor's Identity." *New York Times*, October 10, 2003.

Sherman, Erik. "Walk-by Hacking." *New York Times Magazine*, July 13, 2003.

Surveillance and Society. Ejournal. David Lyon, ed. Surveillance Studies Network, 2001.

Thurman, James N. "Proposed Health Database Has Privacy Advocates in Uproar." *Christian Science Monitor*, July 23, 1998.

Weiser, Benjamin. "The Two Lives of Havelock Woo." *New York Times*, May 6, 2003.

Welly, Kinley. "TIA: Terrorism Information Awareness or Totally Inappropriate?" *Econtent*, October 2003.

Web

"Email: Voice from the Grave." *Salon.com*, October 2002.

"Liquidating Your life." *New York Metro.com*, October 2004.

McCullagh, Declan. "Database Nation: The Upside of 'Zero Privacy.'" *Reason.com*, June 2004.

Mieszkowski, Katharine. "WANTED: Your Name and Number." *Salon.com*, October 2, 2001.

7 CONTINUOUS CITY

DISTANCE YEARNING

dbox concept image for CONTINUOUS CITY.

OPENINGS

At first, sitting in the darkness, audience members perceive only the sound. The same bars of digitized music repeat in a loop, punctured only slightly by the thwap and blip of what turns out to be a game. Lights come up on a little girl sitting alone at a desk onstage, compelled by the computer in front of her, where she interacts with digital versions of Webkinz plush toys with each type and swipe of the keyboard. The simulated homes and parks of her Webkinz appear on her computer and also on a large screen projected in front of her. Behind her, two more computer screens flicker dimly as she plays and cares for her virtual pets. More lights come up, revealing more desks where technicians, actors, and office employees work beneath the shimmering squares.

A man enters, purposeful, affable, ready to access a world before him. "You get them up yet?" he asks someone in the shadows. "Yeah, they're calling now," a technician responds. In front of him on his side of the stage, two more screens appear with a smiling face on each one. "Hey, family, how are you?" the man begins, and he launches a video family chat with the two screens. The screened figures chastise the man for working late in the office ("When are you going to go home?"), but he says he feels happy to be talking to them from his perch on the screen: "This is home. You know that. This is just as good. I got my cousin in London, my nephew in Virginia. Just tell me what's going on at the house." As they finish talking about the antics of the family cat or the contents of the latest care package, more screens of different sizes open around the stage space. The new screens project a close-up on a man in a collared shirt and suit who is walking under the sun along a village road. He passes shanties, wipes his brow, and looks to the right and left before releasing a bewildered exhale.

CONTINUOUS CITY premiered in 2008 at the Krannert Center for the Performing Arts in Urbana, Illinois. It was the culmination of two years of experiments and workshop performances and six weeks of labor-intensive final rehearsals. The relation among analog and digital experiences of the world had already informed the Builders Association's aesthetic, but CONTINUOUS CITY took up a different aspect of that conjunction by exploring the relation between urban and digital expansions. By the first decade of the twenty-first century, social media were entrenched in the everyday lives of a significant portion of the planet's population. Start-up companies touted the promise of social media, promoting a virtual world as a way to stay connected in a physical world that was coming apart.

Weems and Builders collaborators James Gibbs and Harry Sinclair began to reflect on the parameters that would make such a promise possible, as well as those that challenged it. They pressed on the concept of the urban—a zone that was simultaneously expanding and dissolving in what scholars of urban planning call "the megacity." The accelerated dislocation of diasporic communities had placed the world in a state that was fluid geographically and asymmetric economically. How did the experience of distance and dislocation of first-world travelers differ from that of less privileged transnationals? Would all dislocated world citizens be able to gather around the "virtual hearth," as Weems called it? What was the relation between virtual and physical spaces of gathering? Would the former substitute for the latter? Would the virtual redefine the experience of the physical? And how did social media affect intergenerational connection/? How did new communication devices satisfy the deeply felt desire to connect with loved ones at different life stages?

CONTINUOUS CITY was an attempt to roll these and other geosocial issues into a theater production. Weems began to explore such questions first in *Invisible Cities*, a public art project in New York City that was inspired by Italo Calvino's text.[1] She and collaborators John Cleater, Bertie Ferdman, and Peter Norrman worked with students from underresourced New York high schools who were asked to map their experiences of the city, charting their own personal sense of visibility and invisibility in different urban zones. As she and her collaborators gathered more material and pursued new angles, they became increasingly interested in how technological transformations coincided with the globalized expansion of the urban sphere—what Saskia Sassen investigated in a book titled *Global Networks, Linked Cities*.[2] At the same time, Weems was equally compelled by the intimate experience of such networks and the ways that families and loved ones remained tethered to each other, often over great distances. Related to these sociological topics, The Builders also wrestled with a formal and aesthetic one. After years of hearing audience members ask why Builders' productions were not interactive, Weems wanted to open the stage to become a networked space. Was there a way to explore the urban asymmetries of the network and simultaneously stretch beyond the conventional boundaries of the theater? And was there a way for the theater, as an analog experience of collectivity, to offer a counterpoint for reflecting on the nature of digital connection?

R&D

In August 2006, Weems read two key texts that mined the intimacies of the digital and the political economies of the expanding megacity. The first was Sherry Turkle's "Always-on/Always-on-You: The Tethered Self,"[3] which posited that our experiences of distance, intimacy, and home are changing through connective technologies. Turkle's language of "tethering," a term that signaled technological and sociological forms of bonding, appeared in Weems's notes to collaborators and in later program notes. "We are tethered to our "always-on/always-on-us" communication devices," wrote Turkle, "and the people and things we reach through them: people, Web pages, voice mail, games.... These very different objects achieve a certain sameness because of the way we reach them. Animate and inanimate, they live for us through our tethering devices, always ready-to-mind and hand."[4]

The second key text was Mike Davis's *Planet of Slums*, in which he extrapolates on a proposition that had great cultural currency in 2005 and 2006. For the first time, more people lived in cities than in rural environments. This demographic insight was a hot topic in urban studies and in multiple sectors worldwide. It was a frequent subject in digital forums spaces, at TED (Technology, Entertainment, Design) conferences, and at PopTech 2006, where Weems appeared on a panel with the media theorist Stewart Brand. While discussing this recalibration of the urban/rural divide, Mike Davis coined the term *megaslums*, which he used to describe "peripheral cities" on the outskirts of Lagos, Rio de Janeiro, and other rapidly expanding regions in the developing world. But how did the first world respond to these megaslums? One of his answers was both compelling and harrowing, describing a kind of virtual gated community that was separated and suspended over the earth in the digital ether—"The Golden Nowhere ... floating in the superterrestrial topography of money."[5]

Davis's book was both an index and a propeller of a shifting ethos in urban studies and in a variety of globalizing social science fields. Scholars such as Arjun Appadurai, Zygmunt Bauman, Teresa Caldeira, Manuel Castells, Saskia Sassen, and many others worked to understand geographic shifts that were at once economic and political in effect.[6] They came to terms with the gradual weakening of "the nation state" as an economic force and with the rise of "world cities" and "global cities" as financial centers of global capital. Such centralization coexisted with a number of paradoxes, notably the erosion of the quotidian character and cultural specificity of distinctive cities. Additionally, the aspirations and sanitization of the world city existed in counterpoint to the deleterious expansions of the megaslum, or what others came to call "the megacity." Davis described the expanding demographics of these largely unregulated zones in the developing world and the conceptual erosion of any clear divide between center and periphery:

In the sprawling cities of the Third World, "periphery" is a highly relative time-specific term; today's urban edge abutting fields, forest or desert may tomorrow become part of a dense metropolitan core.... Of the 500,000 people who migrate to Delhi each year, it is estimated that fully 400,000 end up in slums; by 2015 India's capital will have a slum population of more than 10 million.... "if such a trend continues unabated," warns planning expert Gautam Chatterjee, "we will have only slums and no cities."

... [In southern China,] the countryside is urbanizing as well as generating epochal migrations: "Villages become more like market towns, and county towns and small cities become more like large cities." Indeed in many cases rural people no longer have to migrate to the city; it migrates to them.[7]

Another effect of such expansion was vast economic inequity that prompted the erection of varieties of "gatekeeping" behaviors, whether in the construction of new walls or in the movement practices of its inhabitants. Davis noted that "On the edges of Mexico City, Buenos Aires, and other Latin American cities, it is common to find shantytowns of new rural migrants next to walled suburbs of middle-class commuters fleeing crime and insecurity in the city center."[8] In 2005, Rem Koolhaas inaugurated a project in Lagos that became a signature case study. He described how, on their first visit to the city, he and his team were too intimidated to get out of the car because the possibility of violence and the perceived level of chaos were completely disorienting. And Saskia Sassen painted a portrait of cross-class indifference and intrusion:

On the one hand, this raises a question of what the city is for international businesspeople: it is a city whose space consists of airports, top-level business districts, top of the line hotels and restaurants—a sort of urban glamour zone, the new hyperspace of international business. On the other hand, there is the difficult task of establishing whether a city that functions as an international business center does in fact recover the costs involved in being such a center.... Perhaps at the other extreme of legitimacy are those who use urban political violence to make their claims on the city.... These claims have, of course, a long history.... The growing weight of "delinquency," for example, smashing cars and shop windows, robbing and burning stores, in some of these uprisings during the last decade in major cities of the developed world, is perhaps an indication of the sharpened inequality. The disparities, as seen and as lived, between the urban glamour zone and the urban war zone have become enormous.[9]

The juxtaposition of glamour zone and war zone was symptomatic of regions where some were entitled to enjoy a "world-class" city at the expense of those who occupied a megacity. Weems wanted to think about the role played by technology in such spaces by asking how people who lived in these peripheral, unregulated cities related to the virtual world. In November 2006, she flew to Glasgow for a discussion with Stewart Laing, a longtime friend and set designer for SUPER VISION, and John McGrath, the author of *Loving Big Brother: Surveillance Culture and Performance Space*, which was influential in the development of the databody in SUPER VISION. She presented her new thoughts regarding the role of technology in globalizing cities, focusing on issues of cultural specificity and economic access in a digital environment. McGrath responded with phrasing that reversed the traditional relationship between analog and digital, between place and network: "Location is an

illusion created by the intersection of network.... the networks are real and the places are illusive."
Weems wrote notes to herself after their conversation: "If I can find some connection between digital
space and the megaslums—then this show is made. Even if they're just showing up on Flickervision—
it's REPRESENTING a world that isn't accessed yet. It could be seen as an intervention into the
insulated world of 'Friendster.'"[10] Her notes from 2006 look dated from the vantage point of 2015. As
Weems noted soon after, both Flickervision and Friendster were subsumed by YouTube and Facebook,
respectively, exemplifying the omnivorous dynamism of what urban theorist Manuel Castell's called
the network's "space of flows."[11] After leaving Glasgow, McGrath wrote a follow-up email that was
both resonant and galvanizing for Weems: "You have some images in your mind that I would almost
describe as living on the frayed edges of the techno-sphere." It was an apt summation of both the
project and the first frayed stages of research and development.

As conceptual questions around the digital and the analog became entangled with those of core
and periphery, Weems and dramaturg James Gibbs found themselves returning to Calvino's *Invisible
Cities*. They read it again with new eyes and new respect for the prescience of this master writer. They
rediscovered Calvino's exploration of multiple cities within a city, of linked cities, of imaginary cities,
and of the character of Marco Polo, who navigates and narrates them. Gibbs felt that the text played
to The Builders' strengths, modeling a mutable stage that might allow for the presentation of multiple
spaces—some virtual, some physical, some as far away as Lagos, and some right next door. In the
Penthesilea section in a chapter titled "Continuous Cities," Calvino describes fluid spaces and defines
the periphery as the new city:

I should begin by describing the entrance to the city. You no doubt imagine seeing a circle of walls rising
from the dusty plane.... you pass beneath an archway and you find yourself within the city.... Penthesilea
is different. You advance for hours and it is not clear to you whether you are already in the city's midst or
still outside it. Penthesilea spreads for miles around, a soupy city diluted in the plane; pale buildings back
to back in mangy fields, among plank fences and corrugated-iron sheds. Every now and then at the edges

of the street a cluster … seems to indicate that from there the city's texture will thicken. But you continue and you find instead other vague spaces, then a rusty suburb of workshops and warehouses, a cemetery, a carnival with Ferris wheel, a shambles; you start down a street of scrawny shops which fades amid patches of leprous countryside.

If you ask the people you meet, "Where is Penthesilea?," they make a broad gesture which may mean "Here," or else "Farther on," or "All around you," or even "In the opposite direction." …

And so you continue, passing from outskirts to outskirts, and the time comes to leave Penthesilea. You ask for the road out of the city; you pass a string of scattered suburbs…. Penthesilea is only the outskirts of itself…. no matter how far you go from the city will you only pass from one limbo to another, never managing to leave it?[12]

With a slight adjustment, Calvino's section title, "Continuous Cities," became the title of the show. His elaboration of the geography of the perpetual outskirt remained an inspiration that also linked this new project to the issues of global travel, global labor, and global locations that had propelled JET LAG and ALLADEEN years earlier.

A final resonant link occurred during an unusual moment of research development. Writer Harry Sinclair saw Weems spending time via Skype with her six-year-old goddaughter Lola, the daughter of Jessica Chalmers, writer of JET LAG and fellow member of The V-Girls. These conversations were part of a regular routine in which Weems asked Lola about her day and read aloud to her on the webcam, helping out Lola's mother, a working single parent. Harry saw the little girl holding the book up to the camera on her computer, pointing to certain pictures, asking about the meaning of specific words. The exchange prompted Sinclair to imagine a businessperson—a first-world traveler who was always moving and always attempting to remain connected to life at home. This character also arose from Calvino's meditations on the historic traveler Marco Polo. Sinclair and Weems began to talk about casting Marco Polo as a traveling businessman who tries to stay in contact with a daughter left at home. In January 2007, Weems shared this idea with Gibbs:

Marianne Weems Skyping with Lola, age five, daughter of collaborator Jessica Chalmers.

There's a kind of Marco Polo character who travels through these cities—cities that are half imagined, half real. Some footage is even spliced in from the city our show is touring in, including people who may or may not be part of Polo's story but who have their own stories to tell which can dovetail with the explorer's. Marco Polo talks about these places to his small daughter, who sits in front of a huge mediascape in a kind of isolated space (evoking a kind of gated community.) Most of what the audience sees is her being told these stories and communicating with him via webcam.[13]

The idea stuck. A moment from Weems's personal history created a particular affective connection to the conceptual ideas of the show. The dynamics of digital intimacy became central to the narrative and the ultimate design. But first, there were more operational details to attend to.

OPERATING SYSTEMS

How does our experience of being constantly connected through technology alter our sense of distance, and of how the world is mapped around us? What does social networking actually signify? No borders. A peripheral world that transcends the physical. A fantasy about an endless network of "friends." ... How does this device intersect with a physical city? The grid—an endless series of networks, infinitely more vast than the physical spaces? How do people use these, and what motivates them to do so? Get a research assistant and reach out to these new little companies, Twitter, Obvious, Kyte, Radar, etc. Add these functions to the Father's phone—the way he (and we all) will communicate.

Marianne Weems journal entry during a Yaddo residency, May 2007

Transcript of advertisement for Kyte TV (a predecessor of Facebook)
[This advertisement was a key to the character of J.V. and the inspiration for The Builders' website, Xubu.]

(A man speaks with megaphone against orange backdrop.)
Anybody out there? *(He whistles with a coach's whistle. Whistle, whistle. Whistle.)*
Is this thing working?
Anybody out— *(He interrupts himself with an airhorn. Then he blows the horn again.)*
Hey, you. You! How are you? Good? Come over here. Check this out. Why aren't you watching TV?
Me neither?
This is my TV.
So, what is this "Kyte" thing?
It's the new TV.
It's your TV.

It's TV on your MySpace.

It's TV on your website, on your blog, on your phone.

It's TV everywhere, and you're the star.

You're the producer, you're the director, it's your TV channel.

Yours, not theirs.

See who's watching, see who's chatting.

You can broadcast your videos, your pictures, music, and share it with the world.

You can take a video of ... this banana ... and immediately the whole world can see it on your TV channel. *(He films a banana.)*

By the way, all of this you can do online with the drag and drop tools.

Add a poll, and broadcast to the world. You're always connected.

You can have your channel on your site, on your friend's site,

on your mobile, on your friend's mobile, everywhere.

You're always connected.

And it doesn't finish there.

In fact, you have just started.

You can invite your friends onto your channel, they can invite their friends, and all of those shows are on your channel.

You think this is boring? *(He shrugs.)*

Click on another show, right down here. *(He gestures to the menu below the video frame.)*

We like 'em.

So what do I need this thing for? *(A TV has appeared out of nowhere. He smashes it with mallet.)*

Title: Kyte. TV out of the box.

Source: KYTE, April 22, 2007, http://www.kyte.tv/home/index.html.

Having benefitted from a residency for SUPER VISION organized by the Mike Ross, director of the Krannert Center for the Performing Arts and the National Center for Supercomputing Applications (NCSA) at the University of Illinois at Urbana-Champaign, The Builders began to realize how well their creative process interfaced with the research ethos of a university setting. Universities offer both a theatrical apparatus and connections to field specialists who work outside the theater—the sociologists, philosophers, engineers, and designers who were key to making a new media piece of relevance to a contemporary moment. The building of CONTINUOUS CITY expanded on that effort, and The Builders sought university partners to help them conduct research and devise systems for the show. Chuck Helm, Director of Performing Arts at The Ohio State University's Wexner Center for the Arts, organized a miniresidency. By this point, Weems, Gibbs, and Sinclair already had a set of ideas that required an operational imagination. Sinclair's articulation laid out two central hopes:

1. A YouTube-like website attached to the piece. People upload their videos before they come to the show. It could be a) a chorus which is a bunch of people kind of "improvising" on a certain length of text—a chorus like the Greek chorus, good Internet analogy. Or b) we write certain bits of text, they "perform" and upload them, but the story isn't resolved until they come to the theater and see how that text fits into the bigger story.

2. Wireless webcams—use the city we're touring in. We either go OUT into the city during the show or use pre-recorded footage but from people in those specific places, etc.

Both of these ideas went far toward unsettling the parameters and boundaries of the proscenium stage by temporally extending the experience to pre- and post-participation, spatially expanding the experience with local engagement at each touring site. Throughout the spring of 2007, Weems continued to brainstorm, testing the limits of her own impulses, wondering whether a theater production was the right format for this project at all. "Maybe we should be doing something more on the Web rather than thinking that the Father will be able to travel to all of these places," she wrote in her journal: "it is 50/50 at this point whether or not we're going to get the funding." Moreover, there were financial, conceptual, and environmental issues involved in engaging a wide range of global cities: "And isn't global travel wasteful at this point? Isn't there anything we can do that doesn't seem so redundant? … Maybe I should be making something more virtual, more open-ended. Somehow when we start on the story it's so inflexible. Maybe Rizwan should really have to react to the audience—to some 'feed,' or something that's happening live."[14]

While at the University of Illinois, The Builders team tried to reckon with the operational contingencies of their philosophical, political, and artistic hopes. They worked with the National Center for Supercomputing Applications and members of its scientific and data visualization group—primarily Donna Cox and Hank Green—on how to picture network flows. Green helped to clarify that the economic position of each character would affect the reach—and hence visualization—of each network. "This man's social connections," he wrote in an email, "could only be in his city, though his work connections are across the oceans and all over the world. The maid's work connections are local in the city, and her social connections are all over the world…. I think one of the great ways to visualize this may be global network flows over time: immigration, transportation, data and compare to social network flows for the businessman and the maid."[15]

In the fall of 2007, some members of the company—Weems, performer Rizwan Mirza, writer Harry Sinclair, video designer Peter Flaherty, and sound designer Dan Dobson—conducted a formative, one-semester residency at the University of California at Berkeley with funding from the Arts Research Center. They worked with students from the departments of Art Practice and Theater, Dance, and Performance Studies to stage a first iteration of the show, simultaneously collaborating with students and faculty from Computer Science, New Media, and the School of Information. As part of the audition, Weems asked undergraduates to present their Facebook profiles, a conceit that remained in the final workshop production. Weems was struck by how willing these members of the millennial generation were to present the details of their pages. They displayed a readiness, even eagerness, to expose themselves through this frame of self-portraiture, teaching Builders artists about the social protocols of social media interaction along the way. Weems used the resources of UC Berkeley to research the intersections between transnational studies and media theory, brainstorming with

CONTINUOUS CITY workshop with students from the University of California, Berkeley.

AnnaLee Saxenian, dean of the School of Information and author of *The New Argonauts: Regional Advantage in a Global Economy*, as well as with researchers at Yahoo! Labs who concentrated on motivations for online participation.[16] Yahoo! researchers David Ayman Shamma and Peter Shafton and graduate students Ryan Shaw and Nick Reid worked with Weems to create a website that became an integral part of the final production, launched under the fictional company name Xubu.

While in the San Francisco Bay Area, Weems also interviewed and sought support from technology companies, seeing if she could improve those 50/50 chances of securing necessary funding. She represented the project as an opportunity to interrupt social networks that are otherwise circumscribed by class, nationality, and geography and to expand social networks by distributing phones or other devices to people in the developing world. "It's an art project, and a social experiment," she found herself saying to representatives of nascent social media companies. She proposed that users in the developing world could upload images of their city, such as a view from the middle of their street or the traffic in front of their buildings. These could be hand-drawn as well as digital materials, which would become a rough way of reimagining geography, a visual "continuous city." She also described their idea of posting excerpts from the performances on the site, embodying Sinclair's concept of a "video chorus," as well as creating specific scenes with dialogue between live actors and uploaded participants. In the midst of discussing this performance of networked globality, however, their questions and concerns still revolved around the hyperlocality of the theater. The Yahoo! contingent asked, "What is the compelling experience for people who are remote and can't come to the theater? What would drive participation?"

While living in Berkeley, California, Weems spoke to a few startup companies both to seek support and to record some of the language that they used and the claims that they made for the possibilities of connecting. Among her interlocutors were Biz Stone and other partners at Twitter, which had been in operation for a year. During a conversation in the company's modest office, Weems noted that Stone used phrases that have now become entrenched in the social media lexicon and spoke about how new mobile technology would allow users to become "citizen journalists" and "create content, not just use it." Weems asked him what made Twitter necessary, and his provocative response focused on the value of quantity: "What makes it valid is the numbers—how many people participate." He used a recent political uprising as an example (this was before the demonstrations in Cairo's Tahrir Square) and described how users sent political information to each other in real time. His elaborations on the social function of Twitter ended with a resonate paradox: "It's trivial until something happens."

As stories, concepts, characters, and models developed, The Builders continued to press on how to embody, access, and visualize a globally connected world. Questioning the physical parameters of the theater, Weems periodically returned to an idea that had arisen earlier in conversation with Stewart Laing and John McGrath—the idea of creating a piece inside a shipping container. Weems had been

Fictional website Xubu. The name has no meaning
but could be associated with many cultures.

struck by an article in *Wired* that defined
the shipping container as a consolidating
metaphor for global labor and global systems:

At its heart, ocean shipping is a
network business, just like airlines and
telecommunications. Passengers, bulk goods,
data—all three represent uniform-size cargo,
shooting through global transport and sorting
systems 24/7/365. Viewed this way, airline
seats, data packets, and 40-foot shipping
containers are much the same—commoditized
units for carrying content.[17]

Around the same time, other artists were
implementing shipping containers in a variety
of installation pieces, capitalizing on the
politics and aesthetics of its form and function.
A traveling public art event called ContainerArt
used large groupings of shipping containers as
a temporary exhibition space as it traversed
the globe. What if this public art model was
translated to a theatrical piece as it toured?
What if the container and the piece accrued
layers created by local artists as it traveled
from location to location? Weems continued to

imagine the formal possibilities of this model, up to the moment that she faced the exigencies of her own professional networks. In a discussion with Brooklyn Academy of Music executive director and coproducer Joe Melillo, he noted that a shipping container would not fit through a stage door. It was one of many moments in Builders' history where the intermedia aspirations of the work confronted the operating systems of a professionalized theatrical medium.

While the container image of global transport receded, other ideas stuck, no matter the technological difficulties. Many of the retained ideas centered on the intimacies of transnational connection. Weems's hope to have Mirza react "to something that's happening live" became a reality in a scene with his character's family several time zones away. Before Skype video conferencing was possible, TBA used a "very buggy" conferencing software called Ooovoo to create the sense of family members who conversed with each other in real time while one of them kept his foot on a theatrical stage. Despite Weems's occasional concerns about the wastefulness of global travel, they decided that the dramatization of global intimacy needed actual juxtaposition between far and near. To create poignant conversations between the traveling businessman and his daughter at home Harry Sinclair (who played Mike DeVries, the father), Weems, and occasionally James Gibbs traveled to global sites (Shanghai, Toronto, Los Angeles, Las Vegas, Tijuana) to create video of the father "video chatting" as he tried to communicate and connect with his little girl. Once again, such an artistic goal required a technological leap of faith. At the time, FaceTime and video smartphones did not offer reliable capabilities, so The Builders filled in the gaps themselves. In every shooting location, they found an interesting setting, and Sinclair filmed himself with the video camera as if it were a camera phone, delivering dialogue to his daughter. He could not see the daughter while looking into a camera, nor could she actually see him. But this early FaceTime prototype—combined with good acting skills—gave the illusion of a digitally intimate connection between father and daughter. Such a dynamic is now accessible to anyone who has a contemporary smartphone, but in 2007, it was quite a feat, both as a filmmaker and as an actor. CONTINUOUS CITY was thus another moment in the long history of aesthetic experiments that have imagined technological innovations before they become ubiquitous.

STORYBOARD

Eventually, these ideas began to coalesce as the story of the father and daughter took shape. The hope was to integrate their relationship into a structure that reflected on the mutability of the expanded city, the rise of social media industries, and the connective promise of mobile tech devices in the developing world. As the content of the script came into focus, they decided to create stories and dialogues on the connections among three domains: (1) the office of Xubu social media, (2) the home of a fictional father, Mike DeVries, and his daughter, Samantha, and (3) the travels abroad of the father, Mike. Harry Sinclair continued to serve as a scriptwriter and as the actor who played Mike.

While in residence together at UC Berkeley, Sinclair worked with Weems and Mirza to draft the office portions of the script. By that point, they had created the parodically named Xubu, a social media company led by J.V. (Mirza), who promised that his new communication platforms would democratize the populations of the world's emerging economies. As an Indian transnational, J.V. peddled his TED-inspired personal story of an Indian grandfather "who started as a pappadum vendor," moved to a city, and eventually started his own business: "This week, broadband Internet transmission towers are being erected in Dharavi, which is the poorest part of the city, right where my grandfather lived. Now imagine if my grandfather had had a cellphone and access to the Internet. His life and his family's life would have been very different." From there, J.V.'s pitch for Xubu expanded to imagine a world of migrant workers who needed to stay tethered to families elsewhere: "Six months from now, Xubu will be a household name. Why? Because there are people out there who need more…. People who are scattered all over the world, uprooted without choice or drawn to expanding cities. These people need to reach out and stay connected with their families in this unstable world." Even as J.V. touted the political potential of virtual connection, he also promoted its personal use for sustaining online romantic relationships with an array of women from around the world. His "virtual hearth" thus had multiple participants. The irony was that, unlike so many other migrant workers who longed to return to home, J.V.'s intimate connections could be sustained only as long as none of them tried to visit his hearth physically.

Daughter (Caroline O'Neill) and Father (Harry Sinclair) communicate remotely.

Although J.V.'s intimacies depended on physical distance, the relationship between a Marco Polo–inspired father and his daughter was strained by it. Scenes from home usually focused on Samantha (Sam), performed by seven-year-old Caroline O'Neill, as she occupied her time during her father's travels. Sam played Webkinz online, forming attachments to virtual characters who grew and changed under her digital care. She searched to see if her father was "online" or "offline" and occasionally called him to chat at inopportune moments during his working (or sleeping) schedule. In one scene, Sam called her father just as he was boarding a plane. After verifying that there was no emergency, the father realized that he had missed his nightly bedtime call to his daughter. "I can't sleep. You didn't call me," she said plaintively over the wires. "Oh, God. I'm sorry. I lost track of time. Look, I'm gonna come right back to you. I'm gonna get rid of this other call, okay? Okay, wait." He fumbled from his seat on the plane, clamping a seat belt, switching from one phone line to another, trying to maintain both a compassionate connection to his daughter and a professional connection to his employer in the space of a few seconds. As he tried to make the best of the situation, he showed Sam the view from his airplane window and described some of the unusual animals he had seen in his travels ("Do you know what a yak is?"). Inevitably, Sam responded with a recurrent question, "When are you coming home?" And just as inevitably, this global voyager's digital communication was curtailed by the exigencies of international travel when an airline attendant instructed him "to turn off all electronic devices." Her father had to end the call too abruptly for Sam, who had hoped he would tell her a bedtime story: "I've gotta go, Sam. I'm sorry. Bye."

Scenes from home also included Sam's prickly relationship with her nanny, Deb, who was played by long-time collaborator Moe Angelos. The nanny monitored the food, sleep, and online activity of a girl who resented that a nanny rather than her father was performing such caregiving tasks. Deb tried somewhat ineptly to address Sam's emotions. She watched from the sidelines as Sam hung up the phone with her father, asking, "Are you OK?" or whether she would like "juice or milk." She also soothed the melancholies of a privileged transnational child by using the financial resources available to privileged transnational families: "'Kendra has a karaoke machine.' 'Yeah, that sounds nice. Should we get you one? ... I'll use your dad's credit card.'" Meanwhile, the storyboard also thematized Deb's life as a displaced worker who was responsible for the offline affective needs of a globalized family while leaving her own family and friends behind. Deb handled the strain of her domestic job by cultivating a blog of her own—"Debinthecity"—where she shared stories of her own life and of the life of her transnational employer to a wider digital and filial network. When Sam asked Deb if she could read her blog, Deb refused saying, "It's private."

The occupants of both office and home constantly tried to keep tabs on Mike DeVries and his travels abroad. Mike appeared exclusively as a screen presence during the final performance, someone who appeared on cell phones (before FaceTime) and live on computer screens (before Skype). The Builders continued a process of scripting, rehearsing, and revising, but they also had to project ahead to decide on a script for the traveling father. Their spare travel budgets meant that they would have only two to three days in which to shoot in Shanghai and Mexico, and the father's dialogue with his daughter, the nanny, and J.V. needed to be finalized ahead of time. As both actor and writer, Harry Sinclair had a variety of investments in the ultimate storyboard. And as a provider of textual material for The Builders Association, he encountered some of the same struggles that other Builders writers had encountered. At first, he began to propose story lines and dialogue that chronicled a legible arc in the father-daughter relationship, including their personal background, a crisis around his disappearance, and the possibility of his return. That arc was rejected by the team. Over time, Sinclair began to understand the role of text as one element in relation to other conceptual and design elements of the show. In a letter to the group, he offered his own reflections on the significance of this working aesthetic. Although the ultimate show did not end with the completely clear feeling that "everything is possible," Sinclair realized that a "theater of ideas" required the creation of "sensations" that resonated deeply with the issues explored. The script needed to understand its relation to other "abstract or symbolic" elements, propelling a show where content, story, and character were "lighter" and part of an "emotional shape" created simultaneously by screen and sound.

Email from Harry Sinclair to Marianne Weems and James Gibbs

The Story of Ideas: February 2008

A Builders show, from what I've seen of them, works in a layered way, the most obvious layer being the narrative. But there is another level of meaning and emotion being expressed that I, if you will indulge me, would like to call The Story of Ideas.

SUPER VISION, for example, had the stories of the characters, and these were on the surface of the work. But there was another more powerful level to do with a building intensity of ideas, of sound, of pictures, of mood. I think this is the most powerful thing that The Builders create, and it's not in any way a conventional theatrical experience where the audience is moved by the drama of the story, of the characters' lives. It's something else. I've come to understand that the reason that my efforts to create storylines that have conventional shapes—like making the central drama out of the father's disappearance—don't entirely appeal to you, my dear collaborators, is that the work is really about something else.

If I may be so bold, it's about trying to find a way to describe the experience of modern lives mediated by technology by creating a sensation in the theater that resonates deeply with this experience. And in the end, this may be achieved by quite abstract or symbolic means.

Now I feel that with a show like SUPER VISION, the effect of this nonnarrative layer of the show was a little static. What if we treated this aspect of the show as a story, too, drawing the audience into a mood that grows and evolves, creating an emotional shape with a powerful climax?

And for me, writing this show, imagining that working allows me to see the narratives of the characters as lighter, like melodies that weave around this central Story of Ideas.

In CONTINUOUS CITY, the basic shape of this story might be, first, a sense of alienation—things aren't working, the father and the daughter aren't communicating. Then the father begins to tell the story, Rizwan's dating explodes, Moe connects with people within the city, the daughter is being creative, we experience the website, and technology seems to be working, transforming lives, dissolving distances.

Then the father disappears, and we experience loss, aloneness, for all the characters. But then the continuous city somehow appears and everything is possible. The father is inside it, with Moe, Rizwan, and the daughter experiencing their own versions of it.

And the final act might be somehow to do with a realization that the continuous city is a mirage, the father never makes it home, etc....

Well, this is a simplistic corny-sounding description—but something like that....

Vedali presto!

Weems, Gibbs, and Sinclair used those principles to craft scenarios for Mike's travels, and onsite, Sinclair improvised based on loosely anticipated scenarios. Mike would have several interactions with J.V., including participating in selling Xubu to potential investors and stopping a call to take one from Sam. In one father-daughter scenario, Mike played hide-and-seek online with his daughter in Toronto. In another, he sat in a Shanghai taxi and tried to say good night, gently reminding her that he was in a different time zone. In still another, Mike took Sam "shopping" to a Mexican market in Tijuana while talking into a camera and interacting with an absent daughter character who—at the time of the shoot—had yet to be cast: "Let's make tacos for lunch. We've got tomatoes.... Oh! Cactuses! Ow! I'm sure they've taken the thorns out. Oh! Hot peppers! But you don't like spicy stuff, do you?" Sinclair's improvisation anticipated moments of connection ("Ow!") as well as moments that displayed the threat of disconnection. "I like spicy now," Sam eventually responded in the final production, prompting an absent father to ask, "Oh, really? Since when?"

These pieces of improvised dialogue were shot on location, were given places in the final storyboard, and actors and designers eventually retrofit a final script around them. These scenarios and retrofitted storyboards did not focus on filling in content or delivering traditional exposition. Audiences never knew the deeper family background of Mike and Sam, for instance, or whether the daughter ever knew her biological mother. Instead, this textual material was performed on-screen and in real time, clustered with other images and sounds to evoke the ebb and flow of digital intimacy and digital alienation.

James Gibbs documenting the Versailles housing development in Tijuana, Mexico.

Collaborator Moe Angelos created a blog that was based on her local interactions in every city the production appeared in. Pictured here: Cowboy grocer in San Francisco, Ramon, trailer park in Champaign, and a Vietnamese family.

Tuesday, November 4, 2008
San Francisco, CA

On a Mission
Headed to the Mission district today and was bombarded with purchase options from everywhere in Latin America. It's muy fantastico over there, and right away I found what I was looking for in one of the many, many produce outlets on Mission.

The guy who owns the produce place was behind the counter, and he was amazing. Check out the giant

original oil painting behind him: the Virgin of Guadalupe appears to the cowboy grocer. Only in the Mission, friends.

I started chatting with the guy behind the counter, Ramon. Ramon, it turns out, is not Latino, though he speaks Spanish and English. He also speaks Farsi—because he is originally from Afghanistan. He asked me if I had voted, and I said yes, and he said he had voted for Obama. "We have to give him a chance," he said. Ramon got the money to open his 99 cent emporium by going back to his country and working for the US Department of Defense. "Good money," he said, "$220,000 a year." I asked him if it was dangerous, and he said "Look, someone can come

here and—boom boom—shoot me. Only God knows when it is your turn to go. And until then God protects me." I hope, Ramon, you are right about that. So far, so good, my friend.

I forgot to ask him what his name was back in his country. I doubt it is Ramon.

This is Deb in the City, sifting through the diasporas, saying adios and salaam and farewell from the Mission.

Wednesday, September 10, 2008
Champaign, IL

A Bao Grows in Champaign
I was toodling around Champaign today on my bike, and I ran into this most awesome trailer park out by the interstate.

The front of the house had gorgeous flowers, and I waved when I saw somebody in the window, and they waved back. That made me bold, and so I went up on the porch and said, "Hi."

These people are from Bao in Vietnam. They have been in Champaign for five years. The son is in fifth grade and does the talking when nice white ladies show up on the front porch. His name is Tuan. His mom's name is Tu.

Tuan and Tu and I had a broken but animated conversation about all the vegetables. She was explaining to me about the mint, and I said, "Yes, like in pho," which is like the national dish of Vietnam. And her eyes opened really wide, and she said in perfect English, "You know pho?" Oh yes, I know pho and pho knows me.

He said that back in Vietnam he was a fisherman and that he had worked the shrimp boats in the Gulf of Mexico out of New Orleans for the first ten years he was here, saving enough money to bring his wife and sponsor her and their son.

As these elements of the storyboard fell into place, The Builders also experimented with more flexible scripting throughout CONTINUOUS CITY, integrating "live" and locally responsive material inside a touring production. Within the script, two diegetic elements were built to have the capacity for extradiegetic connection. First, actor Moe Angelos's blog as "Debinthecity" functioned as an outreach platform to each city on the tour. While on tour, Angelos traveled to each city a few days in advance of the company and worked with a local guide to identify and document local examples of the show's central themes and spaces. She found gated communities where she could live fictionally as Deb the nanny and integrated references to cultural elements that were specific to the town or region. In Liège, Belgium, Deb/Moe talked about the local puppet "Tchantchès," a famous Liègeois whose museum was a central tourist attraction; in Urbana, Illinois, she integrated references to local the Kraft cheese factory plant; in Troy, New York, she recalled the history of the Arrow shirt company and claimed to be living in a gated community called "Sheldon Hills at Half Moon"—"a neighborhood of curving streets, no sidewalks, and a state-of-the-art clubhouse." As part of this platform, seven-year-old Caroline O'Neill also arrived early to have pictures taken of the two of them at identifiably local sites. These photos were then integrated into each production and into Deb's blog, a photomontage that demonstrated that the nanny and daughter had actually left the house "untethered," exploring local cities away from Mike the father's video link.

The second changeable scripted element involved Rizwan Mirza as J.V. Before every show, Mirza and the crew took time to have a video conference call with his nephew in Delhi and his cousin in London. The content of the conversation changed each time, responding to the new city he was in and current events that were unfolding globally at the time. They chatted together about the World Cup and discussed Obama's historic election in 2008. Due to the lack of reliable software for recording video calls at that time, The Builders recorded the Mirza's family conversations early in the day (often coordinating between three time zones) and then quickly edited the recording for use during the performance. Mirza then improvised a script around it, throwing in lines to create an apparently spontaneous dialogue with his prerecorded family. The sensation of "liveness" was once again

The Nanny (Moe Angelos) and Daughter (Caroline O'Neill) at local landmarks, subsequently featured in performances. Pictured here: San Diego, Liege, Copenhagen, Toronto, 2008–2009.

Performer Rizwan Mirza as an entrepreneur pitching his company Xubu.

produced by integrating two technologies—prerecorded video and the honed skills of an actor. Together they offered the illusion that a video chat was happening live in "real time" each night.

REHEARSAL/ASSEMBLY

After two and a half years of research, residency, and rehearsal, The Builders were ready to assemble materials in a final production. In February 2008, they were given space for a design workshop at St. Ann's Warehouse in Brooklyn, where all designers collectively developed the structure for the show. Their central pursuit was to create "a visualization of a network" that could be performed onstage. Weems started the charrette with a summary of the operating principles of the R&D and storyboard thus far, reminding her colleagues of the rhizomatic form of a network that rotates around each of us, tethering us to specific individuals and then to their networks. Some ties are strong, and some take longer to reach us than others. These virtual networks became newly urgent in a globalizing world, where the fragments of

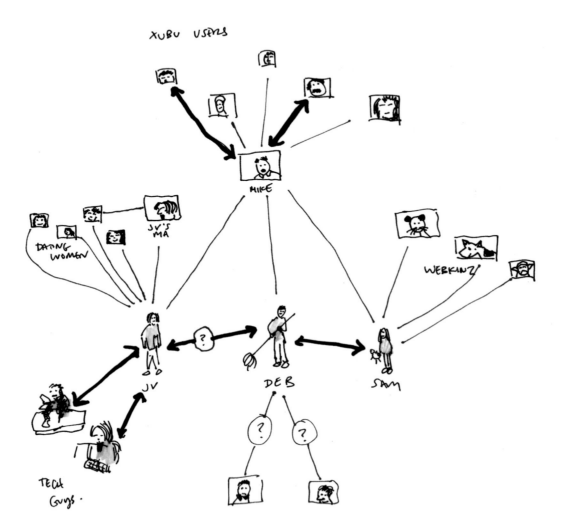

James Gibbs's cocktail napkin concept sketch for a video/set design. Networks form around the production's three central figures.

a vast cityscape—some virtual, some material, some far, some highly proximate—form a network of images that accrue in a meaningful pattern. As video designer Peter Flaherty asserted, "We have to get away from one monumental projection surface. Break apart the screen." James Gibbs agreed and took the idea a step further: "Let's use many screens, the different constellations of screens will define the different networks surrounding (and emanating from) each character. The space needs to be able to shift seamlessly."

Any time anyone said the word *seamlessly*, technical whiz Joe Silovsky knew that he had a new design challenge. He removed himself to another part of the warehouse and, within several hours, returned with a handmade prototype for a series of moving screens. CONTINUOUS CITY thus changed the production apparatus of The Builders yet again. After the serial televisions of MASTER BUILDER, the live film of FAUST, and the monumental screen in each subsequent production, the screen in this show was fragmented, multiple, and flexible. The visualization of a network required many screens to perform relationships that were taking place across phones, computers, clouds, and cities and the tethered imaginations of those who accessed them.

Actualizing this visualization in performance would take some work, however. Drawing from his background as technical director for corporate conventions, Silovsky began devising a version of the collapsible pop-up screens that he had seen at trade shows. He soon discovered that many pop-up models worked well for small to medium-size projection surfaces but were less feasible for a larger surface: "there were too many chances of failure for what we wanted." Thinking through the physics and mechanics of different options, Silovsky eventually came up with the idea of a screen that would open and close like a book and still support a larger surface. "The small prototype worked great," said Silovsky, recalling that it opened and closed with a fresh efficiency. To be visible to all audience members, however, each screen had to be four feet by six feet, and a powerful and dependable means of operation proved challenging. The eventual solution was a pneumatic system that opened and closed the screen by releasing compressed air from cylinders that were controlled by solenoid valves.

Unlike the manually controlled screens from SUPER VISION, this pneumatic system was triggered by a MIDI (musical instrument digital interface) controller.

Adopting Silovsky's system still meant finding a way to convert MIDI commands into the correct voltages necessary to trigger the screen's operation. Silovsky enlisted the help of Eric Singer, the director of the League of Electronic Musical Urban Robots (LEMUR), a Brooklyn collective that was known for creative innovations with electronics for music and performance. Singer was well-versed in using MIDI to control unusual machines and assisted Silovsky in the creation of a custom motherboard and control interface to operate the screens. Ultimately, however, Silovsky and Singer's customized experiment proved too unstable to be put to use live, and The Builders purchased professional MIDI conversion units. Even this solution had its problems because the noise created from its electronic air compressor was too loud during a live play. Instead, Silovsky use two large tanks of compressed air that had to be refilled periodically throughout the run of performances. Although this following approach was more maintenance-intensive than using a compressor, Silovsky's screens opened and closed quietly and efficiently, simulating the seamless ease of an onscreen click. In an example of what Weems calls "the Builders' artisanal technology," the machinations of another highly mechanical, offline process thus produced the liquid smooth effects of digital online experience.[18] As the projection surfaces appeared and disappeared with silent magic, Silovosky and his team refilled air tanks from the sidelines, enacting the material labor necessary to produce a satisfying immaterial encounter.

The thirty screens varied in size (1.5 by 2 feet, 2 feet by 3 feet, 3 feet by 4 feet, 52 inches by 6 feet) and cumulatively filled the stage space with a shifting array of high-resolution digital windows, incarnating the range of images (such as mobile phones, computers, and billboards) that networked citizens encounter each day. In composing a final performance, this multiscreen concept accommodated the entire video design, which used images, stories, and sounds that The Builders had recorded in their travels.

Performer Rizwan Mirza (onstage) communicating with performer Harry Sinclair in Shanghai (on screen).

Other local and global video elements played out on these screens. Before attending the performance, audience members were invited to create personal videos on the topic of how they think about home to upload onto the fictitious website Xubu. The background video screens thus served as an online portal into theater, displaying reflections about home in Japanese, Mandarin, Spanish, Farsi, and English. One figure chronicled a diasporic life: "I'm from Tunisia, but I live in Paris. When I think of home I think of sun. When I think of home, I think of my family. I wish I had all my family near me." Other figures described favorite images and memories from home: "My name is Fatima. I'm from Sri Lanka, and now I live in Canada. When I think of home, I think of many things—maybe the food that we ate there or the fruits that we don't get anywhere. I really miss them."

Some of the self-portraits were recorded during The Builders' travels, which documented the provisional network created in the process of making CONTINOUS CITY. With the aid of a multiscreened projection space, the show returned to that network at transitional moments from scene to scene. After a poignant conversation between Mike and Sam took place on two screens, six or seven more screens opened around them, underscoring the emotional connections between father and daughter by juxtaposing them with a wide field of intimate reflections: "My name is Aiden. I'm from Connecticut, and I live in Connecticut. When I think of home, I think of TV, and I think of a person named Bobo. I wish I had my Xbox 360." In other scenes, audiences were captivated by more reflections on home: "My name is Avery, I'm from upstate New York, and now I live in New York City. When I think of home, I think of our sawmill and chainsaws. I think of my parents, my grandmother, and my aunt. I wish I had the ocean near me" only to realize that the story projections were actually part of J.V.'s presentation to investors: "Isn't that great, isn't that moving? I can't help but think of my grandfather. He was a papadum vendor."

The visualized network of individual memories thus incarnated the attachments of virtual connection at some moments and the alienation of virtual connection at others. Throughout, the stories of home helped to build an ebb and flow of "sensations" around the virtual hearth, offsetting the content of the script to enact the "Theater of Ideas" that Sinclair had hoped for earlier in the scripting process.

CLOSINGS

CONTINUOUS CITY opened in the winter of 2008 at the Krannert Center for the Performing Arts in Urbana, Illinois, and from 2008 to 2010, it toured to international venues such as the Salamanca Festival, London International Festival of Theater (LIFT), Metropolis Festival in Denmark, Luminato Festival in Toronto, and the Brooklyn Academy of Music in New York. The themes and images of the show had been circulating much earlier in conversations with twenty-something technology executives and in online bedtime stories read to a goddaughter hundreds of miles away. They dated even further back to thoughts exchanged with social theorists of urban globalization. Weems recalled one such conversation way back in 2006 in the New York home of Saskia Sassen, a scholar whose *Globalization and Its Discontents* had inspired so much of her thinking. Sassen wrote, "place is seen as neutralized by global communications and the hypermobility of capital.... Even the most advanced information industries have a work process—that is, a complex of workers, machines, and buildings that are more placebound than the imagery of the information economy suggests."[19]

With CONTINUOUS CITY, Weems and The Builders hoped to juxtapose the apparent placelessness of the information economy with the placebounded-ness of the "work process" behind it. Being placebound meant taking seriously a great deal of offline labor and deepening their engagement with the local specificity of a place or region, tracking its ability to engage or resist the homogenizing call of world city status or megacity processes. For Sassen, this on-the-ground activity was not opposed to globalization but was central to its conflicted operation: "Major cities in the highly developed world are the terrain where a multiplicity of globalization processes assume concrete, localized forms. These localized forms are, in good part, what globalization is about. We can then think of cities also as one of the sites for the contradictions of the internationalization of capital, and, more generally, as a strategic terrain for a whole series of conflicts and contradictions."[20]

The international theater festival circuit is a symptom and propeller of urban globalization, and The Builders Association, as a company dependent on it, sought to unsettle its terms. The show rose from a desire to engage the local onstage, said Weems: "to feature local people and sites without it feeling like the worst sort of community theater."[21]

In advance of production, The Builders filmed and incorporated footage from cities and citizens around the world, including Shanghai, Tijuana, New York City, Las Vegas, Los Angeles, and Toronto. They also created an interactive website and branded T-shirts for the show's fictitious company with the tag line "XUBU ... why lose touch?," allowing participants locally and globally to upload stories and images. In addition to having Moe Angelos fly to investigate each local site, they also included messages from audience members from all of their tour stops. "We decided our efforts should be towards engaging with functioning cultural groups in each city who might be working on similar issues," said Weems, who nevertheless wished that they had had more resources: "In the end, I have to admit that this remained unaccomplished, mostly because the role of The Builders would have been overwhelmed by managerial demands. It was enough to keep our own group together." The realities of sustaining an online global network thus proved too much for a company that had to prioritize the offline needs of its immediate family.

Even if Weems and Builders artists had had hopes for deeper local engagement, the process of creating the show and its final product provoked reflection and debate about the intimacies and alienations of global communication for citizen-travelers in its troupe and in its audience. Writing about CONTINUOUS CITY for Urbana's *News Gazette*, critic Patricia Stiller noted, "In the truest sense of theater, this piece encourages audiences to respond independently to the ironies created by the advances of technology, as we ponder the philosophical questions, 'Can we really be everywhere?' and if so, 'Should we?'"[22] Although he felt that "the plot could be better filled out," the *San Francisco Chronicle* theater critic Robert Hurwitt wrote, "The high-tech proficiency of director Marianne Weems and her Builders Association is dazzling and unsettling.... Small and large screens pop up or unfold with videophone, computer or text-message images, or a large face spreads out over the panels of several screens. But it's the low-tech skills of writing and acting that breathe life, humor and poignancy into a provocative exploration of technology as a global force for connection and disconnection."[23] Writing for *Backstage*, Adam Perlman began his review with these comments:

Blue skies and smiling faces. Open windows and open vistas. The whole world is out there—and we'll bring it to you. This is what tech advertising looks and sounds like. It's a promise of freedom that feels a wee bit fascist. That duality is on full display in the imagistic treasure trove of Continuous City.[24]

There were criticisms, too. For Perlman, the ultimate effect of the show reinforced "the potentially alienating effect of technology." For *New York Theater* as well as the *New York Times*, the stories of the central characters needed to go deeper to avoid looking like "an improvisation between strangers," which, at the time of their long distance making, they actually were.[25]

At nearly every turn, The Builders confronted the contrast between the aesthetic of the "information economy" and the intensity of their own "work process." The illusion of easy transnational communication happened only after laborious transnational flights and onsite filming sessions. The maintenance labor of Silovsky's air tanks stood in counterpoint to the seamless screen space that they propelled. Finally, the content and affective sphere of the show thematized the potentials and perils of tethered connection in a digital sphere. The career of the international business traveler required the creation of new familial habits—online bedtime stories and virtual walks through foreign cities. Migrant workers who wished to return home may not have been "empowered" or "democratized" by social media—much less Xubu—but CONTINUOUS CITY presented the fraught and impure role that was played by such media in recalling and sustaining such personal ties. "You know what I always say," J.V. ironically reminded his colleagues: "Family comes first."

ENDNOTES

Artist's Voice: Harry Sinclair, writer

When I first met The Builders, they were all very drunk. I was at a party to celebrate the final night of their season of SUPER VISION at the Brooklyn Academy of Music (BAM) in 2005 and everyone was in a fine mood. After gulping down several glasses of red wine, I felt completely at ease with this charming and funny group of people. I learned that they were about to tour in New Zealand (where I'm from) and that they needed a replacement for an actor who was unable to join them. Two weeks and one audition later, I was on a plane home to perform in SUPER VISION, and I paid my mother a surprise visit as well.

I had worked for many years writing and acting in the theater in New Zealand, and by the time I met Marianne Weems and her cohorts, I had become allergic to the medium. But when I saw SUPER VISION on that fateful night at BAM, I was blown away. Here was live performance taken in a startling new direction—a piece of theater that felt completely modern, a real attempt to describe and invoke the experience of being alive now.

After SUPER VISION, Marianne invited me to be the writer on their next project, CONTINUOUS CITY. The story was about a father who, while traveling around the world on business, talks to his daughter by video phone (something that didn't exist when we created the show). As well as writing, I played the role of the father, videoing my own performance, so the footage could be projected on stage. It was an amazing and at times hilarious challenge to wander the streets of a city like Shanghai, talking to a little camera, leaving spaces for my daughter's lines in our conversation, and watching the puzzled faces of the locals.

One of the most memorable moments in the development of CONTINUOUS CITY was when I saw the set in action for the first time. Until then, I had really no understanding of how the different elements of the show would be brought together, in spite of our many discussions about it. When I saw the thirty or so screens of different sizes opening and closing, with video playing on each one, creating movement and patterns around the stage, I began to understand what we were making. The set was a metaphor for everything that James Gibbs, Marianne, and I had been talking about for a year and a half. The set was telling the story. Nothing in my work as a writer for film or theater had prepared me for this idea that the story could serve the design rather than the other way around.

Theater began to make sense again for me. Now that so much of our lives is spent using technology to connect to people who are physically distant, it feels like there can be a new kind of validity to live performance, a form that's about being in the same space. It feels more and more rare and special to gather together, audience and performers, in one room to share a story. Marianne's work gives her and her collaborators the context in which to discuss the meaning and the feeling of living with digital technology, a discussion that simply would have no resonance on film or TV. At its heart, the work is about presence—about being and not being "here."

In her work, Marianne orchestrates soaring moments where video, sound, music, and live actors weave together in visions of our hyperconnected and thoroughly alienated lives. Working with The Builders Association was a wonderful experience—although I was a little disappointed how sober and hard-working they all turned out to be.

Harry Sinclair writing/
rewriting.

Guest Voice: Joe Melillo, executive producer,
Brooklyn Academy of Music, New York

The 2008 Next Wave Festival presented CONTINUOUS CITY—conceived by Marianne Weems, director; Harry Sinclair, writer; and James Gibbs, dramaturg—in the Harvey Theater here at the Brooklyn Academy of Music (BAM). The production once again demonstrated the extraordinary vision that The Builders Association has for presenting audiences with contemporary issues set within a global landscape in the most original and highly visual contexts.

I am completely captivated by the concept, by the developmental process as the idea grew, by the organic evolution of the material, and ultimately, by the final work of art that they presented in front of a ticket-buying audience. This is theater that is redolent with visual material, and the challenge before the collaborating artists is to authentically devise a story that is harnessed to the idea, while seated within a lush visual environment. Marianne Weems's leadership balances these developmental sensitivities while fearlessly challenging and editing herself and her colleagues to get the right artistic balance. Given the financial, technological, spatial, and human resources limitations of a single producing entity, there are multiple stakeholders in their process. This was readily apparent for the making of this work.

Although BAM does not participate formally in The Builders' developmental process—our role is to provide the company the opportunity to present the result of their artistic process—Marianne and her collaborators are extremely open and eager to receive input and dialogue along the path of creation. It is the marriage of the idea with the process, juxtaposed against a visual and technological wonderland, that yields compelling contemporary theater for audiences everywhere.

People

Conceived by Marianne Weems, director; James Gibbs, dramaturg; and Harry Sinclair, writer

Sound design and original music composition by Dan Dobson

Video design by Peter Flaherty

Lighting design by Jennifer Tipton

Scenic concept and design by James Gibbs, Stewart Laing, and Neal Wilkinson

Performed by

Moe Angelos … Deb

Rizwan Mirza … J.V.

Caroline O'Neill / Olivia Timothee … Sam

Harry Sinclair … Mike

Produced by Claire Hallereau with The Builders Association

Production manager: Neal Wilkinson

Technical design: Joe Silovsky

Technical development: Tom Korder

Touring technical director: Josh Higgason

Costume designer: Chantelle Norton

Video associates: Ed Purver, Austin Switser

Lighting associate: Laura Mroczkowski

Stage manager and company manager: Katie Goodwin

Video footage by

Harry Sinclair (Mike and additional characters)

James Gibbs (Las Vegas, Los Angeles, Tijuana)

Mathieu Borysevicz (Shanghai)

Ed Purver (Toronto)

Deb's blogs by Moe Angelos

Mirza family chats by Nabil Mirza, Rizwan Mirza, and Ariba Sultan

Additional design concepts by dbox

Additional dramaturgy by Jessica Chalmers

Consulting by Donna Cox and the National Center for Supercomputing Applications

Xubu website design and development by Nick Reid and Ryan Shaw

Kim Whitener, executive producer

Other credits:

Jessica Chalmers (small script credit)

John Cleater

David Tacheny

Special thanks: Anne Walsh, Shannon Jackson, Ken Goldberg

Website: Nick Reid, Ryan Shaw

Extra thank you to Jessica Dargo Caplan from Luminato

Video Credits

TIJUANA:

Production coordinator: Laura Irene Arvizu / Teeka Films

On video: Alexis Arias, Laura Irene Arvizu, Marcos Fonesca, Juan Parada (businessman)

TORONTO:

Production coordinator: Melissa Levin

On video: Valda Alleyne, Kidest Ashene, Seifu Tesfaye Belachew, Patricia Burgos, Vanessa Campbell, Ellen Mae Casao, Amanda Christo, Lesia Ciz, Diego Garcia, Peter Gomes, Fathima Hanseer, Mohamed Hanseer, Gaurav Sawhney, Edward Ulzen, Qiyan Uy, Leo Zuniga

Morcel Grant (mango song)

Amanda Christo (busineswoman)

Esther Jun (woman in bar)

Thanks to Cahoots Theater, Canadian Film Makers Distribution Centre (CFMDC), Gladstone Hotel (Chris Mitchell), Regent Park Focus Youth Media Group, Ryerson University Conference Services (Louisa Capetola), Touch Tel Wireless (Little India phone store), Adonis Huggins

Special thanks to Hussein Adan, owner of New Bilan Restaurant Shanghai:

Video production: Matieu Borysevicz

Production assistant: Zhang Mi

Shanghai twins: Zhuang Bin, Zhuang Kai

On video: Stephen Zhao (businessman), Yuan Xuezhi, Feng Jiehui, Lu Jiwei, Chen Feiting, Emily M. Liu Guang (Internet cafe owner)

Special thanks: Raymond Zhou

Venues

2008   Krannert Center for the Performing Arts, Urbana, IL

Walker Art Center, Minneapolis, MN

Yerba Buena Center for the Arts, San Francisco

Brooklyn Academy of Music (BAM) Next Wave Festival, Brooklyn, New York

Experimental Media and Performing Arts Center (EMPAC), Rensselaer, NY

2009   Festival de Leige, Liege, Belgium

Carolina Performing Arts, Chapel Hill, NC

La Jolla Playhouse, La Jolla, CA

Wexner Center for the Arts, Columbus, OH

Salamanca Festival of Theater, Salamanca, Spain

Luminato Festival, Toronto, Ontario

Metropolis Festival, Denmark

2010   LIFT Festival, London, England

Afterparty

Interview with actress Caroline O'Neill

What is your name?

Caroline O'Neill.

How old are you?

Nine.

Who is the character you play?

Sam. Short for Samantha.

What is CONTINUOUS CITY about?

Connecting to people you love.... If you're in one place, you might feel like your family's really far apart, but you have this wonderful technology to connect you.

How does Sam feel when she's on her own?

In the first part, she's a little sad. Then as the show goes on, her mood goes up.

How do you act sad?

I think about my grandpa, who died when I was little.

What was the process of working on a new play like?

It started last spring. Then we took a long break. Then we came back together and did all different things. The script changed completely.

How did you handle that?

Marianne [the director, Marianne Weems]. She's a very good person. She's helped me through the rough parts and easy parts.

What makes this play unique?

The screens. There are about 1,000 of them.

Source: Walker Arts Center Blog 10-21-2008, Emily Zimmer, http://blogs.walkerart.org/performingarts/2008/10/21/the-smallest-building-block.

From a cell phone video that was posted on an audience member's blog immediately after he saw the show at the Wexner Center for the Arts in Columbus, Ohio.

Hi, Andrew. We just … It's me and your sister, and uh, we just left the Wexner Center, and she's driving me home. We saw a great exhibit. I hope it's coming to Chicago. You should probably see it….

(Sister interjects something unintelligible from the driver's seat.)

Right. Anyway, it's about how we're connected all the time but never really there, and anyway, the displays on the stage were like the pictures … like the pictures in my brain at any given moment…. I'll send this to you when I get home.

Script session during rehearsal.

SOME SOURCE MATERIALS FOR THE PRODUCTION

Books

Abani, Chris. *GraceLand.* London: Picador, 2004.

Auge, Marc. *Non-Places: Introduction to an Anthropology of Supermodernity.* New York: Verso, 2009.

Bauman, Zygmunt. *Globalization: The Human Consequences.* New York: Columbia University Press, 1998.

Bauman, Zygmunt. *Wasted Lives: Modernity and Its Outcasts.* Cambridge: Polity Press, 2004.

Betsky, Aaron. *Architecture Must Burn: Manifestoes for the Future of Architecture.* Berkeley, CA: Gingko Press, 2001.

Broeze, Frank. *The Globalisation of the Oceans: Containerisation from the 1950s to the Present.* New York: International Maritime Economic History Association, 2002.

Cudahy, Brian J. *Box Boats: How Container Ships Changed the World.* New York: Fordham University Press, 2006.

Davis, Mike. *Dead Cities: And Other Tales.* New York: New Press, 2002.

Davis, Mike. *Planet of Slums.* New York: New Press, 2006.

Dorrian, Mark, and Gillian Rose, eds. *Deterritorialisations: Revisioning Landscapes and Politics.* London: Black Dog, 2003.

Eggers, Dave. *What Is the Wha? The Autobiography of Valentino Achak Deng.* San Francisco, CA: McSweeney's, 2006.

Levinson, Marc. *The Box: How the Shipping Container Made the World Smaller and the World Economy Bigger.* Princeton, NJ: Princeton University Press, 2006.

Mehta, Suketu. *Maximum City: Bombay Lost And Found.* New York: Vintage, 2004.

Neuwirth, Robert. *Shadow Cities: A Billion Squatters.* New York: Routledge, 2005.

Okri, Ben. *The Famished Road.* New York: Random House, 1991.

Sassen, Saskia, ed. *Deciphering the Global: Its Scales, Spaces, and Subjects.* New York: Routledge, 2008.

Sassen, Saskia. *Globalization and Its Discontents.* New York: New Press, 1998.

Schiller, Nina Glick, and Georges Eugene Fouron. *Georges Woke Up Laughing; Long-Distance Nationalism and the Search for Home.* Durham, NC: Duke University Press, 2001.

Seabrook, Jeremy. *In the Cites of the South: Scenes from a Developing World.* New York: Verso, 1996.

Sieverts, Thomas. *Cities without Cities: An Interpretation of the Zwischenstadt.* New York: Routledge, 1997.

Tomlinson, John. *Globalization and Culture.* Chicago: University of Chicago, 2007.

Virilio, Paul. *City of Panic.* Oxford : Bloomsbury Academic, 2007.

Vladislavic, Ivan. *The Exploded View.* New York: Random House, 2004.

Articles

Murphy, Kate. "Abroad at Home." *New York Times*, January 6, 2007.

Nicholson, Chris. "In Poorer Nations, Cellphones Help Open Up Microfinancing." *New York Times*, July 9, 2007, sec. C6, p. 1.

Pontin, Jason. "From Many Tweets, One Loud Voice on the Internet." *New York Times*, April 22, 2007.

Richtel, Matt, and Brad Stone. "Social Networking Leaves Confines of the Computer." *New York Times*, April 30, 2007.

Richtel, Matt, and Brad Stone. "Web Sites Invite Girls to Come Over to Play." *Times Digest*, June 6, 2007.

Ruskoff, Douglas. "Look at Me: The Other Side of Internet Voyeurism." *Rushkoff.* Blog, March 2001.

Sassen, Saskia. "Naked Cities, Struggle in the Global Slums." *Mute: Culture and Politics after the Net* 2 (3) (1999).

Turkle, Sherry. "Always-on /Always-on-You: The Tethered Self." In *Handbook of Mobile Communication Studies*, ed. James Katz. Cambridge, MA: MIT Press, 2008.

Web

boyd, danah. "Socializing Digitally." Accessed July 5, 2007. http://www.receiver.vodafone.com/article18_1.php.

Ruggeri, Laura. "Palm Springs: Imagineering California in Hong Kong." 1991–1994. http://www.spacing.org.

Shrinking Cities Group. Institute of Urban and Regional Development. University of California, Berkley. Accessed December 12, 2007. http://www-iurd.ced.berkeley.edu/scg.

Other

Koolhaas, Rem. *Lagos Wide and Close: An Interactive Journey into an Exploding City.* Submarine, 2005. DVD

Taking Place. Exhibition and events initiated by Sam Gould, Stephanie Snyder, and Matthew Stadler. Portland, Oregon, July 22–September 12, 2005.

OPENINGS

In the blackness, the sound of orchestra instruments being tuned rises. Streams of violas, violins, and cellos layer on each other, growing from a hum to a cry, a preamble and prophesy that something is about to begin. As wind instruments flutter into the mix, performers appear far upstage and smoothly maneuver large sections of wooden frames and projection surfaces to form the structure of a two-story house. A horizontal band of video appears from on high and lowers to the ground, followed by another horizontal band and another and another. Soon it becomes clear that digital clapboard planks are being projected onto a physical house, creating a structure board by board in a modified game of Lincoln Logs. The music welcomes the creation into existence as projected windows and gables appear. The sound rises to the height of anticipation and then recedes quickly but gently, lightly ceasing as the final physical piece of a house, the pediment, is flown in from above.

The luminescent house suddenly dims when a large video screen lights up behind it. A man with trim brown hair and a "business casual" shirt is being interviewed: "My name is Elan Daniel. I am working in Weinland Park. We're working to revitalize the neighborhood by buying and fixing up houses and selling them to lower- to moderate-income families." He describes one of the houses that his company bought ("1463 North Fourth Street") and the search for its previous owner, apparently a former secretary in manufacturing who could not make the mortgage payments on her home. Daniel then gestures behind him to a wall lined with photos of houses: "So this is my 'ladder of distress,' otherwise known as the 'wall of shame.'" He describes his process for assessing the level of distress and repair to a foreclosed home, tabulating investment and turnaround—that is, the potential for transforming one person's shame into another person's acquisition.

When Daniel finishes, the screen changes again, this time to a vast ochre-colored sky of fog, dust, and wind. The camera pans along the sky as the live twang of a slide guitar follows, setting the scene for an omniscient storyteller, who emerges from the dim house and begins to crank a reel-to-reel tape deck by hand: "To the red country and part of the grey country of Oklahoma, the last rains came gently, and they did not cut the scarred earth. The sky grew pale and cloudless, and the sun glared down." The voice of the narrator of John Steinbeck's *The Grapes of Wrath* fills the theater, slowly evoking a scene in language as spare as the dry plains described: "Men and women huddled, protected in the little houses and outside there was nothing except the dry corn threshing the wind—a dry, rushing sound—and the dust, and the darkening sky. The men were silent and did not move often, and the women worked, cooking from the dwindling stores, and they watched the men, watching to see and feel whether this time the men would break."

HOUSE/DIVIDED was first presented by The Builders Association in workshop form at the Wexner Center for the Arts at The Ohio State University in 2010, premiered professionally at the Wexner the following year, and traveled to the Brooklyn Academy of Music, ArtsEmerson in Boston, and

Eviction scene based on *The Grapes of Wrath*.

An intricately staged scene from the Federal Theater Project Production of *One-Third of a Nation*, Seattle, Washington 1938. Courtesy University of Washington Libraries, Special Collections SOC1109.

other spaces. It addressed themes that were both familiar and startlingly new—the effects of falling markets and housing foreclosures on the lives of US citizens. In many ways, this story of hardship was a familiar American theme. It was endured in the late nineteenth century and in the Great Depression and was chronicled by journalists, novelists, photographers, and theater makers. Artists and craftspeople hired in the 1930s by Franklin Delano Roosevelt's Works Progress Administration mined such stories and devised new documentary aesthetic forms in which to present them. HOUSE/ DIVIDED was The Builders' own documentary response to a twenty-first-century global crisis where the Americanization of markets heightened global risk. It was also, in many ways, a return. This show prompted Builders artists to revisit the canonically American tale of John Steinbeck and also the precarious house and divided set that had launched them as master builders almost twenty years earlier.

R&D

While CONTINUOUS CITY toured in 2008 and 2009, the cast followed alarming news stories of a financial crisis in the interdependent systems of the global financial markets and in the mortgages, retirement funds, and savings of the individuals tied to them. Stocks plummeted, unemployment soared, companies declared bankruptcy, borrowers defaulted, debtors foreclosed, and some banks were declared too big to fail. Between venues on the CONTINUOUS CITY tour, Builders artists thought about the next one, in part because it was almost impossible not to. Weems convened a collective think tank in July 2009 at the upstate home of sound designer Dan Dobson and Chantelle Norton in Cold Spring, New York. Weems sent an exploratory prompt by email:

My immediate thoughts are centering around the housing/foreclosure crisis and what that means in terms of ownership, the American suburban landscape, a revisioning of Master Builder set, etc. However, I'm well aware that by the time this show goes up, the future will be here, and this moment will have faded away. So let's spread the net wide; I'm suggesting we go on a full-frontal literature spree in order to think about the past and the future of domestic space in America. I'd like to spend a good deal of time reading plays and books (out loud) and watching movies or anything else people can bring re: housing.

In Cold Spring, Weems introduced the idea of having The Builders revisit the company's original 1994 piece, MASTER BUILDER, to rethink, repurpose, and recycle the ideas and design elements in that production. They recalled some of the basic technologies that they used to hack and rewire the reproduction of Gordon Matta-Clark's cut house. They recalled the inspiration of critics and artists who thought deeply about our psychic and material relationships to space, including Beatriz Colomina, Laura Mulvey, and Robert Smithson. The memories prompted further reflections on how much the concepts of a house and domicile had changed from 1993 to the foreclosure meltdown of 2007 to 2009. James Gibbs pointed out that "even the idea of owning a house had itself become 'foreclosed,' leaving that part of the American Dream bankrupt." After two days of discussion, Moe Angelos proposed a scenario for exploration of this changing relationship to the house:

We thought about The House as a tragic Hero, a character that is caught in a web of circumstances beyond her/his control, circumstances that can only lead to a downfall which cannot be averted. As the day progressed we talked about the idea of "just buying a foreclosed house" and putting that on stage and creating the play in that house.

They considered how they would get an entire house onstage, and this conversation circled back to the abandoned idea of using shipping containers for the CONTINOUS CITY set. Brooklyn Academy of Music (BAM) executive producer Joe Melillo's warning about what could and could not fit through a stage door rang in their ears.

After brainstorming about the architectural and sculptural form of the set, they turned to researching the themes and text of the show. They found countless online video interviews with foreclosed homeowners and others who were unexpectedly homeless. At this point in time—mid-2009—they found that the prevailing undertone of news reporting was that homeowners or former owners were still largely to blame for their misfortunes, an assumption that shifted in the coming months. At Weems's request, one evening, the group watched the classic John Ford film of John Steinbeck's novel *The Grapes of Wrath* and the next day read passages of the novel aloud to each other. Although most had read it before, they were surprised by the beauty of Steinbeck's language.

Foreclosed house on North Fourth Street
in Columbus, Ohio, 2008.

Research: *Feral House* by James D. Griffoen.

Gibbs was captivated by the omniscient voice, particularly by its scope and capacity to encompass enormous systems, geographies, weather fronts, economic patterns, and migratory patterns. At the end of the workshop, they decided provisionally to sideline other themes and move forward with two thematic domains—*The Grapes of Wrath* text and the current foreclosure crisis. Collaborator Matthew Karges agreed to set up a collective website (which he named "The Jalopy") that would allow each artist to upload research findings and view the contributions of others. They crafted a rough calendar for the development of the show that was, at that point, still titled "Master Builder 2.0." After

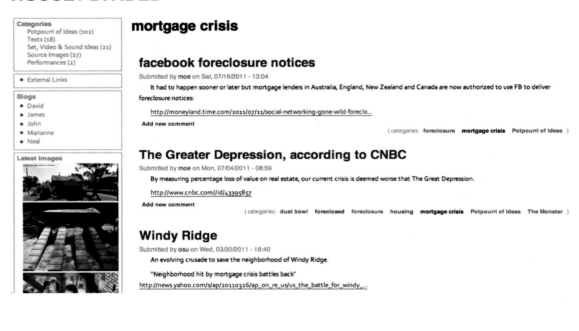

Group research site: The jalopy created by company member Matthew Karges.

committing to the next production dates, they dispersed. Everyone returned to homes and to day jobs, knowing that both were hard to come by for many US citizens.

The process of research and development winnowed down quickly from the abstractions of architectural and philosophical theory—including readings by Walter Benjamin, Gaston Bachelard, and Le Corbusier—toward what Weems called "the matter at hand, foreclosures taking place all around us." In being compelled by the immediate context, their process unintentionally followed that of the Federal Theater Project of the 1930s, a national project that aspired to make use of what its director, Hallie Flanagan, called "the entertainment value of the fact."[1] For The Builders, the overwhelming "facts" of financial disaster were everywhere: "most of the inspiration came screaming out of the pages of the *Times* and endless footage on TV and on YouTube drawn from personal stories of the foreclosure crisis."[2] Nearly eighty years earlier, Flanagan extolled the potential of a theatrical form called The Living Newspaper, which was a flexible, intermedia container that could feature and juxtapose the "screaming" stories of the Great Depression. In a brief to the Federal Patent Commission, she extolled The Living Newspaper as a "terse cinematic, hard-hitting dramatic form [that] deals with contemporary factual material: Agriculture in *Triple-A Ploughed Under*; Labor in the Courts in *Injunction Granted*; Housing in *One Third of a Nation*."[3] As the theatrical arm of an expansive federal program that pressed artists into national service, such plays mined the real-world tales of farmers, workers, and those without homes in the 1930s. Eleanor Roosevelt lauded *One-Third of a Nation* ... for relaying the experience of that era's housing crisis better than any political study: "we couldn't have it shown more truthfully or dramatically."[4]

Perhaps more than any other Builders production thus far, HOUSE/DIVIDED participated in a tradition of documentary theater, and this one was placed within a Federal Theater Project genealogy. As a twenty-first-century version of a Living Newspaper, this piece recalled what *One Third of a Nation*'s director, Arthur Arent, described as a piece "composed in greater or lesser extent of many news events, all bearing on the subject and interlarded with typical but non-factual representations of the effects of these news events on the people to whom the problem is of great importance."[5] Like documentary theaters of the past, HOUSE/DIVIDED artists found themselves embroiled in "facts," assailed by the hyperempiricism of struggle and loss, moved to focus on "actual" events and the "real" stories of individuals who had less patience for aesthetic abstraction. This immersion in the factual paralleled the process of earlier WPA artists, photographers, writers, and theater-makers, and it also transformed mundane realities into representations that were newly luminous. Much as Flanagan, Dorothea Lange, or James Agee used aesthetic skills to gain new perspectives on the "abstractions" of stock market crashes and economic depression, so The Builders found themselves interested in concretizing a twenty-first-century financial crisis, showing the "effect ... on the people to whom the problem is of great importance."[6]

As a new media theater company, The Builders had always resisted easy oppositions between the real and the virtual, between the live and the mediated. However, the goals of documentary art complicated the assumptions of these new media conversations. The values of "truth" and the "factual" had a different urgency in a situation where citizens found themselves bankrupted by deceitful Ponzi schemes. When investors took "risks" in seemingly weightlessly global markets, it seemed important to dramatize the weight of the lives affected. In imagining a twenty-first-century version of a Living Newspaper, The Builders had an expanded array of news formats at their disposal (including YouTube), which in turn expanded the definition of what qualified as cinematic in this journalist aesthetic form. But the compulsion of what Benjamin H. D. Buchloh has called the "factographic" impulse of earlier political art movements played itself out once again here.[7] Recalling earlier traditions—Progressive Era muckraking, Constructivist avant-gardes, New Deal aesthetics— The Builders' pursuit of the dramatized fact shared in the impulse to understand the appeal of both the fact and the construction of the fact, creating an arena that featured but also questioned the reality of the referent it purportedly signified.

In their respective locations, each Builders artist began to collect and upload articles, images, and stories that were related to the foreclosure crisis and to the Depression Era context of Steinbeck's classic novel. Weems, Angelos, and Matt Karges visited a homeless encampment in Cedar Bridge, New Jersey, that was informally supervised by a pastor named Reverend Steve. There, homeless people, including those who had been recently foreclosed on, built an unsanctioned tent city in the woods next to a strip mall. For Angelos, the encampment uncannily recalled the imagery of the Dust Bowl: "They are modern day Joads on the road with no fixed addresses. The 'squatters' have built amazing structures for homes and community spaces using found materials."[8] The same sense of aesthetic reuse in the face of hardship had propelled Steinbeck's *The Grapes of Wrath* as well as *Triple-A Plowed Under* and *One Third of a Nation*, the Federal Theater Project's much earlier intermedia investigations into the plight of dislocated citizens.

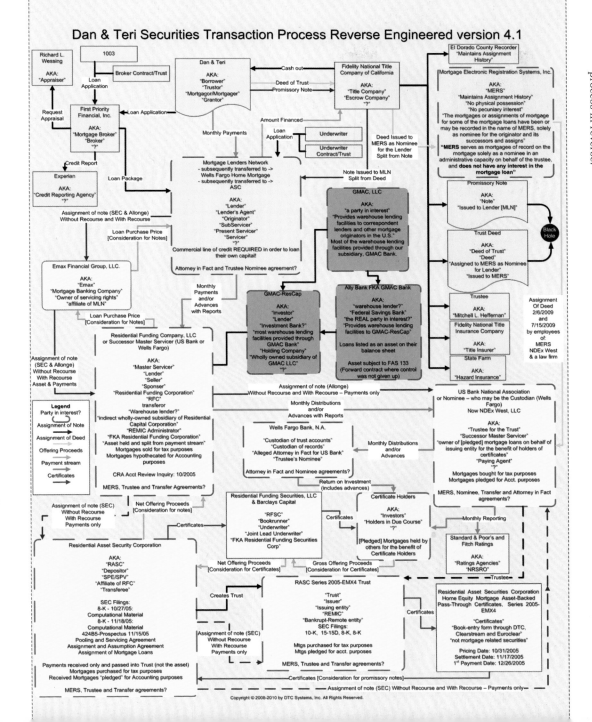

Dan & Teri Securities Transaction Process Reverse Engineered version 4.1

351

A couple's chart of their securities transaction process in reverse.

Cedar Bridge encampment, New Jersey, 2010.

Real estate consultant Elan Daniel tracks local
foreclosed houses.

OPERATING SYSTEMS

A central piece of the R&D for this show was
documentary interviews, and the access and
creation of such interviews was enabled by
a central operating system, a campus arts
residency at the Wexner Center for the Arts at
The Ohio State University in Columbus. The
Wexner Center had already been among the
most stalwart of the Builders' supporters, often
commissioning and consistently presenting
their productions from ALLADEEN on. Chuck
Helm, director of performing arts at the Wexner
Center, took the lead on this production,
applying for and receiving significant funds for
the piece and campus collaboration through
the Creative Campus Innovations Grant
Program funded by the Doris Duke Charitable
Foundation. The goal of the program was to
"foster interdisciplinary exchange on campuses
using the arts as a catalyst."[9]

The process of conceiving a grant
application required—and enabled—more
research. Gibbs, Angelos, Erica Laird, and
Weems made several trips to The Ohio State
University campus in Columbus. They held
exploratory meetings with faculty from across
the campus—including English literature,

theater, landscape architecture, history, agriculture, business, and architecture—seeking overlaps and synergies between The Builders' project and their teaching and research interests. Several professors signed on and began to conceive related workshops and research projects for their students. Weems and Angelos also met students at the Knowlton School of Architecture, led with the help of professors Jane Amidon, Jennifer Evans-Cowley, and Katherine Bennett. The workshop plotted connections among The Builders' emerging concepts and the scholars' expertise in housing and land use. At that time, The Builders found themselves in conversations with graduate students from the Fisher College of Business, one of whom had recently been through the foreclosure process. Excerpts from her articulate and highly emotional portrait of her dilemma in February 2010 became one of the documentary anchors of the show:

My name is Eve Wendzicki, and I am an MBA candidate at the Fisher College of Business. I recently found myself in the foreclosure process in the last year. One of the harder emotional parts is wondering what others think because there's a kind of a stigma you have to fight against. It's like thinking, "Hey, I'm not this person. I never bought a house or entered into a homeowner state knowing that it's not going to work out and that I won't be able to repay my loans." The interesting thing you have to struggle with is "Who am I?" You may have in your head a depiction of who somebody that's homeless is and who somebody who needs assistance or has to visit a food pantry is, and the reality of the unemployment situation especially in an extended circumstance like this is that it's breaking down every preconceived notion because you find that you are that person.

After receiving the Creative Campus grant, The Builders and Chuck Helm at the Wexner Center carried this process forward on many levels, including two more research and educational trips in October 2010 and January 2011. Weems, Gibbs, Angelos, and John Cleater returned to Columbus to visit the project-based classes created to do local research for the show. As they heard more stories of foreclosure, the idea of using a foreclosed house as the basis for a set returned to them. Placing such a resonant infrastructure into the theater space recalled MASTER BUILDER but also underscored the economic systems and housing politics that both enabled Gordon Matta-Clark's patrons to purchase such a home for *Splitting* back in 1974. Weems and Angelos also visited nearby Cleveland, where they talked with urban farmers and activists who worked in half-abandoned sections of the city, often on the deserted plots of foreclosed properties. Many referred to themselves as "guerrilla gardeners." Although in some ways they recalled Dust Bowl farmers of yore, this time they were extracting resources from the earth while manmade structures crumbled around them.

As research continued, a larger team of designers joined the core group: Cleater, Austin Switser, Neal Wilkinson, and others joined another residency in Columbus in January. Following up on research conducted by themselves, students, and faculty, they conducted a series of interviews with citizens in Columbus, Ohio. In addition to speaking with foreclosed former homeowners, they also met several people who held various jobs in the foreclosure industry. It was particularly unexpected and unsettling to meet workers who performed "trash-outs" in foreclosed homes with teams of people who were hired to remove quickly and efficiently all of the personal items left behind when former owners left their homes. They told stories of found clothes, furniture, dolls, photographs, and other mementoes of the intimate life that had been enjoyed in the house. Professor Katherine Bennett introduced them to Elan Daniel, a real estate developer at Wagenbrenner who bought and renovated foreclosed homes in an underresourced section of town that abutted the OSU campus and whose interview ultimately opened the show. Daniel offered to take them around Weinland Park to look at some of the foreclosed homes in his company's portfolio, allowing them also to take video footage for possible use in the show. Angelos recalled an encounter with the remains of a household: "One of the houses has fallen victim to the serial arsonist of the neighborhood and is completely open to the elements. We venture inside and take still photos, with all of the belongings of the last owner laying charred in piles in the front and side yards, covered with snow."[10] In addition to documenting the exteriorized interiors of singular houses, they also filmed the wider neighborhood. Austin Switser documented from the open side door of their rented minivan as they drove through the snowy, deserted streets.

Foreclosed house repurposed
as the set of HOUSE/DIVIDED.

Company members Josh Higgason (above) and Moe Angelos (below) deconstructing the North Fourth Street house.

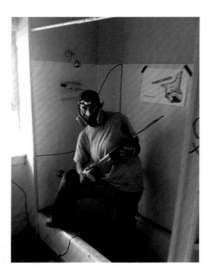

Finding themselves surrounded by objects and structures that were resonant with human loss, The Builders felt acutely the need to place these symbols of stalled domesticity onstage. Whatever the size of any stage door or loading dock, they felt that they wanted to have this highly political and intimately material experience of foreclosure inside the theater, an unavoidably "factographic" remnant of the crisis. Daniel steered them toward two foreclosed houses that had been placed at the bottom of the "ladder of distress" and were slated for demolition. After some quick negotiation and intervention with permits and insurance, Wagenbrenner agreed to give The Builders full access to the two houses, letting them cut away and repurpose walls, windows, gables, and sections of roof from these two abandoned properties. Cleater, Angelos, Switser, Josh Higgason, and Neal Wilkinson entered the foreclosed houses and—in a collective replay of Gordon Matta-Clark's process—cut up the walls, removing whole sections of the bathroom and kitchen, and interior walls. They also uprooted the actual pediment of the house to incarnate Cleater and Wilkinson's master plans for the set. It was an uncanny and emotional redefining of the practice of the trash-out, this time extracting pieces not for resale or landfill but for aesthetic re-assembly. In humid, eighty-degree weather, they spent three days in the houses with no ventilation, also salvaging household objects that had been melted by fire or damaged by rain. Angelos recalled that raccoons and rodents had also contributed to the premises. The company placed the collected parts into a storage unit in Columbus and layered them with antitermite chemicals. The process incarnated the paradox of politically engaged art making. On the one hand, the extraction of these structures embodied an ethic of reuse and recycling, paving the way for them to politicize stories of human loss in the theater. On the other hand, the artists felt intently the politics of appropriating such symbols of human loss, scavenging amid the wreckage of a war.

The mandate to repurpose documentary details and recycle old structures extended to the technology in this production as well. As always, projectors were acquired, and software was upgraded for HOUSE/DIVIDED, but the ethos of the material combined with a tight budget prompted the designers to repurpose old cameras and other gear. In a reversal of his usual approach, sound designer Dan Dobson created music live during the performance, designing and building his own elaborate electric zither, which he played onstage. His music was mixed by a fellow sound engineer, Matt O'Hare, who added additional tracks from the front of house, but ultimately, the zither and the live voices of the actors drove the pace and emotional undercurrent of the show. A reviewer for the *Boston Globe* wrote, "Dobson's compositions and his alternately pulsating and percussive sound design generate an aura of danger and crisis that make you feel like you're witnessing a crime, which in a sense you are."[11]

Around this time, The Builders also began to think inventively—and retrospectively—about how to embody the narrator of the show. They decided to heighten the relationship between past and present by delivering this voice from an old, once-new, media technology—a reel-to-reel tape recorder. The machine was retrofitted with a hand-held crank, and when operated by an actor, the actor's gestures were reminiscent of someone trying to start an old jalopy. Excerpts from the voice of Steinbeck's omniscient narrator (voiced by performer Jess Barbagallo) could be cued on the tape and played by the actors as they cranked the recorder, allowing the voice to unfurl as their arms rotated round and round.

STORYBOARD

After The Builders decided to adapt and perform from a classic text—something that they had not done since IMPERIAL MOTEL (FAUST) and JUMP CUT (FAUST)—the process of storyboarding coincided with the evolving research and operational development of the set. They knew that they wanted to juxtapose the Steinbeck text with documentation of the US foreclosure crisis and with scenes from the global financial sector where investments, currencies, and banking systems were negotiated. After some effort, they received approval from the John Steinbeck estate to use *The Grapes of Wrath* as a source text. The agreement read, in part, as follows:

Owner has agreed to allow Lessee to include the title of the Work
as a subtitle to the Play as follows:
HOUSE/DIVIDED
Inspired by THE GRAPES OF WRATH

Recalling prior struggles over the role played by writers inside the process, they decided to give different artists the chance to contribute to a variety of media forms. The group turned to long-time collaborators actor/researcher Moe Angelos and dramaturg/designer James Gibbs to create the text. "At the beginning I thought, 'I have no idea what this is going to be,' recalled Angelos, "but I'll do it."[12] In Weems's view, the decision was a relief. As artists who saw their artistic contributions as component parts of an intermedia assembly, these two approached the production of text with the same attitude. "Moe and James knew exactly what to write and what to leave unwritten, leaving space for all visuals and set ideas," recalled Weems: "Not one stage direction."[13] Gibbs and Angelos divided the work of writing, passing drafts back and forth. As Gibbs recalls:

For me the script really cohered following the decision to use, as a structuring device, two sets of nonnarrative text: the bigger "superomniscient" narrator from *Grapes of Wrath*, and the transcripts of financial firms' earnings results conference calls. These form the backbone or organizing principle of the text, and they are then interwoven with more character-driven, dialog-based text: the direct dialog of the Joads and that of our portfolio managers, Cliff and Marty, and of the other contemporary characters, operators, and employees trapped in, or complicit in, the recent financial crisis. They led us, in the end, to the FCIC [Financial Crisis Inquiry Commission] testimony of Alan Greenspan, which is, in a way, or synthesis of all of the above: a self-consciously engineered record of conflict and confrontation with a man who sees himself as "above" history even as he attempts to obfuscate and spin the facts and his own record.[14]

To dramatize the global scale of the financial sector, Gibbs listened to and drew from transcripts of earnings results conference calls from Bear Stearns, Lehman Brothers, and Goldman Sachs. Greenspan's testimony was indeed a performance that offered exposition and information while simultaneously embodying the anxious interdependencies of national governance structures and international markets. Gibbs reflects:

I remember one afternoon when I found our first earnings call transcript—the Bear Stearns call from just before the first market collapse—and I met Marianne to discuss it. We were in a cab on the way to her apartment, and I was so excited about the text that I brought it out and started reading it aloud in the cab. The fact that it was direct documentation of the crisis, and the hubris it showed before the fall ... and it really is boastful and unbelievable with the benefit of hindsight ... these things were so exciting and fresh that I knew we'd found one of the keys to the whole piece.[15]

Angelos and Gibbs began crafting dialogue around the experience of foreclosure, drawing inspiration from websites on foreclosed properties, abandoned neighborhoods, and wildlife and

Scene based on Alan Greenspan's testimony before
the FCIC, Sean Donovan as Alan Greenspan.

nuisance control and the transcripts of governmental and bank call centers that negotiated unpaid mortgages and bankruptcies. Initially imagining a family that had a house foreclosed on in California and moved east to Detroit, the text included stories and references to housing depreciation, animal and human invasion, police presence (or lack thereof)—all in an attempt to incarnate the testimonies of shell-shocked homeowners who were in the process of losing their homes.

Unusually for The Builders, these suppliers of textual material created a relatively complete script before the actors began rehearsal. Typically, the text for Builders shows was crafted during rehearsals. In this case, the artists began assembly and performance with a solid text, even though much of the text was reshuffled and deleted. Dan Dobson invoked a musical analogy in relation to textual and intermedia production: "everyone is doing their part of the thing and you need all of them to understand the story."[16] At their first workshop rehearsal at the Performing Garage in New York, they trimmed and refined some scenes, created new ones, and deleted some. Said Angelos, "Sometimes what Marianne thinks is pertinent and sometimes I thought of it as secondary. At some points she was listening from the outside and I was listening from the inside—a performer writing for performers. She would take that material and tailor it to the larger vision. James, working with Marianne in rehearsals, remained on the outside advocating for what parts of the text were critical, what needed to stay in order to keep the structure afloat."[17]

Ultimately, they decided that the storyline of the script (a family that lost its California home to foreclosure and headed back to Detroit) was too "on the nose," too literal an arc and reenactment of the Steinbeck story. They discovered instead that simply "delivering sections of the omniscient narratives in the novel was a satisfying way to guide the story."[18] The recycled Steinbeck text thus became the sole driver of the story and also functioned as a fellow object in the midst of bodies, images, and recycled structures. The decision to use a kind of narrator figure was unusual for The Builders yet familiar to anyone who knew the history of the Federal Theater Project, where the voice of Living Newspapers functioned both to chronicle dramatic action and cajole and comment. Here, however, the juxtaposition of scene and disembodied voice functioned variously and sometimes ambiguously. Steinbeck's narration occupied scenic space as another form of found material, lending uncannily appropriate wisdom from the past while also offering itself as a specimen to be examined, a wondrous historical object brought back to the light of day:

Workshop version of the jalopy, set elements by Neal Wilkinson.

The Bank or the Company—needs—wants—insists—must have—as though the Bank or the Company were a monster, with thought and feeling, which had ensnared them.... The bank—the monster—has to have profits all the time. It can't wait. It'll die. No, taxes go on. When the monster stops growing, it dies. It can't stay one size.[19]

REHEARSAL/ASSEMBLY

The process of assembly leading to the first performance followed an attenuated schedule in 2011—winter in Columbus, Ohio; a May workshop at the Performing Garage in New York; a July workshop at the Baryshnikov Arts Center in New York; and an October premiere at the Wexner Center for the Arts in Columbus, concluding The Ohio State Creative Campus residency. At the Performing Garage, the script was renamed "Road Trip" and still followed a storyline about the uprooting of an upper-middle-class family. Played by long-time collaborators David Pence and Moira Driscoll and their children, Owen Pence (age fifteen) and Mabel Pence (age eleven), the family was forced to leave its Inland Empire McMansion in Bakersfield, California (one of the epicenters of the foreclosure crisis). They moved east toward Detroit after hearing that "they are giving away land" to people who seek an agricultural life in "blighted" urban areas.

These contemporary scenes were interspersed with snippets from *The Grapes of Wrath*, using dialog from the book and requiring the actors to struggle awkwardly with the Okie dialect and directness of the language. "Somewhere in this workshop Stewart Laing (set designer for SUPER VISION) dropped by and read the 'omniscient' voice of the third person chapters in his quiet, wry manner," recalled Weems. Gibbs described these interstitial chapters as "a 'superomniscient' narrator that discusses events and patterns on the scale of the continent and the economic system, discussing principles of governance and revolt, patterns of weather and climate, and the ways these come to affect populations." In any case, Weems said of Laing's reading: "It was immediately clear that Steinbeck's overarching chapters could act as a structuring device."[20]

The John Ford film adaptation of *The Grapes of Wrath* was a central inspiration for the videoscape of the show. Research revealed, however, that the per-minute price tag of using the film ($10,000) was financially prohibitive. Necessity being the mother of invention, video designer Austin Switser appropriated the black-and-white aesthetic of the John Ford film using the same framing devices, giving Builders performers on screen the same ochre sheen and hard-bitten demeanor of the Okies of

In workshop, Moira Driscoll as a middle-class migrant.

Ford's "realistic" Oklahoma Dust Bowl. They thus created a live enactment of the film's classic cinematography.

These scenes were juxtaposed with images from the road in contemporary America (including images of gated communities, foreclosed and abandoned neighborhoods, and Walmart parking lots). The screen cut to local TV newscasters reporting on the growing foreclosure crisis and then moved to YouTube dialogue of teens discussing what they would do with the money they earned by emptying abandoned homes. In his review for the *New York Times*, Charles Isherwood summarized the effect of these narrative details as "mordant" in their resonance:

"House/Divided" finds some surprising nuggets of dark humor in its exploration of the indignities of the foreclosure crisis. At one point one of the performers mimics the automated voice from a call center: "Hello!" it chirps like a metallic bird. "Are you having problems meeting your payments?" Another segment, both funny and chilling, depicts a man whose possessions are being tossed out onto the road calling his bank, only to find that nobody quite knows who owns his house anymore. Mordant too is the scene in which a female banker calls a sheriff, preparing to ask him to clear a house of squatters; before she can pose the question, he nervously blurts out, "I sent it!"—assuming the call was an inquiry into a late payment. He also tells her, with no small satisfaction, that he and his deputies have better things to do than harass desperate people on behalf of a bank.[21]

By July, the plot of the Bakersfield family had been eliminated. The group wanted to find a way to connect the experience of foreclosure with the wider systems of the financial marketplace. While in New York, an interview with stockbroker Mark Hanratty inspired the space and vocabulary of new dialogue from the trading floor. When The Builders worried that they were reproducing stereotypes in peppering the dialogue of traders and portfolio managers with curse words, Hanratty rolled his eyes: "It is like ten times worse."[22] They created a video stream of stock prices flitting colorfully across the top of the stage space as traders quickly and crudely joked, speculating in what Frank Norris might have called "The Pit" below. Their staccato tempo recalled that of other investigative theaters of the market, such as Caryl Churchill's *Serious Money* (1987) and David Hare's *The Power of Yes* (2009).

Returning to Ohio for a last production push, The Builders refined the process of assembly. The preserved housing parts from Weinland Park were removed from storage and constructed/deconstructed into a set, a repurposed structure conceived and installed by set designers John Cleater and Neal Wilkinson and technical designer Josh Higgason. The core structure looked like a classic Midwestern clapboard frame house. The walls of the house were in fact the visual effect of a screen projection, an array of blocked scrims on which different housing structures appeared and disappeared.

Although these intermedia techniques adapted the forms of earlier Builders works, their use in a piece driven by documentary investigation highlighted their connection to the intermedia aesthetic of the Living Newspaper, one whose "techniques handbook" avidly encouraged artists to juxtapose multiple locations and to use the then latest technology to compel spectatorial attention. Hallie Flanagan had developed the intermedia aesthetic of the Living Newspaper after seeing it in operation in the Constructivist theaters of the Soviet Union. It is a reminder of how deeply the journalist impulses of "factographic" art were offset and refracted by the collage aesthetics of intermedia art, which juxtaposed scenes and time frames and used scrims, sound effects, and shadow play to evoke and question different realities. In 1938, the Federal Theater Project compiled a guide called "Techniques Available to the Living Newspaper Dramatist" describing elements that were important to this approach. It includes the recommendation, "The Living Newspaper dramatist should, whenever possible, conceive of his stage as a mobile area, unencumbered by bulky, fixed sets—a stage pliable and subject to swift change."[23] Characteristics of the Living Newspaper productions included quick scene and set changes, flexible stage space, using many levels, rolling and hand-carried scenery, and scrims that established many locations without elaborate constructed sets.[24]

The Builders' intermedia forms were thus in unwitting dialogue with the intermedia forms of earlier documentary theater. Over six weeks of rehearsal, the house was choreographed materially and virtually to divide and deconstruct itself, coming apart as the housing/market crisis wiped out equity and capital all over the country. John Cleater used this collaboration with the Builders to launch his Augmented Reality app, which allowed spectators to view the set through digital fields that were visible inside a smartphone. The show premiered as a conclusion to a campus residency in October 2011 with a title that stuck: HOUSE/DIVIDED.

CLOSINGS

After premiering at the Wexner Center for the Arts in Columbus, Ohio, HOUSE/DIVIDED was remounted at the University of Illinois's Krannert Center for the Performing Arts in Urbana, Illinois, the Brooklyn Academy of Music (just before Hurricane Sandy), and ArtsEmerson in Boston. Reviews were positive about its treatment of the content and its aesthetics of assembly:

The evening's seven performers—Ms. Angelos, Jess Barbagallo, Sean Donovan, Matthew Karges, LaToya Lewis, David Pence, and Mabel Pence—play several roles each. I mean no disrespect in saying that no one

HOUSE/DIVIDED performers Jess Barbagallo and
Sean Donovan as mortgage brokers, Moe Angelos as
Ma Joad (seated at the reel-to-reel tape recorder).

makes a particularly strong impression: this is ensemble work so cleanly executed that the focus always remains on the larger story being told, not any particular individual within it. By the same token, while the contributions of the designers are all terrific—Jennifer Tipton's ever-elegant, ever-unobtrusive lighting; the complex video by Austin Switser; the sets by John Cleater and Neal Wilkinson; the haunting music and sound by Dan Dobson—at no point does one component of the show upstage another. As sophisticated as their contributions are individually, they are so artfully interlaced that they are hard to separate.[25]

Many of the artists played even more roles than were apparent from the stage, with actors serving as writers and designers working across several media at once. The sense of ensemble that was apparent in the show stood in counterpoint to the highly individuated assumptions of the voices that it documented. This mix of form and content allowed The Builders to demonstrate that the financial market was, after all, an interdependent ensemble. Unintentionally, the commitment to ensemble replicated the ethos of the Federal Theater Project: "here is play that has no hero, or heroine, no great figure or fanciful character.... here is a play about you."[26]

At each stop on the tour, the script was updated to reflect the most recent earnings reports, attempting to keep time with an ever-present ticker tape. It was both striking and depressing that the foreclosure crisis was perceived to unfold throughout 2012, in some ways challenging the definition of *crisis*. The logic of crisis assumes an unexpected and seismic shift, an unanticipated shock that hides its connection to a series of decisions and fragile systems that were unfolding long before. Those decisions and systems continued and still continue long after, whether or not the shocking effects of crisis seem to recede. But the obscuring of that continuity allows some texts to appear timely and others to appear dated. Steinbeck's *The Grapes of Wrath* appeared timely in 1939, dated two decades later, and prescient when an apparently new set of circumstances in 2009 echoed the events of the 1930s. Weems had opened The Builders' first think tank worrying about such cycles and acknowledging that "this moment will have faded away" and that soon "the future will be here." Although some might decide that the themes of HOUSE/DIVIDED are now old news, one might wonder about the politics of attributing datedness. Perhaps we will always have to wait for a new "crisis" to expose the timelessness of something that we thought was timely, and the "prescience" of art that knows that the future is likely to be here again.

In performance: Sean Donovan, Moe Angelos, Jess Barbagallo (on video), Josh Higgason.

ENDNOTES

Artist's Voice: John Cleater, set designer

We built the three-story house for MASTER BUILDER to include multiple unfoldings, unpeelings, trap stairs, trap doors, and rotating walls. Given the organic process of making work with The Builders, most of these set tricks were incorporated after the main structure was built. In fact, the final model and drawings were made after the set was completed. After six months of this, we decided that the grand finale ought to be the entire house splitting in half. When I proposed this to our Technical Director, Michael Casselli, he nearly blew his lid. But he did it and the house survived.

In HOUSE/DIVIDED, we again put a very physical two-story house on stage that transforms through space and time. This was a feat of pride for Neal and me. Our foreclosed house from Columbus, Ohio manifests itself as a Walmart parking lot, Peach stand, Trading Floor, Train Car, Court Room and the 1920s home of the Joads. The impulse to re-purpose, re-cycle and re-think the simple architectural frame remains a preoccupation of the Builders.

—edited by Eleanor Bishop

Guest Voice: Kate Valk, founding member, The Wooster Group

I remember seeing MASTER BUILDER, the first piece Marianne directed as The Builders Association. I had worked with her quite closely at the Wooster Group, so I knew about her vision and the nature of her inspiration and yet it was amazing to see that she could fill this giant, vast and cavernous piece of architecture, with a piece of architecture—the house. I loved the way she mixed high and low culture, (which is of course a place that we work from too) but it was great to see it in her style.

MASTER BUILDER was more dimensional than most theater I had seen. It felt like the whole house was taking place in time. Let alone no fourth wall, there were all the walls and all the floors and the grounds around it and the roof. There was a whole world that the theatrical text could live in, animated by these Led Zeppelin songs.

In JET LAG, I saw how huge her vision really is—it can take up quite literally a giant stage, but also large are the themes and the formal devices. In JET LAG, she took us outside of the theater space—it felt like we traveled. Again, it was this great architectural metaphor for the story she was telling. Always the formal elements are just as important as the story, which is something I relate to too, having worked with Liz all these years. Marianne is really, really good at staging an idea. There's always a lot of ideas in the Builders work but it's always very humanist—there's often a small witty story in there too. If you want to say that art is like bread-making then those stories are like the poppy seed on the giant thing she's making.

In the subsequent shows, Marianne and The Builders have continued to develop their own style and vision for staging these huge ideas. They have survived for twenty years, and I can't wait to see what the next twenty years will bring.

People

Conceived by

Marianne Weems, director

James Gibbs, co-creator/writer

Moe Angelos, writer/performer

Dan Dobson, sound design and original music composition

Austin Switser, video design

Jennifer Tipton, lighting design

Laura Mroczkowski, co-lighting design

John Cleater and Neal Wilkinson, scenic concept and design

John Cleater, augmented reality design

Performed by

Moe Angelos

Jess Barbagallo

Sean Donovan

Matthew Karges

LaToya Lewis

David Pence

Mabel Pence

Neal Wilkinson, production manager

Sarah Krohn, assistant director

Joshua Higgason, technical director

Paulina Jurzec, associate video designer

Jesse Garrison, video associate

Matt O'Hare, sound associate

Veronica Falborn, stage manager

Erica Laird, managing director

Additional contributing artists:

Francesca Spedalieri, assistant director (Wexner)

Shiree Houf, costume coordination (Wexner)

Judy Parker, costume coordination (Krannert)

Phil Garrett, performer, video and photo documentation (Wexner)

Brad Steinmetz, assistant sound designer (Wexner)

Divya Murthy, props coordinator

Jirye Lee, performer (Wexner)

Additional thanks to: Katie Brook, Josh Gelb, Ray Sun, Kelly Shaffer, Steve Brady, Willa Fitzgerald, J. R. Gualtieri (animator), Peter Flaherty, Joe Silovsky, Stewart Laing, Brian Morgan, Moira Driscoll, Owen Pence

Touring Venues

2011   Baryshnikov Arts Center, New York, a work-in-progress showing   Wexner Center for the Arts, Columbus, OH, world premier

2012   Krannert Center for the Performing Arts, University of Illinois at Urbana-Champaign, Urbana, IL
Fine Arts Center, University of Massachusetts, Amherst, MA
Next Wave Festival, Brooklyn Academy of Music, Brooklyn, NY

2014   ArtsEmerson: The World Onstage, Emerson College, Boston, MA

Afterparty

Notes on a Life by Dan Dobson, sound designer, founding member of The Builders Association

1997–1998: IMPERIAL MOTEL (FAUST) and JUMP CUT (FAUST)

They built us a theater in Oerlikon Train Station. (I spelled it right.) Schwamendingen. Leffe. Neumarkt
  producers Stephan, that other dude. Ben Rubin. Cecil. Gessnerallee workshop. Drinks at Rote
  Fabrik. Weren't there some issues with Heiner Goebbels?

Meat plate in Munich. That theater.

Munich fleamarket

1998–2000: JET LAG

Munich flea

Rotterdam flea

Budapest flea

Budapest bath

Budapest Cave Club

Food poisoning at a Budapest strip club/hotel

Agna Smisdom. Those Kaai apartments. Passport scam. Izzy Dungan at Kafka Bar.

Oyster mountain in Renne. Massage in Maubuege. That subwoofer show by the Austrians at site visit.
  (Granular Synthesis) Maubuzz.

What was that Georgian singer's name?

Brussels flea

Haunted hotel in Glasgow

Dominique and Ann Carlson

Nantes bonfire at New Year's

2000–2002: XTRAVAGANZA

The ocean in Le Havre. That's a meal.

Peter Norrman crashed. Impressive truck elevator at the Rotterdam opera house.

Meat plate in Strasbourg. That woman.

9/11

2003–2005: ALLADEEN

Lear. WAH center. Surprise birthday.

Turn of The Screw 1.0

Old spices in the ceiling rehearsing at Smackmellon

Peter Flaherty. And Heaven. And Tanya. And bowling.

2005–2006: SUPERVISION

Finding a doctor in Freemantle

Joe humping Charlie Chaplin's grandson at the Spiegeltent. Or sleeping anywhere. Or sawing his hand
   in three.

Playing at the Wellington basketball team's court

Water skiing in New frickin' Zealand. That tattooed crew member.

Jamie ninja crawling onstage during the show to free the screens. Riz. The Standard.

2007–2010: CONTINUOUS CITY

Jeff Morey. Jeff Morey. Jeff Morey. Jeff Morey.

Pneumatic screens. Come on.

Staying at that rented house in the Illinois cornfield. Demolition Derby. Meat. Mafia. Making Morgan
   cry. Katie Morgan! Her name's not Morgan is it?

Computer crashing at the Walker

2010–2013: HOUSE/DIVIDED

That girl who stole a stuffed squirrel

A frozen gulag at Amherst with an adult store that hosted Ron Jeremy while we were there

There was the rented house in Gahanna. What was their name? Parsley? I still have their garage
   door opener.

The Fact Family band. Mabel Pence, keyboard;
David Pence, guitar; Owen Pence, drums. The
Performing Garage, May 2010.

SOME SOURCE MATERIALS FOR THE PRODUCTION

Books

Alexander, Christopher. *The Timeless Way of Building.* New York: Oxford University Press, 1979.

Bachelard, Gaston. *The Poetics of Space.* 1958. Reprint, Boston, MA: Beacon Press, 1994.

Ballard, J. G. *High Rise.* New York: Liverlight, 1975.

Ballard, J. G. *Kingdom Come.* New York: Harper Perennial, 2007.

Berman, Marshall. *All That Is Solid Melts into Air.* New York: Penguin, 1988.

Buck-Morss, Susan. *Dialectics of Seeing.* Cambridge, MA: MIT Press, 1989.

De La Croix, Horst. *Military Considerations in City Planning: Fortifications.* New York: Braziller, 1982.

de Pierrefeu, François (Le Corbusier). *The Home of Man.* Translated by Clive Entwhistle. Princeton, NJ: Architectural Press, 1948.

Eisner, Will. *A Contract with God, and Other Tenement Stories.* New York: Norton, 2006.

Findlen, Paula. *Athanasius Kircher: The Last Man Who Knew Everything.* New York: Routledge, 1994.

Franzen, Jonathan. *The Corrections.* New York: Farrar, Straus and Giroux, 2001.

Hawthorne, Nathaniel. The *House of Seven Gables.* 1851. Reprint, New York: Dover, 1999.

Homer. *The Odyssey.* Translated by Robert Fagles. New York: Penguin, 1996.

Jacobs, Jane. *The Death and Life of Great American Cities.* New York: Random House, 1961.

Lang, Peter, and William Menking. *Superstudio: Life without Objects.* New York: Skira, 2003.

Lippard, Lucy. *The Lure of the Local.* New York: New Press, 1998.

Milton, John. *Paradise Lost.* 1667. Reprint, New York: Dover, 2005.

Poe, Edgar Allan. "A Descent into the Maelstrom." In *Complete Stories and Poems of Edgar Allen Poe.* New York: Doubleday, 1984.

Riis, Jacob. *How The Other Half Lives.* 1890. Reprint, New York: Penguin, 1997.

Ruan. Xian, and Paul Hogben. *Topophilia and Topophobia; Reflections on Twentieth-Century Human Habitat.* New York: Routledge, 2008.

Sadler, Simon. *Archigram: Architecture without Architecture.* Cambridge, MA: MIT Press, 2005.

Schoenauer, Norbert. *Six Thousand Years of Housing.* New York: Norton, 1991.

Steinbeck, John. *The Grapes of Wrath.* 1939. Reprint, New York: Penguin, 1983.

Walker, Lester. *The Tiny Book of Tiny Houses.* New York: Overlook, 1993.

Whyte, William H. *City: Rediscovering the Center.* New York: Doubleday, 1988.

Wright, Gwendolyn. *Building the Dream: The Social History of Housing in America.* Cambridge, MA: MIT Press, 1983.

Yates, Frances. *The Art of Memory.* 1966. Reprint, Chicago: University of Chicago Press, 2001.

Yates, Frances. *Theater of the World.* New York: Routledge, 1987.

Articles

Dixon, Steve. "The Philosophy and Psychology of the Scenographic House in Multimedia Theatre." *International Journal of Performance Arts and DigitalMedia* 6 (1) (2010): 7–24.

Plays

Aeschylus. *The Oresteia.* Translated by Robert Fagles. New York: Penguin, 1966.

Pinter, Harold. *The Caretaker.* 1960. London: Faber & Faber Plays, 1991.

Pinter, Harold. *The Dumbwaiter.* 1957. New York: Samuel French, 1960.

Simon, Neil. *The Prisoner of Second Avenue.* 1971. New York: Samuel French, 2010.

Steinbeck, John. *The Grapes of Wrath.* Adapted by Frank Galati. New York: Dramatists Play Service, 1991.

Strindberg, August. *A Dream Play* and *The Father*. In *Six Plays of Strindberg*. Translated by Elizabeth Sprigge. New York: Doubleday, 1955

Web

Howard, Sidney. Screen play for *Gone with the Wind.* 1939. Based on the novel by Margaret Mitchell. http://www.dailyscript.com/scripts/Gone_With_the_Wind.pdf.

Johnson, Nunally. Screenplay for *The Grapes of Wrath*. 1940. Based on the novel by John Steinbeck. http://www.dailyscript.com/scripts/grapes_of_wrath.html.

Ling, Lisa. "Lisa Ling Investigates a Tent City." February 25, 2009, http://www.oprah.com/oprahshow/Lisa-Ling-Goes-Inside-a-Tent-City.

Ling, Lisa. "Lisa Ling Investigates Foreclosed Homes," February 29, 2009, http://www.oprah.com/oprahshow/Lisa-Ling-Investigates-Foreclosed-Homes.

"Man Says Actions Intended to Send Message to Banks." February 18, 2010, https://www.youtube.com/watch?v=MabgiO9pZDA.

"Mission Hill Housing Project," https://www.youtube.com/watch?v=CgSe8-hA8Ds.

"Stock Market Commentary Live Stock Market Crash Trading Analysis." January 29, 2011, https://www.youtube.com/watch?v=faOgVVL4_HI.

"Stock Market Crash 5/6/10 (Live Panic!) Incredible!!" http://www.youtube.com/watch?v=s3JHBAJ0Kn0.

Film and Television

Basic Bucky: R. Buckminster Fuller. Directed by Robert Snyder. Santa Barbara, CA: Masters & Masterworks, 1990.

Design for Dreaming. Directed by William Beaudine. Detroit, MI: General Motors Company, 1956.

Fahrenheit 451. Directed by François Truffaut. London: Anglo Enterprises, Vineyard Film Ltd., 1966.

Gondry, Michel. Collected videos.

Gone with the Wind. Directed by Victor Fleming. Los Angeles: Selznick International Pictures, Metro-Goldwyn-Mayer, 1939.

The Grapes of Wrath. Directed by John Ford. Los Angeles: Twentieth Century Fox, 1940.

Harris, Hilary. Various films.

House by the River. Directed by Fritz Lang. Los Angeles: Fidelity Pictures Corporation, 1950.

Idiocracy. Directed by Mike Judge. Los Angeles: Twentieth Century Fox, Ternion Pictures, 2006.

Keaton, Buster, performer. "One Week," Joseph M. Schenck Productions, Metro Pictures Corporation, 1920; "The Saphead," Metro Pictures Corporation, 1920; "Neighbors," Joseph M. Schenck Productions, Metro Pictures Corporation, 1920.

The Lady Vanishes. Directed by Alfred Hitchcock. London: Gainsborough Pictures, 1938.

Manufactured Landscapes. Directed by Jennifer Baichwal. Toronto: Edward Burtynsky Photography, 2006.

Matta-Clark, Gordon. Various films.

The Nightcomers. Directed by Michael Winner. London: Elliott Kastner–Jay Kanter–Alan Ladd Jr. Productions, Scimitar Productions, 1971.

The Prisoner. Television series starring Patrick McGoohan. London: Everyman Films, 1967–1968.

Radiant City: Population Restless. Directed by Gary Burns and Jim Brown. Montreal, Quebec: Burns Film Ltd, National Film Board of Canada, 2006.

Rear Window. Directed by Alfred Hitchcock. Los Angeles: Paramount Pictures, Patron Inc., 1954.

"A Report to Home Builders." Stran-Steel Division, Great Lakes Steel Corporation, 1946.

Safe. Directed by Todd Haynes. Los Angeles: American Playhouse Theatrical Films, 1995.

Synecdoche, New York. Directed by Charlie Kaufman. Los Angeles: Sidney Kimmel Entertainment, 2008.

Wall-E. Directed by Andrew Stanton. Los Angeles: Pixar Animation Studios, Walt Disney Pictures, 2008.

"Wino." Directed by Jack Smith. New York, 1977.

"A Wonderful New World of Fords." Television advertisement for the Ford Motor Company, 1960.

Visual Art

Bourgeois, Louise. *Femme Maison* (1947). *He Disappeared into Complete Silence* (1947).

Kiesler, Frederik. *The Endless House* (1958–1959).

Orta, Lucy. *Refuge Wear and Body Architecture* (1992–1998).

Parker, Cornelia. *Cold Dark Matter: An Exploded View* (1991), *Exhaled Schoolhouse* (1996).

Whiteread, Rachel. *House* (1993).

Zittel, Andrea. Various.

Other

Josephine Baker's Château des Milandes and her unbuilt house in Paris that was designed by
Adolf Loos

Bruno

Cicero

Fludd

Langston Hughes

Museum of Modern Art catalog

Springsteen, Bruce. *The Ghost of Tom Joad.* Columbia Records, 1995.

The company begins the next production, ELEMENTS OF OZ, 2014.

EPILOGUE

MEDIATURGY

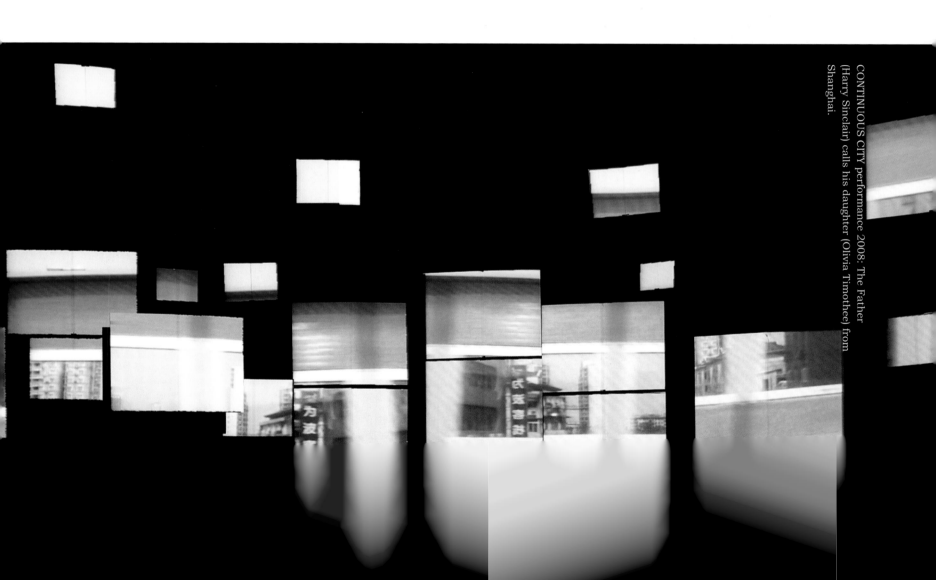

MARIANNE WEEMS IN CONVERSATION WITH
ELEANOR BISHOP

In December 2014 Marianne Weems sat down with me in New York to talk me through the concept of mediaturgy. She had a folder filled with handwritten notes and drawings from throughout The Builders Association's history. The notes chronicled her ideas of how The Builders' use of media has developed over each show and how they invented a new language of theater making.

Eleanor Bishop   What does *mediaturgy* mean?

Marianne Weems   Bonnie Marranca coined the term when she interviewed me for her recent book. The way I think of it is that it's an interweaving between the design of our shows and the dramaturgy. The design springs directly from the idea and expresses it in a way that is different from a lot of other theater because what's onstage is the idea embodied in many different forms—video, sound, architecture, staging, etc. I recently had an insight into how The Builders' media design—the screens, the network, the space, the video and sound—is both the material and the metaphor in each production. The screens are placed in a larger context onstage—a context that might more normally be called *scenography* but in this work is the architecture of invisible information.

It amazes me to look back now and see how my propositions for each show were perfectly, complexly, brilliantly manifested by my collaborators. I would say that what I did was stage the idea inside this complex arrangement. Another way of saying it is that the idea wouldn't make sense without the set and the set wouldn't make sense without the media, and we need it all to tell the story.

EB   The discourse about your work often focuses heavily on The Builders' use of media and technology, but you're saying that the conversation is broader?

MW   Yes, the technology itself is not the point: it's the ideas we're talking about. The proliferation of cell phones is a symptom of what we diagnose or question in the culture. A cell phone leads to a much deeper investigation of what drives our need for the phone—capitalism, social currency, the need for connection, etc. In the bigger

MASTER BUILDER Chris Kondek's sketch of the video system on a cocktail napkin, 1993.

picture, our work delivers a cultural critique by staging the complex relationship between media and personhood in the twenty-first century.

EB   So could you talk about how this "architecture of invisible information" has developed through your work?

MW   All right, I'll give it a try, but I am somewhat reluctant to trace this idea through various shows because it will inevitably seem reductive, but here we go. In MASTER BUILDER, we constructed and deconstructed a house. We used some primitive video and sound as a kind of intercom system between the rooms, which big suburban homes used to have. Did you ever have those?

EB   Yes.

MW   So the sound and video became a kind of skeleton for the house. It was our first foray into staging "the network"—tracing how information circulated in the house.

EB   How do you think that related to the contemporary moment?

MW   We discovered the language of staging people who were separated physically (as one is in a suburban home) but united electronically (as one is in American life).

In JUMP CUT (FAUST), we focused on the historic versions of Faust where he was portrayed as a practitioner of black magic, entranced by the transformative powers of alchemy. It turns out that a lot of early movies used Faust as their subject. So we fell in love with those films, and that literally became the scenario. We would move cameras and screens around, trying to imitate tropes from early cinema (tricks using forced perspective and scale, jump cuts, etc.). The idea was to create the magic of a movie but to do it live in front of the audience by staging our clumsy apparatus of moviemaking. So the design and the story became storyboarding the movie—specifically, our various attempts to reproduce stills drawn from F. W. Murnau's 1926 film *Faust*.

EB   You became theatrical alchemists.

MW   Right!

MW   In JET LAG, again we were focusing on the construction of the screen image, but this time in the context of mass media. In the first half of JET LAG, Jeff Webster as the sailor sits in a small boatlike construction in front of a little screen. On that screen, the audience witnesses him creating images of his journey—which were then reproduced in the British press. He basically programs his backgrounds, saying things like, "I have weathered some terrible storms, survived incredible, terrible, um, tremendous thirty-foot waves, massive walls of water," as we see him swaying on a stool, spraying water on his face, etc. He is writing his narrative through clearly constructing these images using media, which is also what we are doing in the design, the staging, and the whole show.

EB   That sounds like today, where part of our everyday actions is constructing the narratives of our own lives through Instagram and Twitter.

MW   Yes. IN ALLADEEN, the screen became the desktop of a computer. I can't believe that there was a time when this wasn't obvious, but when Chris Kondek suggested that as an image, it was such an inspired, surprising way of dissecting a screen!

EB   How was that different from what you had done before?

MW   We had always used one large screen, essentially delivering one image at a time. But in rehearsal, we were scrolling through the call-center office footage we shot in Bangalore—mostly endless aisles of operators facing computer monitors—and Chris had the idea of complicating The Builders' typical large screen by accommodating

JUMP CUT (FAUST) rehearsal in New York, 1998.

ALLADEEN performance, 2003. Onstage: Rizwan Mirza
as Joey at work in the call center. Screen/desktop
windows: show *Friends*, Douglas Fairbanks, live video
feed, word searches, and advertisements.

many threads of information and having it function like a desktop. So in ALLADEEN, the screen often had three or more windows playing at once. We used live feed of the operator/actors, images from old films of Alladdin, documentary footage from the Bangalore call centers, data that the operator/actors were seeing on their screens (such as the weather report in the caller's location), etc. The choreography of those windows opening and closing directed the audience's attention, and, as always, we created an elaborate dance between what was happening on stage and how it was transformed on the screen. Again, the design both told the story of the show and embodied the story of the show. The action takes place in the context of the desktop.

In SUPER VISION, we started with the idea of the databody. After a long series of experiments in visualizing this form, the designers came up with a beautiful way of expressing how the physical body is enmeshed in data. They created a very narrow playing space—a kind of alley where the actors were squeezed between two projection surfaces. From this compressed physical space, we animated how our data spreads freely and infinitely around us. Jennifer Tipton miraculously lit this five-foot alley while keeping the light off the screens, though she wasn't happy about it at the time.

In CONTINUOUS CITY, we talked about how we remain connected, both in the global flurry of the first world and the global diaspora of the developing world, and how we invest in the idea that our social networks maintain our connections. We were looking for a fluent way to express each character's personalized network, and James [Gibbs] and Peter [Flaherty] came up with a large constellation of small screens that could instantly reconfigure around each character in an ingenious method invented by Joe [Silovksy]. In this show, we finally exploded the large screen and created a fragmented media space that was a portrait of the characters' individual networks and that told their stories partly through the screens popping open and closing, conveying a fleeting sense of fragmentation.

Finally, in HOUSE/DIVIDED, the most obvious expression of the idea is the stock quotes streaming along the tickers onstage. The tickers don't simply frame the house, but there is a real narrative told there. The figures reflect what was happening with stocks involved in the mortgage crisis from 2006 to 2008. The story is being told with those numbers, and people who are financially literate who come to the show actually read it. Also, the set is composed of the clumsily analog pieces of a foreclosed home—the latticework, the bathtub, and the kitchen sink—which are interpolated with many kinds of projection surfaces. Through the course of the show, the house is gradually dismantled—the physical house disappears under the weight of the tickers, under the weight of the financial system. It's also like The Builders blowing up a house.

EB   Wow!

MW   And then there's the AR [augmented reality] world that John Cleater is developing to give the audience the sense that invisible data is streaming around them at every instant. So that, briefly, is the idea.

EB   All right, then let me ask this. HOUSE/DIVIDED is also the coming together of a number of recurring formal concerns. For example, the Bear Stearns quarterly reports are staged as live video chat, like in the Skype conversations that you're staging in ALLADEEN and CONTINUOUS CITY. And then there's the film of *The Grapes of Wrath*—

MW   Well, which we actually couldn't use, so we remade it in the style of—

EB   Which is like what you're doing in JUMP CUT (FAUST)

MW   Right!

EB   You can also trace your productions in correlation to the rise of different kinds of media—from analog to digital.

MW   We went from televisions in MASTER BUILDER and cinema in FAUST to the much more computerized space of ALLADEEN. Then we tracked the digital rise of dataveillance in SUPER VISION and landed in CONTINUOUS CITY in sync with the rise of mobile technology. All of that was just growing alongside the pieces, in dialogue with them.

EB   You were often taking technology that the mainstream hadn't even come to grips with and molding it for your own theatrical purposes. Did that cause any problems?

MW   Absolutely! Computers freezing and crashing at the Melbourne Festival, at the Singapore Lyric Opera, at the Walker Art Center, at the Brooklyn Academy of Music, at the Rotterdam Schouwburg. I could go on. In fact, at one point where we had overloaded every computer just to run SUPER VISION, a good show was one where nothing broke down. That's what happens when you're touring with everything you have and no safety net.

EB   Did you know where this was going to go when you started the company?

Sound designer Dan Dobson in rehearsal.

MW   No! No idea. At the beginning, I could've said, "We're going to stage *The Cherry Orchard* on a mountain of hamburger." I never really thought, "Oh, let's stage technology," but rather, "How do we relate to what is happening now?"

EB   So you didn't set out on this quest to create a lifelong body of work exploring how technology and culture affect one another?

MW   (laughs) No. In fact, I would advise against it.

EB   Because I think what intimidates a lot of young artists is that you look at great people's bodies of work and you feel like they had this grand plan, and thus you feel inadequate.

MW   That's interesting because it was so clearly not that. No, it's just beneath the level of consciousness. If you keep plugged into the culture, then somehow the culture flows into you and into your work. The Builders began working in a period where the accelerating proliferation of screens was launching digital culture. When we started using screens, we were simply looking for the best way to express the idea in the show. We were just using the tools at hand, without consciously saying, "This show is going to be about making a film." We were in a generative moment where a smart audience was rising, with their smartphones, and we were talking to them. That was the atmosphere in which this work was created.

The designers have a very immediate and lively conversation with what is happening in the world. It's a very specific kind of dramaturgy because we are reaching into the digital realm and then staging it. At least, now I understand that we were doing that.

This print [*Musurgia universalis*] has been mine and John Cleater's reference for a lot of shows. It's this etching by Athanasius Kircher (shows print). All of these spaces are interconnected through invisible, supervised means. I think it's really elegant and playful and exactly what we're talking about.

EB   This is a crucial part of the book because while the rest of it deals with the specificities of each show in a unique way (from academic analysis to the realities of being an experimental theater company), this conversation is about reflecting on the innovations of your body of work and the way media, dramaturgy, design, and the cultural moment are coming together.

Athanasius Kircher, *Musurgia universalis* (1650). Credit:
Reproduced by permission of the Librarian, National
University of Ireland Maynooth, from the collections of
St. Patrick's College, Maynooth.

MW   It's great to hear you say that. Because I have always found our conversations about design so satisfying. We were talking about manifesting content in all these different forms and not primarily in text.

EB   I like that there's physical evidence about how fruitful those conversations were—like this napkin with a crazy scheme for HOUSE/DIVIDED right here. I can really picture it.

Ultimately, I think your work shifts the question for theater makers in a really exciting way. We get to move the conversation forward from "How can we tell this story?" to "How can we stage what is living inside this idea?"

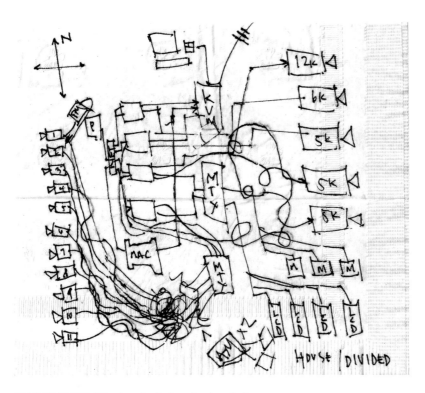

HOUSE/DIVIDED: Austin Switser's sketch for
the video system on a cocktail napkin, 2012.

Notes

PROLOGUE

1. Henrik Ibsen, *The Master Builder*, trans. Michael Meyer (London: Rupert Hart-Davis, 1961), 105.

INTRODUCTION

1. Robert Edmund Jones, *The Dramatic Imagination: Reflections and Speculations on the Art of the Theater* (New York: Routledge, 2004).
2. Slavoj Zizek, *Did Someone Say Totalitarianism? Five Interventions in the (Mis)Use of a Notion* (New York: Verso, 2001).
3. Wendy Hui Kyong Chun, "Introduction," in *New Media/Old Media: A History and Theory Reader*, ed. Wendy Hui Kyong Chun and Thomas Keenan (New York: Routledge, 2006), 8.
4. Ibid., 3.
5. Alisa Solomon, "Off to See the Wizardry," *Village Voice*, April 30, 2002.
6. Ibid.
7. Philip Auslander, "Against Ontology: Making Distinctions between the Live and the Mediatized," *Performance Research* 2, no. 3 (1997): 50–55.
8. Peggy Phelan, *Unmarked: The Politics of Performance* (New York: Routledge, 1993).
9. Freda Chapple and Chiel Kattenbelt, *Intermediality in Theater and Performance* (Amsterdam: Rodopi, 2006).
10. Jay David Bolter and Richard Grusin, *Remediation: Understanding New Media* (Cambridge, MA: MIT Press, 2000): 33.
11. Ibid., 34.

12. Jacques Rancière, *The Politics of Aesthetics: The Distribution of the Sensible*, trans. Gabriel Rockhill (New York: Continuum, 2004), 19.

13. Ibid., 16.

14. Ibid., 18.

15. Charles McNulty, "A Dizzying Global Vision," *Los Angeles Times*, February 28, 2004, http://articles.latimes.com/2004/feb/29/entertainment/ca-mcnulty29.

16. Rancière, *The Politics of Aesthetics*, 18.

17. Johannes Birringer, "Contemporary Performance/Technology," *Theater Journal* 51 (4) (1999): 361–381; Johannes Birringer, *Performance, Technology and Science* (New York: PAJ, 2008).

18. Hans-Thies Lehmann, *Postdramatic Theater*, trans. Karen Jürs-Munby (New York: Routledge, 2006).

19. Elinor Fuchs, *Death of Character: Perspectives on Theater after Modernism* (Bloomington: Indiana University Press, 1996).

20. Lehmann, *Postdramatic Theater*; Fuchs, *Death of Character*; Henry M. Sayre, *The Object of Performance* (Chicago: University of Chicago Press, 1989); Phelan, *Unmarked*; Amelia Jones, *Body Art / Performing the Subject* (Minneapolis: University of Minnesota Press, 1998); Rebecca Schneider, *Performing Remains: Art and War in Times of Theatrical Reenactment* (New York: Routledge, 2011) and *The Explicit Body in Performance* (New York: Routledge, 2013); Shannon Jackson, *Professing Performance: Theater in the Academy from Philology to Performativity* (Cambridge, UK: Cambridge University Press, 2004) and *Social Works: Performing Art, Supporting Publics* (Abingdon Oxon: Routledge, 2011).

21. Wendy Hui Kyong Chun and Thomas Keenan, eds., *New Media, Old Media: A History and Theory Reader* (New York: Routledge, 2006); Lev Manovich, *The Language of New Media* (Cambridge, MA: MIT Press, 2001); Steve Dixon, *Digital Performance: A History of New Media in Theater, Dance, and Performance* (Cambridge, MA: MIT Press, 2007); Susan Kozel, *Closer: Performance, Technologies, Phenomenology* (Cambridge, MA: MIT Press, 2007); Alexander Galloway, *The Interface Effect*

(Cambridge, UK: Polity Press, 2012); N. Katherine Hayles, *How We Became Posthuman: Virtual Bodies in Cybernetics, Literature and Informatics* (Chicago: University of Chicago Press, 1999) and *How We Think: Digital Media and Contemporary Technogenesis* (Chicago: University of Chicago Press, 2012).

22. Arjun Appadurai, *Modernity at Large: Cultural Dimensions of Globalization* (Minneapolis: University of Minnesota Press, 1996); Saskia Sassen, *Territory, Authority, Rights: From Medieval to Global Assemblages* (Princeton, NJ: Princeton University Press, 2006); Hal Foster, *Return of the Real* (Cambridge, MA: MIT Press, 1996); Pamela M. Lee, *Forgetting the Art World* (Cambridge, MA: MIT Press, 2012); Dennis Kennedy, *The Spectator and the Spectacle: Audiences in Modernity and Postmodernity* (Cambridge, UK: Cambridge University Press, 2009); Janelle Reinelt, *After Brecht: British Epic Theater* (Ann Arbor: University of Michigan Press, 1995).

CHAPTER 1: MASTER BUILDER

1. Jeff Webster, "Random Build Thoughts," notes on creating MASTER BUILDER, June 2009.
2. Ibid.
3. Marianne Weems, personal research notes, 1991.
4. Marianne Weems, interview with Shannon Jackson, May 2010.
5. Hans-Thies Lehmann, *Postdramatic Theater* (Abingdon Oxon: Routledge, 2006), 50.
6. David Savran, *Breaking the Rules: The Wooster Group* (New York: Theater Communications Group, 1986); Andrew Quick, *The Wooster Group Work Book* (New York: Routledge, 2007).
7. Walter Benjamin, "Surrealism: The Last Snapshot of the European Intelligentsia," *Selected Writings*, vol. 2, pt. 1 (Cambridge, MA: Harvard University Press, 1999).
8. Elinor Fuchs, *The Death of Character: Perspectives on Theater after Modernism* (Bloomington: Indiana University Press, 1996), 102.
9. Henrik Ibsen, *Six Plays by Henrik Ibsen* (New York: Barnes and Noble Classics, 2003), 785.
10. Rem Koolhaas, "BIGNESS: The Production of LARGE," Weems personal research notes, page 3.
11. Marianne Weems in conversation with Shannon Jackson, January 2009.

12. Marianne Weems, personal production files, The Master Builder (1993).

13. Anne M. Wagner, "Splitting and Doubling: Gordon Matta-Clark and the Body of Sculpture," *Grey Room* 14 (Winter 2004): 36.

14. Pamela Lee, *Object to be Destroyed: The Work of Gordon Matta-Clark,* (Cambridge, MA: MIT Press, 2000), 29.

15. Wagner, "Splitting and Doubling," 28. The quote is from Joan Simon, "Gordon Matta Clark, 1943–1978," *Art in America* (November–December 1978): 13. Simon borrows this phrase from the interview with Matta-Clark conducted by Donald Wall, "Gordon Matta-Clark's Building Dissections." This text of this interview has been reprinted in *Gordon Matta-Clark*, ed. C. Diserens (London: Phaidon, 2003), 181–186.

16. Wagner, "Splitting and Doubling," 36.

17. Wagner, "Splitting and Doubling," 36; Tom McDonough, "How to Do Things with Buildings," *Art in America* (November 2007): 164–169, 237.

18. Wagner, "Splitting and Doubling," 39.

19. Daphne Spain, *Gendered Spaces* (Chapel Hill: University of North Carolina Press, 1992).

20. Beatriz Colomina, "Intimacy and Spectacle: The Interior of Adolf Loos," *AA Files* 20 (1990): 8.

21. Laura Mulvey, "Pandora: Topographies of the Mask and Curiosity," in *Sexuality and Space*, ed. Beatriz Colomina (Princeton, NJ: Princeton Architectural Press, 1992).

22. Weems, Weems Production Files, 1993.

23. Ibsen, *Six Plays by Henrik Ibsen*, 705–825.

24. Martha Baer to Marianne Weems, Weems Production Files, 1993.

25. Walt Whitman, *Leaves of Grass* (Modern Library Series, 2000), 97.

26. Shannon Jackson in conversation with Marianne Weems, June 2008.

27. Marianne Weems, personal research notes, 1993.

28. Fax from Sulan Kolatan to Marianne Weems, Weems personal research notes, 1993.

29. Weems Production Files, June 23, 1994.

30. Ibid., 1994.

31. The Master Builder Project Description, Weems Production Files, January 12 1994.

32. Master Builder Production Materials, Weems Production Files.

33. Then and Now, Budget Files, Weems personal research notes.

34. Shannon Jackson in conversation with Weems, June 2008.

35. Marianne Weems to Jennifer Tipton, June 11, 1994, Master Builder Production Materials, Weems Production Files.

36. Marianne Weems in interview with Shannon Jackson, May 2010.

37. Marianne Weems to Jennifer Tipton, June 11 1994, Master Builder Production Materials, Weems Production Files.

38. Marianne Weems to Valerie Edward, February 16 1994, Weems Production Files.

39. Shannon Jackson in conversation with Marianne Weems, 2010.

40. Marianne Weems, rehearsal notes, 1993.

41. Marianne Weems, journal notes, December 10, 1994.

42. Marianne Weems, journal notes, December 13, 1994.

CHAPTER 2: FAUST

1. Excerpt by playwright John Jesurun from IMPERIAL MOTEL (FAUST).

2. Marianne Weems, production/dramaturgical notes for the company, 1995.

3. Marianne Weems, journal notes, 1995.

4. Michael Kelly, "The Road to Paranoia," *New Yorker*, June 19, 1995, 60–75.

5. Robert D. McFadden, "A Life of Solitude and Obsessions," *New York Times*, May 4, 1995, A1, B12.

6. Pam Belluck, "Suspect Hoarded Bomb Materials, Affidavit Implies," *New York Times*, May 12, 1995, A1, A26.

7. Janet Staiger, *Before Hollywood: Turn-of-the-Century Film from American Archives* (New York: American Federation of Arts, 1986), 138.

8. Ibid., 70.

9. Tom Gunning, "The Cinema of Attractions: Early Film, Its Spectator, and the Avant-Garde," *Wide Angle* 8 (3–4) (Fall 1986): 381–388.

10. Interview with Marianne Weems, "A Magical Meeting of Stage and Screen," *Le Soir*, March 16, 1998.

11. Gunning, "The Cinema of Attractions," 384.

12. Charles Musser, *The Emergence of Cinema: The American Screen to 1907* (Berkeley: University of California, 1990), 15.

13. Gunning, "The Cinema of Attractions," 383.

14. Paul Hammond, *Marvelous Méliès* (New York: St. Martin's Press, 1974), 36.

15. Ibid., 57.

16. Gunning, "The Cinema of Attractions," 382.

17. Ibid., 383.

18. Gertrude Stein, *Lectures in America* (New York: Random House, 1935), 125.

19. Marianne Weems, note to Neumarkt producers Stephan Müller and Volker Hesse, May 13, 1996.

20. Marianne Weems, journal notes, 1996.

21. Jonathan Kalb, JUMP CUT (FAUST), *New York Press*, December 17–23, 1997.

22. Johan Callens, "The Builders: S/he Do the Police in Different Voices," in Johan Callens, ed., *The Wooster Group and Its Traditions* (Berne: Peter Lang, 2004), 253.

23. Christoph Von Kuhn, "Faust in Amerika," *Tages-Anzeiger*, October 21, 1996, 53.

24. Peter von Becker, "Faust Fiction Theater and Video in Zurich," *Die Zeit*, November 1, 1996.

25. Von Kuhn, "Faust in Amerika," 53.

26. Interview with Marianne Weems, "A Magical Meeting of Stage and Screen," *Le Soir*, March 16, 1998.

27. Von Kuhn, "Faust in Amerika," 53.

28. Interview with Marianne Weems, "A Magical Meeting of Stage and Screen," *Le Soir*, March 16, 1998.

29. Jean-Louis Perrier, "Le dialogue des nouvelle technology et de l'art vivant," *Le Monde*, March 25, 1998, 30.

30. Philip Auslander, "Against Ontology: Making Distinctions between the Live and the Mediatized," *Performance Research* 2 (3) (1997): 50–55.

31. Callens, "The Builders," 247–261, 259.

32. Ibid., 258.

33. Von Kuhn, "Faust in Amerika," 53.

34. Jonathan Kalb, "JUMP CUT (FAUST)," *New York Press*, December 17–23, 1997.

35. Jean-Louis Perrier, "Le dialogue des nouvelle technology et de l'art vivant," *Le Monde*, March 25, 1998, 30.

36. Von Kuhn, "Faust in Amerika," 53.

37. Ibid.

CHAPTER 3: JET LAG

1. "A Conversation about *Jet Lag* between Diller & Scofidio, Jessica Chalmers and Marianne Weems," *Performance Research: On Line* 4 (2) (1998): 58.

2. Diller Scofidio + Renfro, *(Monkey) Business Class*, http://www.dsrny.com/#/projects/monkey-business-class.

3. Chris Salter, *Entangled: Technology and the Transformation of Performance* (Cambridge, MA: MIT Press, 2010), 81.

4. Paul Virilio, *The Open Sky*, trans. by Julie Rose (New York: Verso, 1997), 3.

5. Paul Virilio, "The Third Window: An Interview with Paul Virilio," in *Global Television*, ed. Cynthia Schneider and Brian Wallis, trans. Yvonne Shafir (Cambridge, MA: MIT Press, 1988), 196.

6. Jacques Rancière, *The Politics of Aesthetics: The Distribution of the Sensible*, trans. Gabriel Rockhill (London: Continuum, 2004).

7. Herbert Muschamp, "ART/ARCHITECTURE: Exploring Space and Time, Here and Now," *New York Times*, February 6, 2000, http://www.nytimes.com/2000/02/06/theater/art-architecture-exploring-space-and-time-here-and-now.html.

8. Susan Melrose, "Bodies without Bodies," in *Performance and Technology*, ed. Susan Broadhurst and Josephine Machon (London: Palgrave Macmillan, 2006).

9. Ibid., 4.

10. Ibid., 4.

11. Shot list for Brussels, 1998, JET LAG production files.

12. Shannon Jackson interview with Weems, January 2009.

13. Ibid.

14. Ibid.

15. Philip Auslander, *Liveness: Performance in a Mediatized Culture* (Abingdon, Oxon: Routledge, 1999).

16. Elinor Fuchs, *The Death of Character: Perspectives on Theater after Modernism* (Bloomington: Indiana University Press, 1996). For more investigation into the landscape play, see Elinor Fuchs and Una Chaudhuri, eds., *Land/Scape/Theater* (Ann Arbor: University of Michigan Press, 2002); and Una Chaudhuri, *Staging Place: The Geography of Modern Drama* (Ann Arbor: University of Michigan Press, 1997), on space and theater.

17. Hans-Thies Lehmann, *Postdramatic Theater*, trans. Karen Jurs-Munby (New York: Routledge, 2006), 68.

18. RoseLee Goldberg, "Dancing about Architecture: The Genesis of Diller and Scofidio," *Scanning: The Aberrant Architectures of Diller + Scofidio* (New York: Whitney Museum of American Art, 2003).

19. "Jet Lag," *Teater, ET & Kit*, ed. Rikke Rottenstein and Jakob Steen Olsen, *TEATER* 1 (94) (1999): 16–17.

20. Muschamp, "ART/ARCHITECTURE: Exploring Space and Time, Here and Now."

21. Jonathan Romney, "Oceans of Time," *The Guardian*, July 8, 2000, http://www.theguardian.com/books/2000/jul/08/books.guardianreview4.

22. "A Conversation about *Jet Lag* between Diller & Scofidio, Jessica Chalmers and Marianne Weems," 57–60.

23. Ibid., 58.

24. D. J. R. Bruckner, "Technology as a Setting for Isolation and Defeat," *New York Times*, January 14, 2000, http://www.nytimes.com/mem/theater/treview.html?res=9406e4d7153af937a25752c0a9669c8b63&_r=1&.

25. Ibid.

26. Philippa Wehle, "Live Performance and Technology: The Example of *Jet Lag*," *PAJ: A Journal of Performance and Art* 24 (1) (2002): 133–139.

27. Jason Zinoman, "Going Places in a Media-Saturated World," *New York Times*, September 29, 2010, http://www.nytimes.com/2010/09/29/theater/reviews/29jet.html.

28. Ibid.

29. Excerpt from RoseLee Goldberg, "Dancing about Architecture: The Genesis of Diller and Scofidio," *Scanning: The Aberrant Architectures of Diller + Scofidio* (New York: Whitney Museum of American Art, 2003).

CHAPTER 4: XTRAVAGANZA

1. Marianne Weems, interview with Shannon Jackson, June 2008.

2. Charles Musser, *The Emergence of Cinema: The American Screen to 1907* (Berkeley: University of California, 1990), 1, 15.

3. Marianne Weems, journal, quoted from Martin Rubin, *Showstoppers: Busby Berkeley and the Tradition of Spectacle* (New York: Columbia University Press, 1993).

4. Simon Reynolds, *Generation Ecstasy: Into the World of Techno and Rave Culture* (New York: Routledge, 1999), 29.

5. Peter Norrman, interview with Matt O'Hare, 2013.

6. Ibid.

7. Marianne Weems, journal, 2000.

8. Musser, *The Emergence of Cinema*, 8 ("The Edison Manufacturing Company introduced commercial, modern motion pictures to the world. Its owner, Thomas A. Edison, achieved immense influence through both his company's activities and his use of patent litigation as a commercial weapon.").

9. Marianne Weems, interview with Shannon Jackson, 2009.

10. Reynolds, *Generation Ecstasy*, 51.

11. Marianne Weems, journal, April 10, 2001.

12. Marianne Weems, journal, January 2000.

13. Reynolds, *Generation Ecstasy*, 50.

14. Alisa Solomon, "Off to See the Wizardry," *Village Voice*, April 23, 2002, http://www.villagevoice.com/2002-04-23/theater/off-to-see-the-wizardry.

CHAPTER 5: ALLADEEN

1. Pico Iyer, *The Global Soul: Jet Lag, Shopping Malls, and the Search for Home* (New York: Vintage Books, 2001) 140.

2. Tara McPherson, "Reload: Liveness, Mobility and the Web," in *New Media, Old Media: A History and Theory Reader*, ed. Wendy Hui Kyong Chun and Thomas Keenan (New York: Routledge, 2005), 200, 202.

3. Ibid., 202.

4. *The Arabian Nights: Tales of 1001 Nights*, ed. Robert Irwin. Trans. Malcolm Lyons with Ursula Lyons (London: Penguin Classics, 2010).

5. Motiroti website, http://keithkhanassociates.com/about/press/past-press/moti-roti-puttli-chunni.

6. Keith Kahn, interview with Charles McGrath, at RedCat in Los Angeles, 2003E.

7. Marina Warner, *Fantastic Metamorphoses, Other Worlds* (Oxford: Oxford University Press, 2002), 144.

8. Mark Landler, "Hi, I'm in Bangalore (but I Can't Say So)," *New York Times,* March 21, 2001, A1, C4.

9. Ibid., A1, C4.

10. Marianne Weems, in discussion with Shannon Jackson, June 10, 2008.

11. Moe Angelos (performer, Builders Association), in discussion with Shannon Jackson, June 11, 2008.

12. Call Centers—Trip to Bangalore, Weems production files.

13. Hans-Thies Lehmann, *Postdramatic Theater*, trans. Karen Jurs-Munby (New York: Routledge, 2006), 68.

14. Pico Iyer, interview with Dave Weich, powells.com, March 27, 2000, saved and underlined in Weems Production Note Files.

15. Ernesto Laclau and Chantal Mouffe, *Hegemony and Socialist Strategy: Toward a Radical Democratic Politics*, 2nd ed. (London: Verso, 2001), 98–99.

16. Ibid., 111.

17. Hans-Thies Lehmann, *Postdramatic Theater*, trans. Karen Jurs-Munby (New York: Routledge, 2006), 178.

18. Laclau and Mouffe, *Hegemony and Socialist Strategy*, 111.

19. "The Story of 'Ala al-Din (Aladdin) and the Magic Lamp," *The Arabian Nights II: Sinbad and Other Stories,* trans. Husain Haddawy, ed. Muhsin Mahdi (New York: Norton, 1995), 86–88.

20. For a lengthier discussion of such topics in relation to other artists, see Shannon Jackson, *Social Works: Performing Art, Supporting Publics* (New York: Routledge, 2011).

21. Michael Hardt and Antonio Negri, *Multitude: War and Democracy in the Age of Empire* (New York: Penguin, 2004), 108.

22. Saskia Sassen, interviewed by Dale Leorke, "Power, Mobility, and Diaspora in the Global City," *Platform: A Journal of Media and Communication* 1 (July 2009): 103–108.

23. Saskia Sassen, "Embeddedness of Electronic Markets: The Case of Global Capital Markets," in *The Sociology of Financial Markets*, ed. Karin Knorr Cetina and Alex Preda, 17–37 (Cambridge: Oxford University Press, 2005).

24. Hardt and Negri, *Multitude*, 109.

25. Lehmann, *Postdramatic Theater*, 185–186.

26. Early script material for *Alladeen*, April 22, 2002, Weems production files.

27. Marianne Weems, interview with the author, January 20, 2009.

28. *The Arabian Nights II*, 125.

29. The site is now archived with the British Library at http://www.webarchive.org.uk/wayback/archive/20140304210014/http://www.alladeen.com/fullscreen.html.

30. Jennifer Parker-Starbuck, "Lost in Space? Global Placelessness and the Non-Places of *Alladeen*," in *Performance and Place*, ed. Leslie Hill and Helen Paris (London: Palgrave Macmillan, 2006), 162.

31. Ibid., 162.

32. Ibid., 168 n. 32.

33. Lehmann, *Postdramatic Theater*, 186.

34. Margo Jefferson, "The Other End of the Phone, Workers Striped of Their Identities," *New York Times*, December 4, 2003, http://www.nytimes.com/2003/12/04/theater/ theater-review-other-end-phone-workers-stripped-their-identities.html.

35. McPherson, "Reload: Liveness, Mobility and the Web," 202.

CHAPTER 6: SUPER VISION

1. Hedy Weiss, "'Super' Stories Show Someone Has Your Number—Yikes!," *Chicago Sun-Times*, October 16, 2006.

2. Brendan Kiley, "Sleek and Powerful," *Blog the Boards*, November 12, 2005, http://www.artsjournal.com/blogs1/otb/builders.shtml.

3. Dominic Papatola, "For 'Super Vision' Lack of Humanity Is, Isn't Problem," *Pioneer Press*, October 14, 2005.

4. Steven Winn, "Super Vision Scores an All-Too-Familiar Point," *San Francisco Chronicle*, August 19, 2066.

5. Nigel Hawkes, "Patient Records Go on Database," *The Times*, July 21, 2003, http://www.thetimes .co.uk/tto/news/uk/article1955270.ece.

6. Daniel J. Solove, *The Digital Person: Technology and Privacy in the Information Age* (New York: New York University Press, 2004), 170.

7. Ibid., 175, 177.

8. Christian Parenti, *The Soft Cage: Surveillance in America from Slave Passes to the War on Terror* (New York: Basic Books, 2003), 92.

9. John E. McGrath, *Loving Big Brother: Performance, Privacy, and Surveillance Space* (New York: Routledge, 2004), 159.

10. Ibid.

11. James Gibbs. For a particularly thorough documentation of SUPER VISION that has been important for this chapter, see, Nick Kaye, "Screening Presence: The Builders Association and dbox, Supervision (2005)," *Contemporary Theater Review* 17 (4) (2007): 557–577. See also Nick Kaye and Gabriella Giannachi, "Acts of Presence: Performance, Mediation, Virtual Reality," *Drama Review* 55 (4) (2011): 88–95, and *Acts of Presence: Performing Presence, CAVE Scenarios* (Cambridge, MA: MIT Press, 2011) (DVD-ROM). The Builders Association was one of the companies featured in Kaye's The Presence Project, a research project that was led by the University of Exeter's performance studies department in collaboration with the Stanford University's Archaeology Center and the University College London's computer science department from 2005 to 2010. The project explored experiences of presence in multimedia theater, installation, video, new media, and immersive virtual reality environments.

12. Julia Scher, "The Institutional State," *Els Limits Del Museu Catalogue* (Barcelona: Antoni Tapies Foundation, 1995), 188.

13. N. Katherine Hayles, *How We Became Posthuman: Virtual Bodies in Cybernetics, Literature and Informatics* (Chicago: University of Chicago Press, 1999), 290.

14. Michel Foucault, *Discipline and Punish: The Birth of the Prison* (New York: Vintage Books, 1995).

15. Jacques Derrida, *Of Grammatology* (Baltimore: Johns Hopkins University Press, 1998).

16. Hayles, *How We Became Posthuman*, 35.

17. Ibid.

18. Ibid., 290 (italics in the original).

19. Kaye, "Screening Presence," 7.

20. It was reputed to be "one of the most expensive shows ever produced at the Royal Court" when it came to Liverpool, for example. Philip Key, "Supervision/Liverpool," *Liverpool Daily Post*, May 5, 2006.

21. Jason Zinoman, "All the World's a Technology Incubator," *New York Times*, November 20, 2005.

22. Hayles, *How We Became Posthuman*, 31.

23. James Gibbs, interview with Nick Kaye, 2013.

24. Zinoman, "All the World's a Technology Incubator."

25. Marianne Weems, in conversation with Nick Kaye, The Presence Project.

26. All of the above quotations taken from "SUPER VISIONS IMPROVS," a CD of recordings of improvisations dated June 3, 2005. Builders Archives.

27. Jan Hallam, "Supervision," *Sunday Times*, February 15, 2006.

28. Ibid.

29. Weiss, "'Super' Stories Show Someone Has Your Number—Yikes!"

30. Kaye, "Screening Presence," 568–569.

31. Ibid., 567.

32. James Gibbs quoted in Kaye, "Screening Presence," 562.

33. James Gibbs, interview with Nick Kaye, 2013.

34. Dan Dobson quoted in Kaye, "Screening Presence," 570.

35. Kaye, "Screening Presence," 562.

36. Ibid., 563–564.

37. Ibid., 573.

38. Ibid., 569.

39. Ibid.

40. Ibid., 565.

41. Mark Blankenship, "Super Vision," *Variety*, December 1, 2005.

42. Kaye, "Screening Presence," 565.

43. Ibid., 576–577.

44. Hayles, *How We Became Posthuman*, 290.

45. Mark Swed, "The Unblinking Eye of Technology," *Los Angeles Times*, December 8, 2006, http://articles.latimes.com/2006/dec/08/entertainment/et-super8.

46. Winn, "Super Vision Scores an All-Too-Familiar Point."

47. Rohan Preston, "Theater Goes High Tech with 'Super Vision,'" *Star Tribune* (Minneapolis), October 15, 2005.

48. Jan Hallam, "Supervision," *Sunday Times*, February 15, 2006.

49. Pip Christmass, "Digital Doubletake," *West Australian Today*, February 16, 2006, 12.

50. Kiley, "Sleek and Powerful."

51. Mark Blankenship, "Super Vision," *Variety*, December 1, 2005.

52. Ibid.

53. Terry Teachout, "Making Ideas Beautiful," *Wall Street Journal*, December 10–11, 2006.

CHAPTER 7: CONTINUOUS CITY

1. Italo Calvino, *Invisible Cities* (Orlando, FL: Harcourt, 1978).

2. Saskia Sassen, *Global Networks, Linked Cities* (New York: Routledge, 2002).

3. Sherry Turkle, "Always-on/Always-on-You: The Tethered Self," in *Handbook of Mobile Communication Studies*, ed. James E. Katz (Cambridge, MA: MIT Press, 2008).

4. Ibid., 122.

5. Mike Davis, *Planet of Slums* (London: Verso, 2006), 120. Davis is quoting from Jeremy Seabrook's *In the Cities of the South: Scenes from a Developing World* (London: Verso, 1996), 211: "The Third World urban bourgeoisie 'cease to be citizens of their own country and become nomads belonging to, and owing allegiance to, a superterrestrial topography of money; they become patriots of wealth, nationalists of an elusive and golden nowhere.'"

6. For more on economic and political shifts, see Saskia Sassen, *Globalization and Its Discontents* (New York: New Press, 1998); Zygmunt Bauman, *Globalization:The Human Consequences* (New York: Columbia University Press, 1998); Teresa Caldeira, *City of Walls: Crime, Segregation and Citizenship in São Paulo* (Berkeley: University of California Press, 2001); Manuel Castells, *The Rise of the Network Society* (Oxford: Blackwell, 2000) and *City and Grassroots: A Cross-Cultural Theory of Urban Social Movements* (Berkeley: University of California Press, 1985); Arjun Appadurai, *Modernity at Large: Cultural Dimensions of Globalization* (Minneapolis: University of Minnesota Press, 1996); and AnnaLee Saxenian, *The New Argonauts: Regional Advantage in a Global Economy* (Cambridge, MA: Harvard University Press, 2007).

7. Davis, *Planet of Slums*, 8–9.

8. Ibid., 46.

9. Saskia Sassen, "Whose City Is It? Globalization and the Formation of New Claims," *Public Culture* 8 (2) (1996): 220–221, reprinted as the introduction to Sassen, *Globalization and Its Discontents*, xxxiii.

10. Marianne Weems, journal entry, November 2006.

11. Manuel Castells, *The Rise of the Network Society* (Oxford: Blackwell, 2000).

12. Calvino, *Invisible Cities*, 156–158.

13. Marianne Weems, in conversation with James Gibbs, 2007.

14. Marianne Weems, journal entry, May 2007.

15. Hank Green, National Center for Supercomputing Applications, in an email to Marianne Weems, August 2007.

16. AnnaLee Saxenian, *The New Argonauts: Regional Advantage in a Global Economy* (Cambridge, MA: Harvard University Press, 2007).

17. Stewart Taggart, "The Twenty-Ton Packet," *Wired* 7 (10) (October 1999), http://archive.wired .com/wired/archive/7.10/ports.html.

18. Weems email to Shannon Jackson, January 2009.

19. Sassen, *Globalization and Its Discontents*, xxi–xxii.

20. Ibid., xxv.

21. Weems in conversation with Shannon Jackson, 2009.

22. Patricia Stiller, "'Continuous City' Offers Lots to Ponder," *Urbana News Gazette*, 2008.

23. Robert Hurwitt, "Theater Review: 'Continuous City,'" *San Francisco Chronicle*, November 8, 2008.

24. Adam R. Perlman, "Continuous City," *Backstage*, November 19, 2008.

25. Stan Richardson, "Continuous City," *New York Theater*, November 18, 2008, http://www .nytheatre.com/Review/stan-richardson-2008-11-18-continuous-city. In the *New York Times* on November 21, 2008, Jason Zinoman wrote: "Ms. Weems, to her credit, goes against the grain of the usual gloomy, Orwellian portraits of technology. But in her attempt to dramatize real, human connection, the flaws of the script are exposed. Mike and, for that matter, his daughter remain thinly drawn and remote; their crucial scenes together seem lazily written, like an improvisation between strangers. Technology is a vivid character in this play, but you wish it weren't the only one." http://www.nytimes.com/2008/11/21/theater/reviews/21cont.html.

CHAPTER 8: HOUSE/DIVIDED

1. Hallie Flanagan, *Arena* (New York: Duell, Sloan and Pearce, 1940), 70.

2. Marianne Weems, email to the company, June 1, 2009.

3. Hallie Flanagan, brief delivered before the US House of Representatives, February 8, 1938, p. 8, Library of Congress Federal Theater Project, http://memory.loc.gov/cgi-bin/ ampage?collId=ftscript&fileName=farbf/00040002/ftscript.db&recNum=0. The quote retains Flanagan's spelling for the production *Triple-A Plowed Under*.

4. "My Day," *New York World Telegraph*, March 4, 1938.

5. John W. Casson, "Living Newspaper: Theatre and Therapy," *Drama Review* 44 (2) (Summer 2000): 107–122, at 116.

6. Ibid.

7. Benjamin H. D. Buchloh, "From Faktura to Factography," *October* 30 (Autumn 1984): 82–119.

8. Moe Angelos, notes on the Jalopy, group blog for the production, September 10, 2011.

9. Doris Duke Charitable Foundation,www.ddcf.org.

10. Moe Angelos, email to Marianne Weems, May 2014.

11. Don Aucoin, "'House/Divided': The Wrath of the Great Recession," *Boston Globe*, January 13, 2014.

12. Ibid.

13. Marianne Weems, correspondence to Shannon Jackson, June 2014.

14. James Gibbs, email to Marianne Weems, June 2014.

15. Ibid.

16. Dan Dobson, in conversation with Matt O'Hare, 2013.

17. Moe Angelos, email to Marianne Weems, June 14, 2014.

18. Ibid.

19. John Steinbeck, *The Grapes of Wrath* (New York: Penguin, 2006), 31–32.

20. Marianne Weems, correspondence to Shannon Jackson, June 2014.

21. Charles Isherwood, "Dispossessed Progeny of Ma and Pa Joad," *New York Times,* October 25, 2012, C3, http://www.nytimes.com/2012/10/26/theater/reviews/builders-associations-house-divided-at-bam.html.

22. Mark Hanratty, interview with James Gibbs, May 2011.

23. Stuart Cosgrove, *The Living Newspaper: History, Production and Form* (Yorkshire: University of Hull, 1982), 237–244. The quote comes from page 239 where this guide, compiled by the Federal

Theatre Project, has been reprinted as Appendix 1 in Cosgrove's dissertation. The paragraph continues:

Furthermore, he should often conceive of the entire theatre as a single unit, as opposed to the concept of a stage separated from its audience by that invisible fourth wall which is arched by the proscenium. In most theatres the audience has paid to attend and watch the spectacle of a group of characters undergoing some experience which the author has created. The characters may have the sympathy of the audience but there is a conscious effort to retain their own identity as something separate from the observers.

24. Ibid.
25. Isherwood, "Dispossessed Progeny of Ma and Pa Joad."
26. Cosgrove, *The Living Newspaper*, xvii. This quote appears in Cosgrove's introduction and comes from promotional materials for Seattle's production of the Living Newspaper *Power*.

Illustration Credits

40   Photos by Peter Norrman, 1994.

42   Courtesy of Ben Rubin, 1994.

45   "Method Study Your Kitchen," *The Practical Householder*, June 1958, 707.

48   Performer Emma Strahs, 1993. Photo by Peter Norrman.

50   Photo by Peter Norrman, 1994.

51   Photo by Peter Norrman, 1994.

52   Photo by Peter Norrman, 1994.

54   Courtesy of John Cleater, 1993.

54   Photo by Peter Norrman, 1994.

55   Courtesy of Marianne Weems, 1993.

57   Photo by Peter Norrman, 1993.

62   Courtesy of Susan Sontag, 1994.

64   Courtesy of Marianne Weems, 1994.

CHAPTER 2: FAUST

69   Performers on stage: Jeff Webster and Susanne-Marie Wrage. On video: Susanne-Marie Wrage, Jeff Webster, and Michael Neuenschwander. Theater Neumarkt, 1996. Courtesy of Koni Nordmann.

74   Three texts from Weems's dramaturgical research: Transcript of Susanna Margaretha Brandt's 1772 trial. Sources: Siegfried Birkner, *The Life and Death of the Child Murderess Susanna Margaretha Brandt* (Frankfurt: Insel Verlag, 1973); Johann Wolfgang von Goethe, *Faust* (1828) (Translated by Philip Wayne [New York: Penguin, 1949]), John Jesurun, "The Trial of Rhonda Gretchen Kindermoerd" (1996).

77   Photos by Marianne Weems.

78   Georges Méliès's children.

84   Sketch by John Cleater, 1995.

86   Courtesy of Koni Nordmann, 1996.

91 JUMP CUT (FAUST) production photo. Thread Waxing Space, 1998. Photo by Peter Norrman.

94 JUMP CUT (FAUST) production photo. Thread Waxing Space, 1998. Photo by Peter Norrman.

95 Friedrich-Wilhelm-Murnau-Foundation, 1926.

96 Library of Congress MBRS Division, 1909.

98 Thread Waxing Space, 1998. Photo by Peter Norrman.

99 JUMP CUT (FAUST) production photo, 1997. Photo by Peter Norrman.

100 Von Christoph Kuhn "Faust in Amerika—cool und medial," *Tages-Anzeiger*, October 21, 1996. Courtesy of Tages-Anzeiger.

109 Courtesy of Marianne Weems, 1995.

CHAPTER 3: JET LAG

115 JET LAG performances at Peak Performances@Montclair, 2012. Photo by James Gibbs.

118 Courtesy of *The London Times* (left).

118 Courtesy of *The London Times* (right).

122 Courtesy of Brussels Airport Personnel.

123 Photo by Marianne Weems, 1998.

125 JET LAG production photo. Peak Performances@Monclair, 2012. Photo by James Gibbs.

127 Courtesy of Jessica Chalmers, 1998.

129 Photo by Marianne Weems, 1998.

134–139 Diller + Scofidio, "Jet Lag," in *ec art S: #1–99: site de recherche et d'expérimentation*, ed. Eric Sadin (Paris: Ecarts, 1999). Courtesy of ec/art.

145 JET LAG at Peak Performances@Montclair, 2012. Photo by James Gibbs.

146 Photo by Marianne Weems, 2000.

147 Photo by Chris Kondek, 1998.

154 Courtesy of Marianne Weems, 2001.

CHAPTER 4: XTRAVAGANZA

157   XTRAVAGANZA production photo, St. Ann's Warehouse, New York, 2001. Courtesy of © Paula Court.

160   Underwood & Underwood/Corbis.

161   Graphic by Peter Norrman.

164   XTRAVAGANZA production photo 1999. Photo by Peter Norrman.

167   Courtesy of Dan Dobson, 1999.

168   Forbes Co., Lithographer, c. 1872–1890. Courtesy of Library of Congress.

171   The Falk Studio. Courtesy of Library of Congress.

175   Photo by Peter Norrman.

177   Painting by Frederick Childe Hassam, 1893 (left).

177   Copyright © (1884) Scientific American, Inc. All rights reserved (right).

178   The Falk Studio. Courtesy of Library of Congress (left).

178   Photo by Peter Norrman, 2000 (right).

180   XTRAVAGANZA production photo. Performers left to right Bravo LaFortune, Aimée Guillot, Moe Angelos, Heaven Phillips, 2000. Courtesy of © Paula Court.

190   XTRAVAGANZA production photo. Jeff Webster dancing with a video skirt projection, designed by Ellen McCartney. In the background, Aimée Guillot and Moe Angelos, 2000. Photo by Peter Norrman.

CHAPTER 5: ALLADEEN

195   ALLADEEN production photo. Opening scene, 2003. Courtesy of Simone Lynn.

198   Peter Norrman and Ali Zaidi, 2003.

200   Performers, left to right: Heaven Phillips, Rizwan Mirza, Jeff Webster, Jasmine Simhalan. On video: Jasmine Simhalan (image by Ali Zaidi), 2003. Courtesy of Simone Lynn.

201   Performers, left to right: Tanya Selvaratnam, Heaven Phillips, Rizwan Mirza. On video: Tanya Selvaratnam, Heaven Phillips (image by Ali Zaidi), 2003. Courtesy of Simone Lynn.

206   Photos by Peter Norrman, 2003.

CHAPTER 6: SUPER VISION

271   Clockwise: Photo Courtesy of Marianne Weems. Storyboard Courtesy of Stewart Laing. Design render: dbox, inc., after a design by Stewart Laing, 2005.

272   Photo by Marianne Weems, 2010.

274   SUPER VISION rehearsal. Photos by Marianne Weems.

286   Photo by Claire Hallereau.

CHAPTER 7: CONTINUOUS CITY

291   Courtesy of dbox, inc., 2008.

299   Courtesy of Jessica Chalmers, 2007.

304   Students from the department of theater, dance, and performance studies during a residency with The Builders Association, 2008. Courtesy of Marianne Weems.

306   Nick Reed, 2008.

309   Production photo. Brooklyn Academy of Music, 2008. Photo by James Gibbs.

314   Photo by Marianne Weems, 2007.

315   Photos by Moe Angelos, 2008.

316   Photo by Moe Angelos, 2008.

317   Photo by Moe Angelos, 2008.

319   Photos by Moe Angelos, 2008–2009.

320   Rehearsal at the Krannert Center for the Performing Arts, 2007. Photo by Marianne Weems.

321   Photo by James Gibbs.

324   Krannert Center for the Performing Arts, 2008. Photo by James Gibbs.

330   Rehearsals at the Krannert Center for the Performing Arts, 2008. Courtesy of Valerie A Oliveiro.

336   Rehearsals at the Krannert Center for the Performing Arts 2008. Courtesy of Valerie A Oliveiro.

CHAPTER 8: HOUSE/DIVIDED

341   Photo by James Gibbs, 2012.

343   Eviction scene from *The Grapes of Wrath*. Performers Jess Barbagallo, Matt Karges, Sean Donovan. Video design Austin Switser, 2012. Photo by James Gibbs.

344 Courtesy University of Washington Libraries, Special Collections SOC1109.

347 Courtesy of James D. Griffoen (left).

347 Photo by Moe Angelos, 2008 (right).

348 Courtesy of Matthew Karges.

351 Dan & Teri Securities Transaction Process Reverse Engineered version 4.1. Courtesy of DTC systems, 2008–2010.

352 Photos by Moe Angelos, 2010.

355 Photo by Moe Angelos, 2010.

356 Photo by Moe Angelos, 2011 (left).

356 Photo by Austin Switser, 2011 (right).

360 Performers left to right: Jess Barbagallo, Phil Garrett, LaToya Lewis, Moe Angelos, and Sean Donovan as Alan Greenspan, 2012. Photo by James Gibbs.

362 Photo by Marianne Weems, 2010.

364 Photo by Marianne Weems, 2010.

367 Photo by James Gibbs, 2012.

369 Photo by James Gibbs, 2012.

376 Photo by Marianne Weems, 2010.

382 Photo by Erica Laird, 2014.

EPILOGUE

383 Photo by James Gibbs, 2008.

385 Courtesy of Chris Kondek, 1993.

387 Photo by Marianne Weems, 1998.

388 Courtesy of Simone Lynn, 2003.

391 Photo by Marianne Weems, 2010.

392 Photo by James Gibbs, 2008.

394 Reproduced by permission of the Librarian, National University of Ireland Maynooth, from the collections of St. Patrick's College, Maynooth.

395 Courtesy of Austin Switser, 2012.

Index